THE HEARTBEAT OF WOUNDED KNEE

THE HEARTBEAT OF WOUNDED KNEE

Life in Native America

DAVID TREUER

ADAPTED BY **SHEILA KEENAN**

VIKING

In Memory

—

Margaret Seelye Treuer, Robert Treuer,
Sean Fahrlander, Dan Jones

VIKING
An imprint of Penguin Random House LLC, New York

First published in the United States of America by Viking,
an imprint of Penguin Random House LLC, 2022

LIBRARY OF CONGRESS CATALOGING-IN-PUBLICATION DATA
Names: Treuer, David, author. | Keenan, Sheila, adapter.
Title: The heartbeat of Wounded Knee : life in Native America / David Treuer ; adapted by Sheila Keenan.
Description: New York : Viking, 2022. | Includes bibliographical references and index. | Audience: Ages 12
and up | Audience: Grades 10–12 | Summary: "Since the late 1800s, it has been believed that Native Ameri-
can civilization has been wiped from the United States. The Heartbeat of Wounded Knee argues that Native
American culture is far from defeated—if anything, it is thriving as much today as it was one hundred years ago.
The Heartbeat of Wounded Knee looks at Native American culture as it exists today—and the fight to preserve
language and traditions"—Provided by publisher. Identifiers: LCCN 2022021907 (print) | LCCN 2022021908
(ebook) | ISBN 9780593203477 (hardcover) | ISBN 9780593203484 (ebook) | Subjects: LCSH: Indians of
North America—History—20th century—Juvenile literature. | Indians of North America—Social conditions—
20th century—Juvenile literature. Classification: LCC E77.4 .T743 2022 (print) | LCC E77.4 (ebook) | DDC
970.004/97—dc23/eng/20220518 LC record available at https://lccn.loc.gov/2022021907 LC ebook record
available at https://lccn.loc.gov/2022021908

Printed in the United States of America

ISBN 9780593203477

2nd Printing

LSCH

Design by Lucia Baez · Text set in TT Norms Pro

For Elsina, Noka, and Bine,
as always and forever

CONTENTS

PROLOGUE

❖❖❖❖❖❖❖❖❖❖

THIS BOOK TELLS THE STORY of what Indians in the United States have been up to in the 130 years since the infamous massacre at Wounded Knee Creek in South Dakota: what we've done, what's happened to us, and what our lives have been like.[1] It is adamantly, unashamedly, about Indian life rather than Indian death. That we even *have* lives—that Indians have been living in, have been shaped by, and in turn have shaped the modern world—is news to most people. The usual story told about us—or rather, about "the Indian"—is one of decline and death. Our story begins in unchecked freedom and communion with the earth and ends in confinement and perpetual suffering on reservations. Wounded Knee has come to stand in for much of that history.

But what were the actual circumstances of this event that has taken on so much symbolic weight?

In the 1860s, the U.S. government had been trying to solve the "Indian problem" on the Great Plains with a three-pronged approach: negotiation, starvation, and warfare. Open war on its own had not been going too well. The Plains Indians had won decisive victories and forced the government to the treaty table. In 1868 the Lakota secured a large homeland on the Great Sioux Reservation in southwestern South Dakota and northern Nebraska.

---

[1] Throughout this book, I use the word "Indian" to refer to Indigenous people within the United States. I also use "Indigenous," "Native," and "American Indian." These terms have come in and out of favor over the years, and different tribes, not to mention different people, have different preferences. My own choices of usage are governed by a desire for economy, speed, flow, and verisimilitude. A good rule of thumb for outsiders: ask the Native people you're talking to what they prefer.

Then gold was discovered in the Black Hills of South Dakota. The Lakota tried to enforce the terms of the 1868 treaty and throw out the gold-seekers who rushed in. Their attempts led, directly, to the Battle of the Little Bighorn, where George Armstrong Custer and the Seventh Cavalry were wiped out on June 25, 1876. During the final hours of the battle, the Lakota and Cheyenne dismounted, put away their guns, and killed the remaining cavalry with their war clubs and tomahawks in a ritual slaughter. Some Dakota women, armed with buffalo[2] jawbones, were given the honor of dispatching the soldiers with a sharp blow behind the ear.

After that defeat, the U.S. government switched tactics. Instead of confronting the Indians head-on, it encouraged widespread encroachment by settlers, reneged on treaty promises of food and clothing, and funded the wholesale destruction of the once vast buffalo herds of the Plains. By the late 1870s, an estimated five thousand bison were being killed per day.

Without the bison, the Lakota and other Plains tribes could not hope to survive, at least not as they had been surviving. Their reservations might have been designed as prisons, but now they became places of refuge. With the vast buffalo herds gone and a growing white population of ranchers, hunters, railroad workers, prospectors, homesteaders, and soldiers hemming them in, the Plains Indians did what many disenfranchised people have done when threatened on all sides: they turned to God. The Indians, however, turned to God in the form of the Ghost Dance.

The Ghost Dance religion started among the Paiute in Nevada. It promised a payoff: if Indians lived lives of harmony, worked hard, and danced the Ghost Dance, they would find peace on earth and be reunited with the spirits of their ancestors in the afterlife.

As the religion spread from Nevada, it changed. The Lakota believed

---

[2] Throughout this book, I sometimes go with the common usage of *buffalo* to refer to the American bison (as the animal is known scientifically).

if they did the Ghost Dance the right way and lived by its rules, they would find peace in this world and the next *and* all the white people would be washed away. If Indians returned to their traditional ways of life and forms of religious observance, the natural world would be restored and returned to them.

The Ghost Dance movement brought Indians together in large numbers. This greatly alarmed the U.S. government, which redoubled its ongoing efforts to disrupt Indian lives and break up Indian families. It dismantled the Great Sioux Reservation into five smaller reservations, including Standing Rock and Pine Ridge. The Ghost Dance religion was banned, and government troops near the Pine Ridge Reservation were increased.

Trouble came. In December 1890, Sitting Bull, who had led his people to victories against the U.S. military and who had helped wipe out Custer's Seventh Cavalry at the Little Bighorn, was arrested on the Standing Rock Reservation. Authorities feared that the famous Hunkpapa Lakota chief would use his considerable influence to promote the Ghost Dance. In a scuffle during the arrest, Sitting Bull was shot and killed by Indian police officers who had been sent in by the reservation's Indian agent, a white U.S. government official. Hearing this news, Spotted Elk (also known as Chief Big Foot) grew afraid for his life and the life of his Lakota band, which also lived at Standing Rock. Spotted Elk and 350 followers left the reservation. They headed for the sanctuary of Pine Ridge.

En route, Spotted Elk and his band were intercepted by a detachment of the Seventh Cavalry and escorted five miles to a camping spot on Wounded Knee Creek. It was bitterly cold. Before dawn the next day, the rest of the Seventh showed up and set up four rapid-fire cannons around the Indians. The soldiers searched the camp and rounded up thirty-eight weapons. One of the young Lakota men got upset and urged others not to give up their guns so easily; a fight broke out.

What happened next is unclear. Some reported that the Indians opened fire on the government soldiers. Others said that a deaf elder didn't understand the command to give up his rifle; a soldier grabbed the gun to take it away and it went off. Then five young warriors shrugged off their blankets and exposed concealed rifles. They shot at the soldiers. The soldiers opened fire on the entire camp with their rifles and the cannons. The Indian men put up a desperate resistance but were mowed down. Spotted Elk was killed. The rain of fire from U.S. troops also claimed the lives of many of the soldiers, in one of the deadliest incidents of friendly fire in U.S. military history.

The Lakota women and children took off running down the frozen creek bed. The soldiers mounted their horses, chased them down, and killed them. The fighting lasted an hour, and when it was over, more than 150 Lakota lay dead or dying in the snow. The actual number of dead is still in dispute, with some putting the number at over three hundred. More than half were women and children. A cavalry general toured the scene of the carnage after a three-day blizzard had shrouded the dead in snow. He was shocked by what he saw. "Helpless children and women with babes in their arms had been chased as far as two miles . . . Judging by the slaughter on the battlefield, it was suggested that the soldiers simply went berserk. For who could explain such a merciless disregard for life?"

The massacre at Wounded Knee Creek was covered by more than twenty newspapers. Response to the killings represented something more than sympathy for Indians on the one hand, and bitter and bloody American progress on the other. Rather, both sides saw the massacre as the end not just of the Indians who had died but of "the Indian," period. The frontier was closed, Indians were confined to reservations. The clash of civilizations seemed to have wound down. The myths and meaning of America had been firmly established. Perhaps this is why the massacre at Wounded Knee became so emblematic. It neatly symbolized the accepted version of reality: an Indian past and an American present and future.

This version of history remained largely unquestioned through World War I, the Great Depression, World War II, and the 1950s. Then came the 1960s: as the fight for civil rights heated up, so did protests against the American involvement in the Vietnam War. Activists grew concerned about the environment and the toxic effects of industrialization and consumerism. Some people questioned whether mainstream culture was the *only* culture; interest in a counterculture spread—and the story of "the Indian" surfaced with new intensity in the American consciousness. This awareness was popularized by a highly influential book.

Published in 1970, eighty years after the massacre, *Bury My Heart at Wounded Knee: An Indian History of the American West* appeared as news reports of Indian activism were playing out on TV screens across the country, and at a time when many Americans were looking for some other way of being. The book, written by Dee Brown, a white academic librarian, was an enormous success. To date it has sold more than four million copies, and has been published in seventeen languages. It has never gone out of print.

The "greatest concentration of recorded experience and observation" of Indian lives and history, wrote Brown in the opening pages, "came out of the thirty-year span between 1860 and 1890 . . . It was an incredible era of violence, greed, audacity, sentimentality, undirected exuberance, and an almost reverential attitude toward the ideal of personal freedom for those who already had it. During that time the culture and civilization of the American Indian was destroyed." Beneath Brown's effort to speak truth to power, however, he relied on and revived the same old sad story of the "dead Indian." Our history and our continued existence came down to a list of the tragedies we had somehow outlived without really living. As for present-day Native life,

Brown wrote only: "If the readers of this book should ever chance to see the poverty, the hopelessness, and the squalor of a modern Indian reservation, they may find it possible to truly understand the reasons why."

I remember, vividly, reading that passage while in college in 1991, and I was doubly dismayed by Brown's telling. I was far from home, on a distant coast. I was homesick—for the Minnesota Northwoods, for my Ojibwe reservation, for the only place on earth I truly loved. I was also dismayed because I felt so insignificant in the face of the authority and power with which Brown explained us Indians to the world. He had hundreds of years of history behind him, the most powerful cultural myths of America as evidence, and a command of English I could only dream of. All I had was the small hot point of hope that I mattered, that where I was from mattered, and that someday I would be able to explain—to myself and to others—why.

This book is a counternarrative to the story that has been told about us, but it is something more as well: it is an attempt to confront the ways we Indians ourselves understand our place in the world. We carry within us stories of our origins, and ideas about what our families, clans, and communities mean. But too often we agree with the ways in which we are read by outsiders. Despite how much I missed home and how much I had come to love where I was from, old habits of thought were hard to shake: for too many years I understood my home, the Leech Lake Reservation, only as a place of abject suffering, a "nowhere place" where nothing happened and good ideas went to die. I saw it as *in* America but not *of* America. I saw myself and my tribe as a ruined people whose greatness lay behind us.

The evidence seemed to be all around me. A brilliant uncle (*the smartest man I ever knew*, said my mother) was perpetually stoned, and eventually died of an overdose. Another uncle was shot twice in the chest after firing an arrow through the open window of a police cruiser. A cousin was hit by an RV, and another cousin was so thoroughly shot up by the cops that his body leaked through the unstopped holes when

I was asked to shift it in the coffin at his funeral. Our Ojibwe tribal chairman was investigated for robbing our casino at gunpoint. The first Indian elected to the state legislature was convicted of theft and fraud. All this drama and trauma was refracted by the attitudes I heard expressed around me. On a field trip to the state capitol during a protest, my high school band teacher muttered to the class that all Indians were on welfare and we should go back to Canada where we came from. My best friend's mother told him that I'd gotten into Princeton University and he hadn't because I was Indian. A high school friend told me that her parents, who owned property in a nearby town, wouldn't rent to Indians because we were dirty and dangerous. I protested weakly that *I* wasn't dirty, *I* wasn't dangerous. *Oh, well, you're not* really *Indian*, she said. To be "really" Indian, evidently, was to be those things.

By the time I graduated from high school, I was ready to leave the reservation and never come back. In my mind, nothing good came from my Indian life. I was tired of the poverty and the dusty roads that no one saw fit to pave. I was sick of the late-night calls and the trips to the hospital to witness the damage we were doing to ourselves. I looked ahead to the green, leafy excellence of Princeton. Nothing was clearer to me than the conviction that my past lay behind me, on the reservation, and the future awaited me beyond our borders, in America. So I left.

As soon as I was gone, I missed it. I missed what I hadn't known was my Indian life, our collective Indian life. I missed the Mississippi River, which flows through my reservation as a tiny thing, little more than a stream I could walk across. I missed the ways the pine tree scratched the window screens at night. I missed my uncle Davey's antics, and I missed his love and I missed how he loved me: completely, without judgment, without measure, without censure. I missed the Memorial Day gatherings at the cemetery with my aunt and uncles and cousins, the sandwiches of canned ham mixed with Miracle Whip and relish on white dinner rolls. The yearning for home was rooted in nostalgia, but I was also trying to grow beyond it, toward a place approaching true knowledge.

As kids do when they leave home, I began to see my parents more clearly. I saw how my mother, born into the meanest of circumstances, had gone to nursing school and then to law school and then—quietly, without self-promotion—had returned to the reservation to practice. Indians had been appearing in court for centuries, but for most of my mother's clients, it was the first time they had shown up with an Indian lawyer by their side, arguing for dignity, for fairness, for justice.

I saw, too, how my father—who was Jewish and had just barely survived the Holocaust—had adopted the Leech Lake Reservation as his home and our causes as his own. I asked him how he had come to feel so comfortable on the reservation. *I was a refugee, I was an outsider. I was told throughout my life I wasn't enough, I wasn't good enough, I didn't belong. When I came here, I felt at home. I felt like people understood me.* My father taught high school on our Ojibwe reservation and then worked for the tribe. One summer I picked up a woman I was dating from her aunt's house on the reservation. She told me her aunt wanted me to say hi to my father for her. Evidently, on Saturday afternoons back in the 1950s, my father would drive to the small village where the aunt lived. He picked up all the Indian kids hanging out there, dropped them off in a larger town where there was more for them to do, then picked them up later when he was done in town and drove them home. *He was the only white man who even thought about us, and went out of his way to give us something to do, something to look forward to*, the aunt said.

I started in my own haphazard way to think about our collective Indian past and present, and how the story of it was told. I decided on anthropology as my undergraduate major. In the 1980s and 1990s, anthropology was reckoning with its colonial past and its past practices, especially with regard to Indigenous people around the world. Anthropology was also a great place to have arguments, and for better or worse, I loved having arguments.

Around that time, I also launched my life as a fiction writer. I detested the publishing industry's pressure to make multicultural fiction engage in cultural show-and-tell. As a result, I wrote novels where the characters never, ever talked about their spirituality or culture; where nary a feather was to be found. Instead, I tried (and often failed) to create complex, fully realized characters. I went on to get my PhD in anthropology, publish a few novels, and write a nonfiction book about reservation life. It was a hybrid like me: part history, part reportage, part memoir.

Through it all, I came to see we Indians often get ourselves wrong. My lack of regard for my own origins and those of my community began to trouble me, and troubles me still. If I could not see myself and my homelands more expansively, more intimately, more deeply than many non-Indians do, then how could I hope that the future of my people would be any different from the story of "the Indian" we've always been told and keep telling? Many of us have lived bitter and difficult lives, and we have brought the ghost of our modern afterlife inside ourselves, where it sits judging us, shaping us, putting its fingers over our eyes so that all we can see, all we can feel, is that we were once great people but are great no more, and that we are no longer capable of greatness. We may feel that Dee Brown was right: what we have now is not a civilization, not a culture, not even real selves, but rather a collection of conditions—poverty, squalor, hopelessness—and that these are the conditions in which we live, and the state of our spirit.

This is a narrative that must be laid to rest.

I conceived of a book with a new Indian story, the untold story of the past 130 years. It would reveal the broader and deeper currents of Indian life that have too long been obscured. It would explore the opposite thesis of *Bury My Heart at Wounded Knee*: The year 1890 was *not* the end of us, our cultures, our civilizations. It was a cruel, low, painful point, yes—maybe even the lowest point since Europeans arrived in the so-called New World—but a low point from which much of modern Indian and American life has emerged.

To tell that story, I embarked on three journeys. I traveled back into our prehistory and up through the early days of colonialism in North America. I also spent the better part of four years traveling the country—Montana, Washington state, New Mexico, Arizona, California, New York, Florida, and everywhere in between. And as I traveled to Indian homelands across the country, researching and writing about our long history, I listened to Indians telling me what they and their people had experienced, what they had done, what their lives meant to them. I did my best to pair their beautiful lives and beautiful struggles with the recorded past, to link them to the chain of cause and effect, action and response, thought and deed, that is our collective living history. Last, I also continued my inward journey, and included it here. I could not in good conscience ask other Indian people to expose themselves in service to my project, to *trust* me, if I didn't take the same risks. I can't shake the knowledge—and this is perhaps the only place where my anthropological training and my culture actually meet and agree—that it is impossible to separate the teller from the telling. Whatever I say about Indian lives is a way of saying something about myself.

This book is a result of those journeys. As such, it is not a catalog of broken treaties, massacres, and names and dates, of moments when things might have turned out differently. There are, of course, treaties and battles and names and dates. It's a history book, after all. But it also traces the stories of ordinary Indian people whose lives remind us of the richness and diversity of Indian life today and whose words show us the complexity with which we Indians understand our own past, present, and future. It's a work of history, but it also includes journalism and reportage, and the deeply personal and deeply felt stories of Indians across the country, mine among them.

This book is written out of the simple, fierce conviction that our Indian cultures are not dead and our civilizations have not been destroyed. It is written with the understanding that our present tense is evolving as rapidly and creatively as everyone else's.

In a sense, writing this book is a selfish project. I want—I need—to see Indian life as more than a legacy of loss and pain, because I want to pass on to my beautiful children a rich heritage and an embracing vision of who we were and who we are. But I have not created alternative, falsely hopeful realities to make up for a traumatic past or to imagine a better future.

Looking beyond the blinders of the "dead Indian" story means reckoning with relentless attacks on our sovereignty and the suffering that has created. But it also reveals the ingenious and resourceful counterattacks we have mounted over the decades: the resistance to the lives the government would have us live; the many varied paths Indians forged where old ones were closed off or obscured.

This book is about the history we've made and the tools with which we've made it. Indians are not little ghosts in living color, stippling the landscape of the past and popping up in the present only to warn contemporary Americans to behave (to do better by the environment) or to provide examples of superior spirituality.

To treat the lives lost on that cold South Dakota day in 1890 as merely symbolic is to disrespect those lives. It is also to disrespect the more than two hundred Lakota who survived Wounded Knee and lived on—to experience the pain of loss, yes, but much else as well. They survived to live and grow, to get married and have babies. They survived to hold on to their Lakota ways or to convert to Christianity. They survived to settle on the reservation and, later, to move to cities. They survived to go to school and to college and to work. They survived to make mistakes and recover from them. They survived to make history, to make meaning, to make *life*. This book is about them. And it is about the Indians of other communities and tribes around the country, who survived their own holocausts and went on to make their own lives and their own histories, and in so doing, to make and remake the story of America itself.

FATAL ENCOUNTERS
10,000 BCE–1890

◈◆◈◆◈◆◈◆◈◆◈

WHEN MY BROTHER AND I talk, joke, or sing in Ojibwe, we are speaking in a language thousands of years old, once used by hundreds of thousands of people in America, and still spoken by many. When I walk through Bena, our ancestral village on the Leech Lake Reservation in Minnesota, or along the trails on the banks of the Mississippi River by my house, I am following the tracks laid down by my ancestors. The story of Native peoples and our very existence are older than anything else in this country. But ours has long been an invisible American history.

But the story of Native folk I learned in school always began *in 1492 when Columbus sailed the ocean blue*. Like many origin myths, this is a fiction. So is the idea that the European settlement of North America, and the corresponding decimation of Indian tribes and cultures, was sudden and inevitable. It was neither. Christopher Columbus sailed west for money. The colonists came for money and they stayed for money. Indigenous peoples—the lords of the North American continent, the controllers of all its shores and interior—resisted, helped, hindered, and constantly negotiated the changes brought by white people.

From the 1490s through the 1590s, there was a wave of European exploration, followed by many attempts at colonization in North America. These early attempts failed for a number of reasons: disease, starvation, attack by Indigenous tribes, and attacks from other colonial powers. Many of the early European settlements in North America floundered because they were looking for a quick buck: gold, people to enslave and export. Others succeeded when they cultivated the slow buck: cotton, tobacco, timber, furs, gems, and gold and silver from mines worked by enslaved people.

By the beginning of the seventeenth century, the four dominant European colonizing powers had roughly divided the continent: The Spanish had been relegated to Mexico and parts of what is today the American South. The English controlled the main section of the Eastern Seaboard. The Dutch were clinging to parts of New York and New Jersey. And the French had secured much of what is now eastern Canada.

All the colonial powers used violence, strategic dependency, inter-marriage, and religious conversion to create and maintain control. They also wielded another powerful weapon: language. European coloniz-ers created a narrative that said they deserved to stake claim to lands they "discovered." They justified that story by filling it in with details of Indian aggression, lawlessness, laziness, and paganism. The Euro-peans ignored the true story in front of them: that they had arrived in a vast land with a varied cultural landscape that had been evolving for thousands of years.

The earliest verified archaeological evidence of the settlement of North America comes from two distinct sites, both excavated in the 1970s: the Meadowcroft Rockshelter, near Pittsburgh, Pennsylva-nia, and Monte Verde in Chile. Tools, bones, campsites, and personal effects were recovered at Meadowcroft, along with evidence of early farming of squash, corn, and beans. The Monte Verde site is a rare find: a relatively complete village preserved by a peat bog. Both sites may stretch back nineteen thousand years. Together they show that there were people in North America well before the Bering land bridge formed about ten thousand years ago. This throws into dispute the theory that North America was settled primarily by Asiatic wanderers over the bridge.

Most Indians do not see themselves as merely the first in a long series of arrivals to North America; they see themselves as Indigenous.

Indian stories about our own origins almost all claim we came into being in our native lands. Belief in our Indigenous origin is crucial to understanding modern Indian realities. The argument that Indians are just one group of travelers with no greater stake than any other migrating people clashes with Indians' cultural understanding that we have always been here and that our control over our place in this world has been deeply and unjustly eroded.

North America is uniformly seen as an Indian homeland that has shaped and been shaped by the Indians living there then and now. Various empires and nation-states—Spanish, British, French, Dutch, and, later, American—have crawled over these homelands, mapping and claiming as they went. But these maps and conquests have not eradicated the fact that immigrants built their homes and villages and towns and cities *on top of* Indian homelands. History, technologies, and people with distinct, deep concepts of themselves and their place in the world were already here.

THE SOUTHEAST

The Europeans who first arrived on the Atlantic coast landed on an incredibly fertile homeland settled by hundreds of tribes. It seems that, in this period in North America, coastal Indians lived in small villages of about 150 people. They were fairly mobile, spending part of the year on the coast, part farther inland, and getting most of their calories from fish, game, and harvested nuts and berries. Archaeological evidence suggests that between 2500 and 2000 BCE, tribal groups began making clay pots, which indicate food surplus, a need for storage, and a more sedentary lifestyle. (In anthropology, *sedentary* means living in one place for a long time.) Some villages seem to have been fortified by wooden palisades. Tribes did fight and kill one another.

The Ais, Alafay, Amacano, Apalachee, Bomto, Calusa, Chatot, Chine, Guale, Jororo, Luca, Mayaca, Mayaimi, Mocoso, Pacara, Pensacola,

Pohoy, Surruque, Tequesta, Timicua, and Viscayno, to name but a few, had been living in what is now Florida for at least twelve thousand years before Ponce de León arrived there in 1513 to explore and settle the region on behalf of the Spanish monarchy.

Spanish colonization was driven first by the search for treasure, then by a quest for people to enslave, and later by religious missionary zeal. Almost every Spanish attempt at exploration and colonization was attacked and impeded by the tribes encountered. In the sixteenth century, the Spanish finally succeeded in establishing missions in Florida and Georgia. Indians were conscripted and enslaved. They were forced to work, live, and die in deplorable, disease-ridden conditions.

Disease, slavery, starvation, disruption: what happened in Florida would be repeated over much of the Indian homeland of North America. As a consequence, previously distinct cultures and peoples were mixed together, forming new tribal identities. This occurred in what would become the states of Florida, Georgia, South and North Carolina, Kentucky, and Tennessee. By the end of the Revolutionary War era, what had once been the homeland of hundreds of distinct tribes was now in the control of a few "supertribes," such as the Seminole, Creek, Muscogee, Chickasaw, and Cherokee.

The colonization of North America is often seen as a struggle between Indians and settlers. But conflict occurred along multiple fronts. Tribes banded together with other tribes and fought yet others. Colonial powers made alliances, pitting Indian against Indian and against other colonial powers. Different branches of the U.S. federal government joined in. Rulings from John Marshall's Supreme Court favored tribes against states. President Andrew Jackson's executive branch took an opposite stance and supported states against tribes. Some tribes committed genocide against their neighbors. But while the conflicts in the Southeast weren't necessarily linear, the trajectory was more or less clear: tribes were diminished through disease and warfare. Two moments stand out in the sordid history of the

American Southeast—Indian removal and the Seminole Wars.

Founding Father Thomas Jefferson saw the few supertribes remaining in the southeast as impediments to the American nation. He wrote that it was important "to encourage them to abandon hunting, to apply to the raising [of] stock, to agriculture and domestic manufactures, and thereby prove to themselves that less land and labor will maintain them in this, better than in their former mode of living." The problem was that by the beginning of the eighteenth century, the Indians were already doing just that in small villages and settlements where they grew yams, beans, corn, and squash. They had seats of government and centers of power. After the colonists arrived, they began cultivating cotton and other export crops, which they farmed plantation style. Many Cherokee and other tribal people bought and enslaved Black people, as did Jefferson himself.

In 1802 Georgia had agreed to give up claims to land in what would become Alabama and Mississippi if the federal government would remove or reduce the Indians in Georgia. Basically, Georgia would give up land outside the state in order to secure more land within its borders. After Jackson assumed the presidency in 1829, he was happy to oblige.

The Cherokee invoked the tribes' long control over their land as well as the treaties, alliances, and decrees that stipulated that only the federal government had the ability to negotiate with tribes. Cherokee chief John Ross brought his people's case to the U.S. Supreme Court. In a series of rulings known as the Marshall Trilogy, the court affirmed the rights of the Cherokee and ruled the removal of Indians unlawful. It was revolutionary that the Supreme Court sided with Native people against federal policy and the states in the Southeast. President Andrew Jackson did it anyway. Between 1830 and 1850 more than 125,000 Indians of the Southeast were forcibly removed to territory west of the Mississippi, mostly on foot and in wintertime. At least thirty-five hundred Creek, five thousand Cherokee, and many from other tribes died along the way. Many more starved to death when they reached their new lands.

The Seminole were also, in part, subject to removal. They were an amalgam of Creek Choctaw, who had fled south from Georgia and Alabama during the eighteenth century and settled in northern Florida. The Seminole learned how to draw sustenance from Florida's swamps and lowlands, and they traded deer hides for weapons, metal, and other goods.

In 1818 Andrew Jackson (not yet president) mounted a military campaign in Florida to put down the Seminole, recover enslaved runaways, and shake out the Spanish. This was the First Seminole War. When it was over, the United States secured all of northern Florida, some twenty-eight million acres. The 1823 Treaty of Moultrie Creek then moved the Seminoles into a four-million-acre reservation on poor land in central Florida. Another fraudulent treaty, the Treaty of Payne's Landing (1832), was signed by a few non-representative "chiefs," and promised the

Seminole chief Osceola, a young warrior who fiercely opposed government attempts to direct the destiny of his tribe, vowed, "I will make the white man red with blood and then blacken him in the sun and rain, where the wolf shall smell his bones and the vulture live upon his flesh." This 1838 print is the work of George Caitlin, an American artist noted for his portraits of Native Americans.

Seminole land west of the Mississippi. In 1835 the government moved in to enforce that treaty. They were met with resistance.

On December 28, 1835, an American army column moved into Seminole territory near Fort Brooke, but the irascible Chief Osceola and his warriors were waiting for them. The Seminole rose from the tall grass on either side of the trail and opened fire. After the first volley, half the soldiers lay dead or dying. In the ensuing months, the Seminole attacked and burned down twenty-one plantations, along with army forts and even the Cape Florida lighthouse. It took the U.S. government a long time to bring the violence with the Seminole to a close. Even after the arrest of Osceola, the Seminole continued to attack and then melt away. The army could not fight effectively in the Florida swamps. But attrition finally had its way, and the wars wound down in 1842 at a cost of nearly sixty million dollars for the second war alone. The captured Seminole were moved west to Indian Territory, though many remained.

In the 1850s, the Seminole once again attacked settlers moving onto their land. The Third Seminole War ensued and violence swept Florida. Many of the Indian combatants were removed west and on May 8, 1858, the United States declared the war was over. The Seminole made no such pronouncement. The remaining Indians, numbering fewer than a thousand, resumed life in the backcountry and swamps of Florida, and there they remained, never having surrendered and never having been defeated. The Southeast was never entirely freed of Indians. They lived on in the swamps of Florida, the hills of southern Appalachia, the bayous of Alabama and Louisiana.

THE NORTHEAST

The prehistoric tribes of the American Northeast stretched from Virginia all the way up to the Saint Lawrence River and were as diverse as their homeland. The tribes seem to have kept close to the shores and life appears to have been particularly good for them from about 3000 BCE to 700 BCE. The ocean provided seals and swordfish and cod. The innumerable rivers and streams ran with smelt, alewife, salmon, and herring. The warming of the climate helped create vast shellfish beds from Manhattan Island north to Maine. Dependable calories caused a population boom, which in turn supported cultural growth. Villages grew in size. Funeral rites and burials became more elaborate. By about 1000 BCE, pottery was widespread.

Around 700 BCE, the climate cooled again, calories became scarce, and the prehistoric tribes fractured into smaller groups that seem to have relied more on inland hunting. During this era, maize (corn) began its slow crawl north as a domesticated food source from Mexico. It reached the Northeast and was in robust production by 1200 CE. By the time of contact with European fishing fleets in the early sixteenth century, there was a distinct division between what had become the inland tribes of the Iroquois Confederacy and the collection of Algon-quian tribes scattered along the Atlantic coast.

The coastal Algonquian-speaking tribes included the Powhatan, Nanticoke, Pennacook, Massachuset, Mohegan, Delaware, Mahican, Abenake, Mi'kmaq, Pequot, Wampanoag, and scores of other small tribes. Fishing, foraging, and hunting large game farther from shore encouraged the growth of numerous small seasonal villages of no more than a few hundred, organized by clan. The tribes spent the sum-mer catching birds and harvesting berries and nuts near the sea. In the fall, they moved to other temporary villages better situated to net spawning fish. In the winter, they congregated in larger villages and lived in multifamily longhouses to conserve heat, water, and mate-rial for shelter. Their slash-and-burn methods dictated moving to new planting grounds every few years.

The five original tribes of the Iroquois Confederacy—the Cayuga, Oneida, Seneca, Onondaga, and Mohawk—lived in the region between the eastern Great Lakes and the Appalachian Mountains. By the end of the Woodland period (around 1100 CE), the separate Iroquoian tribes of the area had fought one another often for hunting and fishing grounds. Then corn arrived. This crop required intensive cultivation and a kind of seasonal stability not possible with constant, even if low-grade, conflict. The Iroquois built protected villages inland, surrounded by cornfields and acres of squash and beans. By the time of European contact, the Onondaga, Mohawk, Seneca, Oneida, and Cayuga were living this way.

First contact in the Northeast is often presented as the story of Pilgrims arriving in Plymouth, Massachusetts, in November 1620, while the Indigenous Wampanoag stood by and watched the *Mayflower*'s sails grow nearer. In reality, many tribes had intricate social networks that followed well-established trade routes and waterways. It's likely that northeastern Indians had heard of the English, French, Spanish, and Portuguese fishing and exploration fleets, which had started arriving in the early 1500s, long before they encountered Europeans themselves: coastal tribes had been trading with them for decades. The first import to the New World was surely rumor.

More disastrously, European diseases often arrived well in advance of Europeans and ravaged Indian populations even more ruthlessly, especially when paired with slavery. In 1592, before the Seneca had direct and prolonged contact with Europeans, a measles epidemic spread among the tribe, killing many thousands within a decade. The Pequot, Wampanoag, and other New England tribes were laid low by an epidemic of leptospirosis, a bacterial disease. Between 1616 and 1619, as much as 90 percent of the New England tribes were wiped out. Rather than welcoming the *Mayflower* with open arms, precious few Indians remained alive on the Eastern Seaboard to lift their arms at all.

As the Pilgrims and subsequent settlers flooded into New England, the tribes (and some of the settlers) tried to forge alliances and understandings that would benefit them all. These efforts failed. In the 1630s, when Indian populations had rebounded to some extent, the Pequot launched an all-out war. It was crushed by the Pilgrims, and the remaining Pequot were sold into slavery. The Pequot were exterminated from the land and from memory: uttering the tribe's very name was forbidden. By 1890 all Indian lands in coastal New England had long since been taken over. Most remaining Indians had been assimilated into other tribes, relocated, or killed. Most, but not all. Wampanoag, Mashantucket, Mi'kmaq, Abenake, and others made peace and endured. As in the Southeast, total war had not yielded total extermination. Indians remained.

THE GREAT LAKES AND OHIO RIVER VALLEY

The Great Lakes region includes the Ohio River valley, the area around the lakes themselves, and the Mississippi basin up to the edge of the Great Plains.

The Great Lakes are the confluence of a far-reaching network of waterways. This network was a hub for Indians as far back as twelve thousand years ago. By the beginning of the Woodland period in 500 BCE, knowledge spread via a vast cultural and technological network that followed the water. The use of the bow and arrow, pottery, plant domestication, architecture, and burial practices flowed from the Gulf of Mexico all the way up to north of Lake Ontario and back again. In the Middle Woodland period, what is commonly known as the Hopewell culture arose. The Hopewell cultures typically made their homes in or near river areas that seasonally replenished rich planting grounds, aquatic food sources, and waterfowl. Villages could reach significant size and were surrounded by mounds that were one of the hallmarks of the culture. The Hopewell Ceremonial Earthworks near Chillicothe, Ohio, measures 1,254 feet long and connects thirty-eight mounds within an earthen rectangle measuring more than one hundred acres.

Most, but not all, mounds contained burials of staggering richness. The deceased were placed inside the shelter and buried with an abundance of trade goods. In Ohio some mounds were found to contain thousands of freshwater pearls, mica, tortoise shells, Knife River flint from North Dakota, and conch from Mexico. One burial mound at the Mound City site in Ross County, Ohio, contained more than two hundred intricately carved smoking pipes. The finds indicate that these communities were both well-off and well-connected.

Around 500 CE, the Hopewell culture disappeared. No one knows why, exactly. Populations may have declined because of war, a shortage of game as the climate grew colder, or overhunting as weapons improved. During the later Mississippian period (1100 to 1541 CE), there was a shift from gathering to intensive agriculture. Large villages replaced small seasonal camps, and there is evidence of the bow, small projectile points, and pottery. The largest Mississippian village was surely Cahokia, situated at the confluence of the Mississippi and Missouri Rivers near present-day St. Louis. At its peak around 1050–1250 CE, Cahokia spread over five square miles; its population is estimated at about thirty thousand. Whatever the cause, by the time Europeans arrived in the region in the mid–seventeenth century, Cahokia and similar settlements had been long abandoned.

The Iroquois Confederacy maintained a stranglehold on travel into the interior and trade via the Great Lakes waterways. They had access to trade goods: metal traps, kettles, axes, blankets, guns, shot, powder, and knives. This gave them a decided military advantage. Between the end of the sixteenth century and the full blossoming of the fur trade, the Iroquois were engaged in endless wars with their tribal neighbors to the east. They also managed to negotiate lucrative trade deals with the French along the Saint Lawrence and the English down the Hudson River.

The Shawnee, Odawa, Potawatomi, Ojibwe, Meskwaki (Sac and

Fox), Menominee, Ho-Chunk (Winnebago), Osage, Miami, Dakota, Cree, Mandan, Arikara, Hidatsa, and Huron, to name but a few of the tribes to the west of the Iroquois, were numerous and powerful but were spread out over a vast territory. The Huron, whose population numbered twenty thousand to forty thousand or more, lived in large agricultural settlements on the north side of Lake Ontario and later near Georgian Bay. Most western Great Lakes tribes, however, were broken into small mobile villages of around 150 to 300 people, organized by kinship ties. These were the Indians of storybook legend: paddling through the woodlands in birchbark canoes and treading the hushed forests in moccasins. They were primarily hunter-gatherers, though they, too, grew corn, beans, and squash. More westerly tribes such as the Ojibwe had also begun harvesting and cultivating naturally occurring wild rice, a swampy aquatic plant in the oat family that provided a very stable and nutrient-rich food source.

In 1608 French explorer Samuel de Champlain pushed deeper into the Saint Lawrence and landed at what would become Quebec, Canada. The French hoped to take up dealing in furs coming out of the northland and thereby bypass the British to the east and the Spanish creeping up the Mississippi from the south. The French preferred to trade rather than to settle. Their new outpost of Quebec was deep in Indian country; to survive, it needed the help of its neighbors. The French began trading metal goods and guns with the Huron in exchange for their surplus corn. The Huron did not have access to furs themselves, but they maintained good trade relations with their Algonquian neighbors who did, the Odawa and Ojibwe.

As they say: location, location, location. At this time the Odawa and Ojibwe were located around Michilimackinac, which sat at the straits that separated Lake Michigan from Lake Huron. Control the straits and you controlled travel and trade for the majority of the continent. The location also suited the cultural needs of the unique Algonquian clan system. Children took the clan of their fathers and typically married out of their village into nearby villages and even other tribes. As a result, "family" pulled populations of mobile and separate tribes into durable and useful relationships over great distances. This well-woven network was a boon to trade and a backup during war.

Michilimackinac also offered access to reliable food sources. The microclimate of lakes in all directions allowed for corn production well north of its usual limit and supported an incredible diversity of plants and trees. The fall spawn of whitefish was said to be so intense that you could walk across the straits on the backs of the fish. Villages in this area tended to be seasonal and small. Groups of usually no more than 150 relatives mainly lived in single-family reed- or bark-covered wigwams. Populations shifted between winter hunting grounds, spring fishing sites, sugar bush, and summer berrying locations. In summer, when insects were at their worst, villages shifted to high bluffs or rocky promontories to catch the breeze. In winter, when temperatures dropped below zero, as in the Northeast, families often consolidated into larger wigwams or lodges to conserve resources and heat.

The Great Lakes Indians also had the benefit of timing: they were there at the beginning of the seventeenth century, when the fur trade exploded into the first—and for centuries the most important—global industry. Their strong position allowed the allied Algonquian tribes (Odawa, Ojibwe, Potawatomi) to play the French colonists off the British colonists. With such leverage, the fate of the Great Lakes Indians came to differ radically from that of Indians in tribal homelands everywhere else in North America. The population of the Odawa, Ojibwe, and Potawatomi quadrupled between 1600 and 1800. The land base of the northern Algonquians grew twenty times larger. Material culture, arts, and religion flourished.

After the Revolutionary War, the Americans remained the sole colonial force in the Great Lakes region. This was the worst possible outcome for the Indians there. By the mid-1800s the beaver was extinct east of the Mississippi. The lucrative fur trade drew to a close. The Americans were free to force Great Lakes tribes into punishing treaties that reduced their territories, confined many to reservations, relocated others to Indian Territory (in what is now Oklahoma), and further eroded Indian influence. But while it lasted, the power of the Great Lakes tribes was immense. Their cultural habit of negotiation, even from positions of relative powerlessness, persisted through the treaty period of 1830–1865. For this reason, as of 1891, Odawa, Potawatomi, Ho-Chunk (Winnebago), Oneida, Meskwaki (Sac and Fox), and Ojibwe tribes remained in their homelands around the Great Lakes in the same geographical range they had at the height of their power.

THE SOUTHWEST

The Southwest, an area bounded by the Rio Grande to the south and the Cimarron River in the north, is a collection of radically different landscapes that supported four major prehistoric cultures. It is still the homeland of a diversity of modern tribal people.

Around 2,300 years ago a small band of wanderers traveled north through the Sonoran Desert and settled on the Gila River, about thirty miles from modern-day Phoenix. They built single-family dwellings of branches and mud and promptly began digging canals that siphoned off the river a few miles upstream. The canals they dug would be in use for more than a thousand years. Within a couple hundred years, the entire flatlands between the Gila and Salt Rivers were laced with waterways, providing irrigation to upward of a hundred thousand acres. The Hohokam, as the people of this area were called, were master cultivators who grew corn, cotton, warty squash, and agave, as well as tepary, sieva, and jack beans.

By 750 CE, the Hohokam peoples had evolved cultures that crafted beautiful ornate pottery, laid out ball courts half the size of football fields, and held complex rituals in the high ceremonial structures they built. But just as quickly as it arose, the Hohokam culture fell. It is unclear why, but the Hohokam scattered into small bands and found new lands and new ways of life. According to oral tradition, they became the Tohono O'odham (People of the Desert) and the Akimel O'odham (People of the River) in the region that is now Arizona.

The prehistoric Mogollon culture of southern Arizona, New Mexico, and much of northern Mexico was another ancient society that emerged from the desert as foragers and hunters and transformed into farmers. The earliest Mogollon villages were a handful of pit houses, dwellings dug into the ground and roofed at ground level with beams, branches, and earth. Five hundred years later, the pit houses gave way to freestanding adobe structures; complex fortified cliff dwellings like those found at Cueva de las Ventanas followed later. But around 1400 CE, like the Hohokam, the Mogollon culture vanished, although the people certainly did not. The western Pueblo (Zuni and Acoma) as well as the Hopi trace their ancestry to the Mogollon.

The most dramatic of the prehistoric southwestern "supercultures" was probably that of the Násaazí (Anasazi), whose homeland was the Four Corners area, a rocky, canyon-scoured landscape of indescribable beauty in Arizona, New Mexico, Colorado, and Utah.

The Násaazí started out as hunter-gatherers, much like the Hohokam and Mogollon. They were introduced to domesticated crops from the south and began farming intensively. By 300 CE, the advent of pottery meant better storage for food and seeds; this in turn fueled an agricultural revolution. Modest pit houses gave way to what can be seen as a prehistoric middle-class way of life, with complex adobe structures of interconnected rooms accessed by ladders dropped down from roofs. At Chaco Canyon, Mesa Verde, and Bandelier, the Násaazí built "stone palaces." These great houses could hold more than five thousand people, though most of the space was used for food storage. The rooms were carved out of the rock under over-hanging cliffs, which offered protection from the weather and from enemies. These stone palaces, still solid to this day, were also incredibly advanced in terms of ecological engineering, with many of them facing south to take advantage of the sun's warmth.

Pueblo Bonito, a set of multistory dwellings in Chaco Canyon, New Mexico, has been deemed "one of the cleverest bits of passive solar architecture anywhere," with efficiency unsurpassed by modern methods.

Yet by 1400 CE or so, these beautiful and sophisticated dwellings were abandoned as well. The Násaazí people took what they could carry and migrated along the rivers. They formed the basis for present-day Pueblo peoples, including the Hopi, Cochiti, Zia, Santa Ana, San Felipe, Santo Domingo, and Taos.

Around 1200 CE, a wave of Athabascan newcomers arrived from what is now Alaska and British Columbia. They would change the Southwest forever. These small groups of Athabascan-speaking peoples were subarctic hunters and gatherers. As they traveled south over the course of a few centuries, they picked up various skills—pottery making, basket weaving, the use of the bow and arrow. By the time of their arrival in the Southwest between 1300 and 1500 CE, the

Hohokam, the Mogollon, and the Násaazí had disbanded and scattered. The Athabascan found ample room for settlement. In doing so, they came into being as distinct peoples. Those who called themselves Diné (Navajo) spread over the Four Corners area. The future Western Apache (Tonto, Chiricahua, White Mountain) set up on the western side of the Rio Grande. The Mescalero Apache settled between the Rio Grande and the southwestern edge of the Llano Estacado, which straddles northwestern Texas and eastern New Mexico. The Jicarilla Apache moved into northern New Mexico northeast of the Rio Grande. Other Athabascans swung farther east and adapted to the Plains. They would become the Kiowa and Lipan people.

In 1540 the Spanish, led by Francisco de Coronado, first ventured into New Mexico looking for gold. They found a well-populated, well-demarcated Indian homeland that had been settled for thousands of years by constantly evolving tribal groups, among them the Diné, Pueblo (who themselves included the Zuni, Acoma, Cochiti, Taos, and more), Pima, O'odham, and Apache. It should be emphasized again that wherever the Indian groups came from or whomever they descended from, they were defined more by their spiritual and cultural genesis in the lands that sustained them than by their wanderings. All Indian creation stories are significant, not just as folklore, and not just for Native people; such stories explain how Indian peoples and Indian homelands came to define each other. They also explain why the Spanish were met by Indians ready to protect those homelands.

In 1600 the first real attempts at settlement took place. Spanish colonists moved into areas bordering the Pueblos. This land was bare and dry, with hardly enough forage for sheep and horses, so the Spaniards began encroaching on Pueblo land. The Spanish Franciscans who were there to convert Indians didn't behave much better. They conscripted Indian labor and forced the Indians to build the missions while at the same time whipping Indian spiritual leaders, smashing idols and ceremonial objects, and banning dances and ceremonies as devil worship. This was the face of Spanish settlement: slavery, subjugation, and extermination.

For more than 150 years after first contact, the Pueblo, Pima, Diné, Apache, and (later) Tohono O'odham were buffeted by settlers, the Catholic Church, and the Spanish military—and increasingly by one another. The introduction of horses and sheep had a profound effect on intertribal relations. By the late seventeenth century, smaller tribes were being raided regularly by mounted Apache and Diné. Pueblo people in turn raided the Diné. Diné enslaved Hopi people. The Hopi did the same thing to other Indians. (Slavery was a damning practice in many cultures, but it would be Europeans who made it a global phenomenon.) For the first time wealth—in the form of cattle and sheep—could be captured and kept.

In 1675 the Spanish military, along with the Franciscans there, publicly whipped forty-seven Pueblo ceremonial leaders. Four of them died and the rest were imprisoned temporarily. The atrocity brought home to the Pueblo people, forcefully and finally, that the Spanish colonial presence in the Southwest was an assault on their way of life. Within days of their release, one of the leaders—Popé from San Juan Pueblo—returned home and began plotting in concert with other Pueblo. Dozens of communities with significant cultural differences united. On August 12, 1680, they struck.

Sweeping down from the north, the Pueblo attacked haciendas, churches, and settlements, killing men, women, and children. The Spanish settlers fled and then gathered in the walled plaza adjacent to the governor's mansion in Santa Fe. For the next few days, Pueblo Indians bombarded the plaza with arrows and rocks. They diverted the Santa Fe River to deprive the colonists of water. After a week or so, the Pueblo let the Spanish leave. They had accomplished what they wanted: the departure of the Spanish, who had to content themselves with pushing west to California. But other forces they had set in motion came into play.

The horse, which the Spanish had loosed upon the Plains and in the Southwest, changed life in those regions forever. Formerly scattered and relatively small bands of Apache, Comanche, and Ute mounted up. On horseback, they became mobile and grew richer. As a result, their tribes became larger. Now the region was subject to shifting alliances among tribes and even the Spanish.

Meanwhile, over to the west in Arizona, the Jesuits rather than the Franciscans made contact with and settled in among the Tohono O'odham and Pima. The Jesuits did not, as a rule, conscript Indians to build missions or torture them. Instead, they brought livestock and seed. They learned the Indian languages of the region and even seemed to enjoy the company of the people they were intent on converting. A kinder, gentler sort of assault, but an assault nonetheless.

In the mid-1800s the annexation of Texas and the outcome of the Mexican-American War ended Spanish and Mexican control of what we now think of as the Southwest. Per the terms of the Gadsden Purchase in 1853, the United States paid Mexico ten million dollars for nearly thirty thousand acres of what had been Mexican land but would become part of Arizona and New Mexico. And with the Americans came new land grabs and cultural assaults. Southwest tribes charted different courses, which led to different fates.

The Pueblos of the Rio Grande and the Hopi, for example, allied themselves with the United States against northern raiders, principally the Apache and Comanche. In 1848 the United States recognized Spanish land grants, including those made to the Pueblos. This meant that much of the Pueblo homelands remained intact. So, too, did their government and ceremonial structures, a combination of chiefhood, representative democracy, and clan systems.

The Diné suffered horribly. By the time the Americans began

administering the Southwest in 1848, the Diné and Apache were well horsed and numerous. They killed the village-bound Pueblo and mestizo (mixed race) New Mexicans regularly. For their part, the Pueblo and New Mexicans raided and killed the Diné and stole women and children to sell into slavery. When the Americans arrived, they began grazing their horses and livestock on the homelands of the Apache and Diné. They tried to force the Diné into harsh treaty arrangements, and in countless ways attempted to impose their American will on an already fraught cultural and political landscape. Negotiations with the Diné were also complicated by the apparent lack of a centralized government. Different clans and bands of Diné took their own counsel, and there was no single government, much less a spokesperson, for the thousands of Diné living within the borders of their four sacred mountains. In 1846 and again in 1849, the U.S. government sent military detachments into Diné country, bearing treaties. The treaties were signed both times, but they were not recognized by the Diné bands and leaders who were not present at the signings. The Diné largely resisted. The Americans pushed back by building forts in their homelands. The forts were attacked and burned.

In 1863 the military launched a series of campaigns against the Diné to force them into the jurisdiction of the United States. This effort was masterminded and led by frontiersman and Indian agent Kit Carson. Instead of direct conflict or battles, the U.S. Army systematically destroyed flocks and crops. (This would become a signature of U.S. military action in the Southwest and, later, on the Plains).

The Diné could perhaps flee and hide, but their corn, orchards, and sheep could not. Many Diné surrendered until only some holdouts were left, who made Canyon de Chelly their "last stand." They persisted there for weeks while Carson and his militia destroyed century-old peach trees and orchards in the canyon—a wound that, for the Diné, has not yet healed. Once these last fighters were captured, all the Diné were marched to Bosque Redondo, three hundred miles away in eastern New Mexico, for resettlement. Bosque Redondo had sustenance for only half the number of Indians who arrived. Wood for fuel and shelter was scant and water from its river caused intestinal disease. And it was peopled by Mescalero Apache, longtime enemies of the Diné. It was, in short, a hell. Smallpox arrived, taking even more lives. The relocation was, even according to the U.S. government, a failure. After five hard years, the Diné were able to return to a portion of their homelands to live a version of the lives they had lived before they were marched to "the suffering place."

By 1891, just after the massacre at Wounded Knee, life was hard in the Southwest. But there was life. The Pueblos had their village, ceremonial, and political structures. The Diné were back in their homelands, much the poorer but still in possession of the land within the four sacred mountains. The Apaches were largely where they had first made their homelands in Arizona and New Mexico, though their territory had shrunk drastically. The Tohono and Akimel O'odham, having passed between the warring Spanish on one side and the northern raiders on the other, remained in Arizona. With every wave of immigration—Spanish, Mexican, American—Indians still shaped the culture and fabric of the place. To be in the Southwest is to feel the continued lived presence of Native America to a degree not found in most other homelands in the United States.

CALIFORNIA

It is estimated that more Indians lived in California than in the rest of the United States combined when the Spanish first made contact in 1542. There were more than five hundred distinct tribes, who spoke three hundred dialects of one hundred different languages. The region was more densely settled than most places in Europe at the time. Indian people had called the place home for more than seventeen thousand years. Tribes themselves were small, rarely consisting of more than a hundred members. They made the most of the abundant aquatic food supply; further inland, game like elk, grizzly bear, deer, and bison was plentiful. Food was so available that once a tribe had carved out its own small territory, it rarely left. The Indians of California encouraged low-intensity fires, which in turn facilitated the loose rotation of crops such as nuts, berries, and yucca. Basketry and canoe making were both high art and utilitarian pursuits.

California was at the farthest point in North America from Europe, so change came, but not quickly. Easily exploitable wealth wasn't uncovered during the contact period. The mountains and desert of California's eastern topography isolated it from the rest of North America. California was a place apart.

It wasn't until the late eighteenth century that the Spanish began trying to colonize and settle California in earnest. They sailed around the Baja peninsula and trekked in overland from present-day Arizona. These attempts were disastrous. Early expeditions between 1769 and 1776 were chronically short of food. The next colonial expeditions, which included Jesuit priests, remedied this: they brought large herds of goats, cows, and sheep with them. European livestock quickly overgrazed the grasslands. Invasive species took root and displaced native plants. A million acres of land were seized for each one of the Spanish colonial religious settlements called missions. Twenty-one missions were constructed about thirty miles apart (a day's ride), along with forts or presidios. Doing so wreaked ecological and cultural disaster and caused famine for the people Indigenous to the area. Soon, Indians began flocking to the missions. They came not because they had heard the word of God or recognized the superiority of European ways, but in search of food and safety.

The missions meant forced conversions, conscripted labor, and a system of patronage and control. When California passed to Mexico as a possession in 1822, it disbanded and secularized the missions—now called ranchos—but essentially kept the system intact, administering it even more poorly than the Spanish had. For the Indians, there was no other place to go. The ranchos often controlled all of the Indians' former homelands. It is estimated that in 1770 nearly 133,000 Californian Indians lived in and around the missions. By 1832 that number was fourteen thousand. Their working conditions were so poor and disease so rampant that Indian deaths far exceeded births. Things only got worse after California passed into American control in 1847. And then gold was discovered at Sutter's Mill on January 24, 1848.

When the Gold Rush started, there were about nine thousand non-Indian people in California; in 1849 alone, ninety thousand new settlers arrived from all over the globe. The land, already stressed by overgrazing and overpopulation, was damaged further by sluicing, hydraulic mining, dredging, and other gold mining techniques.

The degree of violence in the "Golden State" can't be overemphasized. In order to open up more land for mining, tribes in the interior were systematically and brutally exterminated. The state of California appropriated funds between 1850 and 1860 to hire militia to hunt down and kill Indians.

The brutality that marked the Indian experience in California, from Spanish conquest on through the mission system, Mexican rule, and into the modern age of statehood, had an even more disastrous effect on the Indians of the region than it might have because of the size of most tribes there. Unlike, for example, the southwestern Diné, whose numbers were such that they could survive assaults and raids, and even a harsh relocation and repatriation, many of the Californian tribes were too small to make it. Hundreds of tribes existed in California at contact; as of the 1890 census fewer than fifty were counted. This number undoubtedly underrepresented the actual number of bands, reservations, mission groups, communities, and tribes. But it was a far cry from the beautiful, densely settled, multiethnic patchwork that had once been an Indian paradise.

THE PACIFIC NORTHWEST AND COLUMBIAN PLATEAU

Nearly constant rain encourages rampant growth, making the Pacific Northwest a primeval landscape, old and ever changing. It is also one of the richest ecosystems in the world, supplying abundant material for food and shelter.

It is clear that prehistoric Indian people lived along the Pacific Northwest coast and on the western side of the Rockies. The most ancient signs of coastal settlement date from around 8000 BCE. Farther inland, evidence is emerging from the Paisley Caves in Oregon that suggests robust settlement as early as 14,500 BCE.

Signs of pit houses from 1500 BCE have been found in British Columbia; axe-like stone adzes suggest that wooden structures were also built. Prehistoric weirs or fishing traps are abundant. Tools made from stone quarried far inland have been found on the coast, which suggests a thriving trade between coastal and highland Indians. As elsewhere in North America, rich food sources led to increased population, which in turn led to war. Skeletal remains of (mostly) young men killed by heavy blows to the upper body suggest warfare with clubs; traces of slat armor made of wood and hide have also been detected.

By 500 CE, the cultures of the Northwest Coast were in full swing. Tribal crafts were unmatched in beauty and expressiveness. Even the most utilitarian objects—bentwood baskets, boxes, and household items, hand tools, houses, and canoes—were works of art. Weapons of war were ornately carved of stone and whalebone.

The Europeans came late to this region and were greeted by tribal cultures unlike any others on the continent. In 1500 there was little to no agriculture in the Northwest; all the tribes were primarily hunter-gatherers. They stayed in one place for a long time in large villages centered around architectural traditions, such as cedar bark–covered longhouses and elaborate carvings, including the misnamed "totem poles." They lived in hierarchical societies. Lineages were recounted or sung in the manner of Norse sagas. The chiefs and their groups owned large houses and also held the right to use certain songs and display certain ceremonial objects. They also controlled the rights to local resources, such as fishing, berrying, and hunting grounds.

In the 1780s and early 1790s, the Spanish and English—aided by

In 1938 the U.S. Forest Service and the Civilian Conservation Corps worked with indigenous woodcarvers to repair and reproduce Tlingit and Haida "totem poles" and a clan house in what is now Totem Bight State Historical Park near Ketchikan, Alaska.

better technology and closer ports—made inroads in the region, often running into each other in sheltered bays. Ultimately, the Spanish were confined mainly to California, while the British had a secure hold on the Northwest from Oregon up to Alaska.

From 1792 to 1794, British naval officer George Vancouver traveled and mapped much of the area, from Puget Sound up through the Strait of Georgia and along the coast of what is now British Columbia. The tribes he would have met at the time were numerous, densely packed, and diverse. Along the coast there were the Tlingit, Nisga'a, Haida, Gitxsan, Tsimshian, Nuxalk, Heiltsuk, Wuikinuxv, Nuu-chah-nulth,

Kwakwaka'wakw, Makah, Coast Salish, Quileute, Willapa, Tillamook, and Chinook, among others. The tribes of the Northwest Plateau, enjoying a different climate and topography, were as numerous: the Kathlamet, Clackamas, Clatsop, Multnomah, Wasco-Wishram, Watlata, Flathead, Nespelem, Okanagan, Coeur d'Alene, Wenatchi, Nez Perce, Umatilla, Yakama, Klickitat, Cayuse, Kootenai, Nisqually, Kalapuya, and Modoc, among others. They were less dependent on marine life, though the salmon runs were important to them. When the horse spread across the Plains in the seventeenth century, tribes like the Nez Perce and Flathead adapted quickly and rode far after bison, elk, and deer.

The British were keen to buy furs and trade with coastal tribes. In exchange they offloaded smallpox and measles and other diseases that spread quickly in the communal longhouses and through the densely settled villages. By the time Meriwether Lewis and William Clark's Corps of Discovery reached the Pacific coast in November 1805, the Indians' numbers were greatly reduced. The Corps of Discovery introduced a host of new diseases, including chlamydia and syphilis. Coastal Indian populations that had been around two hundred thousand in 1774 had been reduced to fewer than forty thousand a century later.

Great Britain and the new United States struggled for power in the region. After 1818, the two countries agreed to administer the region jointly. The fur trade fell and the timber industry rose in its place. Tribal control of land was further eroded, yet never fully extinguished, by a treaty-making spree that occurred between 1840 and 1870.

In 1836 two American missionaries, Marcus and Narcissa Whitman, established a mission near present-day Walla Walla, Washington. The Whitmans built a gristmill and a school and introduced the concept of irrigation—all of this for the benefit of the Cayuse people, who had had no need for Jesus, grain cultivation, American-style education, or water. By 1843, more than a thousand settlers and prospectors roamed freely over Cayuse territory, plowing up the ground, and harvesting the salmon, game, and berries on which the Cayuse depended. Tensions rose. In 1847 a measles epidemic unleashed by the settlers killed more than half the Cayuse. The remainder of the tribe attacked the mission, destroying it and killing the Whitmans and some dozen other settlers. This sparked a war that raged for seven years in the region between the Cascades and the Rocky Mountains. All but done in, the Cayuse agreed to a punishing treaty in 1855, which created the Confederated Tribes of the Umatilla Indian Reservation. Still, the Cayuse War had forced the U.S. government to realize it could not afford to make war with tribes across the West. It was cheaper to strong-arm treaty signings and let the unending tide of settlers take care of the rest.

To the north, tribes, principally the Yakama, had entered into a series of treaties for a large tract of their lands. But treaties can be ratified only by the U.S. Senate. While the treaty worked its way through Congress, gold was discovered in Yakama territory, and prospectors flooded into the region. Hostilities erupted all over the territory followed by an all-out war. The Yakama War eventually ground to a halt in 1858 after a serious Indian defeat near Latah Creek. The resulting "peace" treaty moved the remaining Indians to reservations scattered throughout the territory.

THE GREAT BASIN

The Great Basin, a gorgeous, varied land of hot and cold deserts and junipers and Joshua trees, encompasses most of Nevada and parts of Utah, Oregon, Idaho, and California.

Humans have made their home in the Great Basin for about ten thousand years. Prehistoric Indians of the basin seem to have come from the south and clustered around waterways and lakes, where they killed camels, horses, mammoths, and bison along with migrating waterfowl—but seemingly not each other. They were a small group with a large range who were continually hunting and foraging for food. There must have been too few of them to fight over so little.

The prehistoric Indians made nets they used on land and water and even constructed decoys to draw birds closer. They also used digging sticks to unearth tubers and seem to have relied heavily on grass seed, which they collected, roasted, and crushed into a meal. They were highly nomadic people and didn't develop large systems, settlements, or structures. They adopted the bow and arrow around 500 BCE, began living in pit houses (but never year-round), and in some places cultivated maize. These Indians split and split again, becoming the Shoshone, Ute, Mono, and Northern Paiute tribes we know today. Some offshoot bands traveled east over the Rockies, changing along the way into the Comanche and other Plains tribes.

A series of treaties, first with Spain, then Britain and Mexico, brought the entire region under American control by 1848. It was around this time that the first permanent Great Basin settlement was created at Salt Lake. But it was the Mormons, rather than the American government, who would settle the area with force and with consequence.

The Mormon religion began in upstate New York in 1820. Its members traveled through Ohio, Missouri, and Illinois, where they were received poorly, so they kept heading west to create a kingdom in the Utah wilderness.

The government was deeply concerned about the Mormon theocracy growing in the Great Basin and by the practice of polygamy, which allowed Mormon leaders to have more than one wife at once. In 1857 President James Buchanan sent an army to Utah to bring the Mormons to heel. At the same time, the Baker-Fancher wagon train from the Arkansas territory, headed to California with around two hundred well-outfitted settlers, reached Salt Lake. The Mormons would not sell them provisions. They were concerned that the wagon train was in some way connected to Buchanan's troops. The Baker-Fancher settlers rolled away from Salt Lake southwest to Mountain Meadows, a resting spot on the trail west. They spent the better part of the summer in the highlands not far from Salt Lake, feeding their cattle and fortifying themselves to cross the mountains into California. However, spurred on by rumor and paranoia, the Mormons decided not to let them go.

On September 7, 1857, Mormon militiamen dressed as Indians attacked the Baker-Fancher party at their camp in Mountain Meadows. The siege wore on for several days; the settlers ran low on food, water, and ammunition. On September 11, members of the militia approached the wagon train and told the settlers that the "Paiute enemy" had agreed to let them go, so long as the settlers left all their cattle and supplies behind. The exhausted settlers agreed. The adult men were separated from the women and children; 120 men, women, and children of the Baker-Fancher party were then murdered by the Mormon militia. (Seventeen young children were spared and adopted by local families.) The Mormons agreed amongst themselves to blame everything on the Paiute.

Mormon leader Brigham Young himself led an investigation into the massacre. The report sent to the commissioner of Indian affairs said that the attack had been perpetrated by Indians. The U.S. government, not quite believing Young's tale, sent its own investigators, but the Civil War intervened. The truth about the Baker-Fancher massacre didn't come out for twenty years. By that time the Mormons were deeply embedded in Paiute land. It was the Paiute who had to pay for the Mormons' horrible crime and who continue to pay by way of dispossession.

In the 1860s and 1870s the Shoshone, Ute, and Paiute engaged in a series of wars. The results were similar to battles elsewhere: exhaustion and defeat and confinement to reservations. Yet they, like Indians of other tribes and regions, held on.

THE SOUTHERN GREAT PLAINS:
TEXAS AND OKLAHOMA

The Great Plains have captured the American imagination like no other landscape. Roughly five hundred miles wide and two thousand miles long, the Great Plains stretches over more than 1.3 million square miles in ten states (or rather, ten states were laid over the range): Wyoming, Texas, South Dakota, North Dakota, Kansas, Nebraska, Montana, Colorado, eastern New Mexico, and Oklahoma. Its terrain is immense, mostly flat but with a climate that ranges from the humid subtropical zone of Oklahoma and parts of Texas to the cold steppe of North Dakota. What holds it all together, in reality and mythology, is grass, buffalo, and Indians.

Buffalo grass, blue grama, and big bluestem grass had dominated the landscape since the last ice age and encouraged a dizzying variety and density of life. But American bison were the species that defined the place. Before 1800, it is estimated, more than sixty million buffalo roamed the Plains. By 1900 only 541 of these animals existed on the earth. This story of life, loss, and change is best told by contrasting the fate of the Indians in Texas with those in Oklahoma.

In prehistoric times, the Texas area was, like the Southwest, home to three supercultures: the Mound Builders in the east, Mesoamerican cultures in central-south Texas, and the Násaazí of the western Rio Grande. By 1500 CE, as elsewhere, these prehistoric cultures had become agriculturalists more than hunter-gatherers. To the east, the Caddo and Wichita (descended from the Mound Builders) lived in sedentary villages. The Caddo grew corn, sunflowers, and pumpkins, domesticated wild turkeys, and hunted large game in the lowlands of the Rio Grande. To the northeast of the river, the Pueblo people lived much as their counterparts did in New Mexico. Only in central and southern Texas were Indian tribes like the Tonkawa and Coahuiltecan truly hunter-gatherers. They lived in small, loosely formed tribal groups, each probably some version of an extended family. These tribes plied the lowlands of south and central Texas and harvested wild mesquite beans, maguey root, prickly pear, pecans, and acorns.

The first Europeans to travel through Texas in the sixteenth century were, of course, the Spanish. The Spanish wouldn't come back there in force until the late seventeenth century. But by then, as always, new winds were sweeping the Plains.

After the Pueblo Revolt, where the Indians drove the Spanish out of Santa Fe in 1680, horses were unleashed on the Plains. Until then, the animals had been almost exclusively controlled by the Spanish. Horses became both a kind of currency on the Plains and a prime shaper of its landscape. Rather suddenly, the tribes bordering on or living in the Plains—the Diné, Apache, Shoshone, Kiowa, and Pawnee—could fight and hunt by horseback in ways never before imaginable. But perhaps no other tribe took to horses like the Comanche.

Once the Comanche started acquiring horses in the late seventeenth century, they pushed east and south in search of bison. They also ran roughshod over any other Indians in their way. By 1700 the Comanche had spread into Oklahoma, New Mexico, and as far south as central Texas. They soon had everything: easy access to food, the ability to attack and defend themselves, and a steady influx of captured enemies, including Spanish and New Mexican settlers as well as other tribal people. The tribe's numbers swelled. By the end of the eighteenth century, there were about two million wild horses in the "Comancheria," the new Comanche homelands that included all of West Texas, eastern New Mexico, western Oklahoma, and southwestern Kansas. By the early nineteenth century, the tribe numbered forty thousand. Like other tribes, the Comanche lacked a central authority or governing body; they were split into as many as thirty distinct bands, each with its own hierarchy and leaders.

The Comanche were universally feared. Texas could not protect, or even define, its western border against them. The whole of Comancheria, as well as surrounding areas, was a battleground for the better part of two centuries. During the Civil War, the Comanche, Apache, and other Indian tribes (sometimes in alliance and sometimes acting singly) pushed back the "civilized" frontier hundreds of miles, burning homesteads and seizing cattle, horses, and captives. While the story

of American expansion is largely one of "Westward ho!" the historical reality shows that many tribes successfully repelled settlers, and
that sometimes resettlement took decades, if it happened at all. But
eventually many Indians of the Great Plains were defeated by disease
and by the systematic extermination of the buffalo on which they
depended, including the Comanche, whose empire came to an end in
1875. By that time, its population had dropped to around three thousand and its remaining members retired to reservations in Oklahoma.

Oklahoma was and is a strange exception to the very concept
of Indian homelands. Originally, it had been the domain of Caddo,
Lipan Apache, Kiowa, and Osage, among others. They were mainly
agriculturalists to the east and hunter-gatherers to the west. But all of
that was upended after the Louisiana Purchase in 1803 during Thomas
Jefferson's presidency, and the establishment of "Indian Territory" that
followed in the 1830s. Jefferson intended what became Indian Territory
as a relocation site for all the eastern Indians, so they would be out of the
way of American farmer-settlers. The original Indian Territory was huge,
but when Indians began to be sent there after the passage of the Indian
Removal Act of 1830, it was reduced in size almost immediately and
started to resemble present-day Oklahoma. Relocated Indians were
forced to move there anyway, on top of those Indigenous to the region.
By 1888 more than thirty tribes from all over the country were resettled
in Oklahoma, including Cherokee, Choctaw, Chickasaw, Seminole,
Seneca, Delaware, Meskwaki (Sac and Fox), Ho-Chunk (Winnebago),
Creek, Ottawa, Potawatomi, Ponca, Cheyenne, Arapaho, and Pawnee.
Crowded together, enemies became neighbors.

Indian Territory was a chaotic mess, but it was a homeland of sorts.
At first, it seemed more secure than the ones many tribes left behind.
That didn't last. As the cattle industry got under way in Texas in the
1870s and 1880s, Texas ranchers needed a route on which to herd their
beef to rail lines in Kansas. Indian Territory was in the way. The cattle
drives still moved forward.

Some tribes, like the Osage, found ways to resist. They originated in the Ohio River valley but were pushed out during the Iroquois Wars in the seventeenth and eighteenth centuries and made a new homeland in what is now Kansas, Missouri, Arkansas, and northeastern Oklahoma. There they became a power to be reckoned with. But after the Civil War, the Osage—who had variously sided with both the Union and the Confederates—faced removal and reduction. They were forced to sell their reservation lands in Kansas. With the proceeds, they bought themselves a new reservation in Oklahoma. The Osage were unique among the many Indian tribes facing the growing might of the American republic. When they purchased the land in northeastern Oklahoma, the Osage insisted they retain headrights to any mineral wealth in the area under their new reservation. Oil was discovered there in the late nineteenth century and the Osage profited. By the 1920s, they were the wealthiest people in the world per capita. In other negotiations, the Osage demanded treaty annuities and supplies come to them directly, rather than be paid to middleman traders who skimmed off the top. Clearly the Osage were not only militarily and physically strong; they were fierce and effective negotiators as well. And they remain such.

The Osage Council and other Osage traveled to Washington, D.C., to meet with the Commissioner of Indian Affairs about mineral and oil rights on tribal land. Photo undated, circa 1909–1932.

THE NORTHERN PLAINS

The Indians of the northern Great Plains—Mandan, Arikara, Hidatsa, Lakota, Dakota, Crow, Cheyenne, Arapaho, Blackfeet, Assiniboine, Cree, Saulteaux, and Plains Ojibwe—lived in one of the last regions of North America to be settled by Europeans. Broad expanses of the High Plains were too cold for too much of the year to be farmed easily, and the Plains tribes were unusually resistant to the colonizers.

The Plains Wars waged between 1850 and 1890 and played out in front of a national audience in the young republic of the United States. New forms of print and photographic technology made these wars the first Anglo-Indian conflicts witnessed by a wide range of Americans. The drama on the Plains was covered in magazines, newspapers, and illustrated weeklies. The journalism and published images of the time helped raise an urgent, defining question: Was America a democratic country that respected the rights of individuals, or was it just another greedy power in disguise?

Indian resistance, as we have seen, took many shapes across the United States. But rarely was resistance so widespread, successful, and brutal as it was during the Plains Wars. Two very powerful forces came together and changed that struggle: horses and firearms.

Indian hunter-gatherers appeared on the northern Great Plains about eighteen thousand years ago. There isn't a lot of archaeological evidence of how these prehistoric people lived. What we do know from studying Native languages is that tribal offshoots from Mexico, Canada, and the Rocky Mountains trickled out into the vast grasslands and made their lives there. There were no huge settlements or concentrations of population because the northern Plains didn't support the same density of habitation that could be found elsewhere on the continent. The tribes that emerged—Crow, Cheyenne, Arapaho—lived in small bands centered around family. They were highly mobile, sheltered in animal-skin-covered teepees, and hauled their belongings from place to place in travois (a type of framed sledge), following the buffalo. Everything revolved around the buffalo.

In their stories, the Cheyenne looked to the Black Hills and the buffalo herds that surrounded them as their birthplace, spiritual home, and spiritual center. The Blackfeet were, similarly, migrants who settled against the spine of the Rockies. In the early seventeenth century, refugees from the bloody struggles of the Iroquois and the Great Lakes Algonquians that squeezed everyone else out began to arrive from the east. Woodlands tribes of Wisconsin and Minnesota, such as the Mandan, Hidatsa, Arikara, Dakota, and Lakota, fled out onto the Plains to rebuild a way of life there.

It wasn't long, however, before the former woodland people and the Blackfeet took to the horse. Around the same time, the French had been making inroads north of the Great Lakes through Canada in their ever-expanding quest for furs. And while the British were loath to arm Indians, the French had no such qualms. Guns were prevalent by the beginning of the eighteenth century and only became more so. Within a few decades of journeying to the Plains, the Blackfeet, Crow, Arikara, Mandan, Cheyenne, Lakota, Dakota, Nakota, Cree, and Assiniboine were armed and horsed. They were, for a while, indomitable.

There were more than thirty distinct tribes with many sub-bands on the northern Plains at the beginning of the eighteenth century. The horse and the gun bonded together small roving bands into the horse cultures of the Plains. With easy mobility and steady access to food, populations swelled. Infant mortality went down, life spans increased, birth rates went up.

By the early nineteenth century, the Plains tribes were the people we recognize today. They lived on horseback and hunted buffalo. Their ceremonial lives were organized into "societies," and were governed by the sacred pipe. The horse was the key to this renaissance in Plains cultures. It made everything possible: new art forms, new religions, new societies, and new thinking.

Contrary to popular misconception, tribes didn't wither in the face of "superior" European technology, thinking, religion, and culture or merely succumb to European diseases. In the Plains in particular, tribes took what Europeans brought and made it wholly their own. When the Americans began showing up in force there in the early and middle nineteenth century, they were greeted with armed and mounted Indian armies, the likes of which—in terms of dress, technology, and tactics—had not been seen before on the continent.

The territory west of the Mississippi (but excluding the Northwest and California and portions of the Southwest) passed from France to the United States as a result of the Louisiana Purchase in 1803. A little more than a decade later, settlers bound for California trekked across the Great Plains. They came in steady if not extravagant numbers from the 1820s through 1840s, but the California Gold Rush of 1848 changed all that. Tens and eventually hundreds of thousands of people crossed the northern Plains to the gold fields. Wagon trains tore up the ground and disrupted the buffalo. With each new wave of travelers came another wave of disease. These travelers had nothing to offer the Indians. Tribes began attacking them. Even this was a primarily economic rather than military action: raiding (and killing) had long been a cultural norm on the northern Plains. However, intertribal raiding generally left a low body count and was seen by many Plains tribes as a quasi-spiritual activity wherein boys grew into men. By attacking the American wagon trains and stealing horses, flour, iron, gunpowder, lead, and other hard-to-obtain items, the Plains tribes were simply responding to unwelcome pressure and continuing a way of life that was fairly stable.

The U.S. government, however, didn't see things that way. Violence on the trail was bad for American business and it needed to end. But the government didn't have a military force strong enough to take on the tens of thousands of efficient and mounted warriors on the Plains. The U.S. Army would certainly lose. Instead, government officials resorted to treaty making.

In 1851 the Cheyenne, Lakota, Arapaho, Assiniboine, Crow, Mandan,

Gros Ventre, Shoshone, Arikara, and Hidatsa signed the first Treaty of Fort Laramie. The provisions were, on paper, good for both sides. The United States was assured that settlers would be allowed to pass through the Indian homelands safely, and that the government could build forts and supply depots to provision and reprovision the travelers. In return, the tribes' title to the land itself was affirmed, and they were guaranteed fifty thousand dollars in annuities per year for the right of way.

Settlers began to move in and stay, regardless of the Treaties of Fort Laramie or the Treaties of Fort Benton or the many other pacts signed by Plains tribes but violated immediately by the government and the citizens of the United States. The result: war.

Beginning in 1850 but escalating in the 1860s and 1870s, the Plains Indian Wars drew in almost every single Plains tribe and involved settlers, militia, and the U.S. Army. It is estimated that at least twenty thousand Indians and eight thousand Anglo settlers and soldiers died in twenty-five years of warfare, although the figure for Indian deaths, based on U.S. Army records, should almost certainly be higher. Every time the Indians fought back against clear violations of the treaties they had signed in good faith, punishing violence was unleashed upon them. America did not conquer the West through superior technology, nor did it demonstrate the advantages of democracy. America "won" the West by blood, brutality, and terror.

The second Treaty of Fort Laramie (1868) created the Great Sioux Reservation. The Lakota were also guaranteed the right to hunt in the unceded territory as far as the Sandhills of Nebraska. But the arrangement was too good to last. Trespass continued unabated and intensified after gold was discovered in the Black Hills in 1874 and the Indians of the area pushed back. Lieutenant Colonel George Armstrong Custer led punitive winter campaigns against the Lakota.

Lakota and other tribal leaders saw that they would have to deliver a resounding defeat to the U.S. Army and sent runners from tribe to tribe, reforged old alliances, strengthened friendships, and plotted. They built a formidable army of Lakota, northern Cheyenne, and Arapaho. Meanwhile, the U.S. Army conducted a summer campaign to round up all Indians who had refused to settle on the Great Sioux Reservation.

At dawn on June 25, 1876, Custer and his men spotted a large encampment of Indians near the Little Bighorn River in what is now southern Montana. He thought it was perhaps a band or two, a big and fatal mistake. Thousands of warriors had actually amassed, all ready for battle. Custer, ignoring the advice of his scouts, attacked. The army was quickly surrounded by Lakota, Cheyenne, and Arapaho, as planned by Hunkpapa Lakota leader Sitting Bull and the other chiefs. After a two-day battle, Custer's entire command was wiped out.

Seven weeks later, the U.S. military mounted retaliatory attacks, but other tactics proved more decisive. The U.S. refused to send provisions and payments due to the Lakota per the 1868 Treaty of Fort Laramie until they ceded the Black Hills to the Americans. Soon after, hundreds

Somewhere between thirty and sixty million buffalo roamed in the mid-1800s; by the end of the century, there were only three hundred of the animals left in the wild. The mountain of bison skulls that dwarfs the men in this 1892 photo suggests the scale of the slaughter.

of buffalo hunters enabled by the government descended on the High Plains and began ruthlessly slaughtering the great bison herds. With the destruction of their traditional food source and the denial of their guaranteed annuities and provisions, the Lakota and their allies were starved into submission. Now the reservation period began for these unhappy few as well.

1890

And so, by the end of 1890, after the massacre at Wounded Knee, it must have seemed that everything was over. In four hundred years, Indians had lost control of 100 percent of the United States and remained only in small clusters scattered like freckles over the face of the country. The federal government had stopped making treaties with Indian nations in the 1870s, and by 1890 the frontier was officially closed. The ways of life that tribes from Florida to Washington and Maine to Montana had evolved over thousands of years were gone. So were the buffalo. Tribal government had been replaced by the dismal and crushing paternalism of the federal bureaucracy: the Office of Indian Affairs, the government body created to "administer" the Native nations inside the United States. The European colonial powers and later the American government had shown themselves to be feckless, cruel, shortsighted, hypocritical, and shameful in their dealings with the original owners of the country. Indians were nearly wiped out from the East Coast, and far on the other side of the country, they lived as tattered remnants around former mission communities in California. The entire United States had been "settled," and Indians had been broken, removed, and safely "settled," too—on reservations where they were expected to either die or "become" Americans by way of cultural death via assimilation.

And yet: Indians remained. The Seminole still called the swamps and bayous of Florida home and emerged to join the burgeoning ranching trade in the Panhandle. On Martha's Vineyard and elsewhere in New England, Indian settlements—Christian but still tribal—were growing. Niagara Falls, Rochester, and Syracuse, New York, sprang up around Iroquois settlements that remained after hundreds of years. In the Southwest, cultures arose that were a blend of Anglo, Mexican, and Indian. Pueblo men still met in kivas, their underground rooms for ritual and other important gatherings. The Tewa, Diné, and Apache languages were all still in use. The Plains tribes, ever resourceful, adapted to a land without buffalo. The Indians of the Great Lakes, unlike their western neighbors, could still do what they had always done: trap, harvest wild rice, hunt, and ply the waters much as they had for centuries. The small coastal tribes of the Pacific Northwest traveled, traded, and became loggers and fishermen.

The 1890 U.S. Census Bureau tabulated that there were fewer than two hundred thousand Indians left alive, of populations that had likely numbered over twenty million. But there were Indians left in all the corners of the country. Some had held on to their homelands, others had been removed and relocated and made new homelands.

In 1891 the Indians who remained poked their heads aboveground, surveyed the desolation of their homelands, and echoed the question Indians had been asking since the beginning: What can we do next to survive?

THE "INDIAN PROBLEM"
1891–1934

❖◆❖◆❖◆❖◆❖◆❖

KEVIN WASHBURN SLIPS OFF HIS cowboy boots and puts on his running shoes before we engage in a "walk and talk" around the golf course at the University of New Mexico in Albuquerque, where he was a professor of law at the time. I wanted to talk to Washburn because he served as the assistant secretary of the interior for Indian affairs in the Obama administration and because, as a Chickasaw, he was one of very few Indians to serve Indians and the government in that capacity.

Kevin has a quick smile and is about the friendliest former government official you could hope to meet, although under all that cheer is something deep and fierce. Washburn grew up in the Chickasaw Nation and earned his BA in economics with honors from the University of Oklahoma in 1989. "I had a powerful, strong-willed mom. She was a single mother for much of my childhood. My mom was 'the divorcée' in a small town in Oklahoma. She was the first woman to be Chamber of Commerce president. At that time, she had a children's clothing store because she thought, 'If I own a clothing store at least my kids will be clothed.' I got my drive and work ethic from her."

Washburn enrolled in the University of Oklahoma and then attended Yale Law School. He graduated from clerkship to trial attorney for the Department of Justice to assistant U.S. attorney for New Mexico to dean of a law school. Still his tribe and Indian people across the country have always been on his mind.

"You know," he says, "we [Chickasaw] feel that we chose our own destiny. Even today, our tribal seal includes the words 'Unconquered and Unconquerable.'"

This belief in the intelligence and capability of Indian people was on ample display between 2012 and 2015, when Washburn served as an assistant secretary of the interior, a federal position that put him in charge of the Bureau of Indian Affairs, among other agencies.

The Bureau of Indian Affairs has a long and not always illustrious history. As early as 1775, the Second Continental Congress created two, then three agencies to oversee agreements, settlements, annuities, and trade with Indian tribes. The colonists were concerned that Indians—who vastly outnumbered them—would side with the British during the Revolutionary War. Many tribes, notably most of the Iroquois Confederacy, sided with the British anyway; they seemed a stronger force than the colonists. In response, in 1779, General George Washington, whom the Iroquois called Hanodaganears, or "Devourer of Towns," ordered an offensive against the tribe to be mounted. More than forty villages were destroyed, driving most of the confederacy from the Finger Lakes region north to Buffalo, Rochester, and Syracuse, New York. The Oneida, despite being a member of the Iroquois Confederacy, sided with the Americans and fought alongside the colonists at the battles of Oriskany and Saratoga, among others.

This engraving was printed in 1857, eighty years after the Battle of Oriskany, New York. Han Yerry Tehawengaragwen led a band of Oneida who joined forces with the Americans at Oriskany. His wife, Sara Tyonajanegen, was among the Oneida fighters.

During the winter of 1777–1778, when Washington and his troops were starving at Valley Forge, Pennsylvania, the Oneida marched down and provided much-needed supplies and support. Polly Cooper, an Oneida woman, cared for the sick and showed Continental Army soldiers how to prepare Indian corn, which helped prevent famine. After the war Congress signed a treaty with the Oneida in 1784 in recognition of their contributions to American victory: "The United States acknowledges the lands reserved to the Oneida . . . to be their property; and the United States will never claim the same . . ." A mere thirty years later, the promises that had been made to the Oneida, as well as their homelands, had faded away.

After the Revolutionary War, the new American government's relations with eastern tribes shifted from military concerns to economic ones. An Office of Indian Trade was created within the newly established U.S. War Department to regulate commerce with tribes. The office worked with the "factory system," a network of federally operated trading posts that had been established by an act of Congress in 1796. Indian factories helped maintain political stability. They often functioned as forts and could host military detachments as needed.

The factory system remained in effect until 1822, by which point the fur trade had waned and the Louisiana Purchase and the War of 1812 had established more or less agreed-upon borders to the United States. In 1824 the government established the Office of Indian Affairs (the OIA name was changed to the Bureau of Indian Affairs in 1947). Scores of treaties had been signed that defined Indians' rights and homeland borders, and included provisions for annuity payments in the form of cash, seed, iron, trade goods, and blankets. Thus the U.S. government, long an overbearing trading partner and military threat to the tribes, had added yet another role: trustee of annuity money and goods promised to the Indians by treaty.

In 1832 Congress created the position of commissioner of Indian affairs, and in 1849 the Office of Indian Affairs was moved from the War Department to the Department of the Interior. The office's origins in trade and war, however, continued to define its role.

In 1869 Ely S. Parker became the first Indian to be placed in charge of the Office of Indian Affairs. He was something of a nineteenth-century Indian all-star. A Seneca, he was born and raised on the Tonawanda Reservation in upstate New York. Ely had been brought up as a Baptist, although he, like many others, also participated in Seneca Longhouse ceremonies and had a Seneca name: Hasanoanda. When Ely came of age his parents sent him to a missionary boarding school, where he learned English; his bilingualism would later help his band negotiate a number of treaties regarding land claims upstate.

In his mid-twenties, Parker was appointed to an important political and ceremonial position within the Seneca Longhouse. He used that position and his connections to fight federal, state, and private interests trying to gobble up Tonawanda land and relocate his Seneca band out west. In 1857 the Tonawanda signed a new treaty with the government that preserved a large portion of their original reservation. Other Seneca communities—such as the reservation at Buffalo Creek—disappeared.

Parker graduated from the prestigious Rensselaer Polytechnic Institute, and then worked as an engineer, helping to improve the Erie Canal. In Illinois, he befriended Ulysses S. Grant, who had returned there to work after his military service in the Mexican-American War. When the Civil War broke out, Parker tried to muster a company of Iroquois soldiers for the Union, but the governor of New York refused because they weren't Americans. (Most American Indians wouldn't be considered citizens until 1924.) Parker then tried to enlist on his own, noting that there was a shortage of engineers in the Union Army, but again he was turned down. In desperation he wrote to Grant, who vouched for him; Parker was commissioned as a captain in May 1863. Eventually, he served as Grant's adjutant and secretary and was present at Confederate general Robert E. Lee's surrender at Appomattox in April 1865. It was Parker who helped draft and produce the final copy of the articles of surrender that ended the Civil War.

Brigadier General Ely Parker (seated, left) with General Ulysses Grant (seated, center) during the Civil War, sometime between 1861 and 1865.

Ulysses S. Grant was inaugurated as president in 1869. His administration was marred by corruption and graft, but it represented a welcome change in the ways the federal government worked with Indian tribes. One of Grant's first moves was to appoint Parker as commissioner of Indian affairs. At Parker's urging, Grant steered the federal government away from a policy of war with the tribes and toward one of peace. Together they established a Board of Indian Commissioners, charged with addressing "what should be the legal status of the Indians; a definition of their rights and obligations under the laws of the United States, of the States and territories and treaty stipulations; whether any more treaties shall be stipulated with the Indians . . . should Indians be placed upon reservation and what is the best method to accomplish this." The findings of the board should have been encouraging to Indians across the country: "The first aggressions have been made by the white man . . . There is a large class of professedly reputable men who use every means in their power to bring on Indian wars, for the sake of profit . . ."

Despite his affection for Parker and his apparent concern for Indian interests, President Grant arrived at a disastrous solution to the problem the board had described. If the Indian service was rife with opportunists and ne'er-do-wells and warmongers, Grant would find a new source of administrators. In his second annual message to Congress, in December 1870, the president unveiled his plan. Indian affairs would come under the control of a handful of religious orders. This plan would have dire ramifications for every aspect of Indians' daily life.

In 1871 Ely Parker resigned from the Office of Indian Affairs, calling it a "thankless position." The end of his service was the end of an era: on March 3, 1871, Congress passed the Indian Appropriations Act. This small piece of legislation was meant to appropriate around fifteen hundred dollars for the relief of the Lakota, who were experiencing serious hardship at the time. However, a rider was attached to the congressional bill. It read, in part: "No Indian nation or tribe within the territory of the United States shall be acknowledged or recognized as an independent nation, tribe, or power with whom the United States may contract by treaty; but no obligation of any treaty lawfully made and ratified with any such Indian nation or tribe prior to March 3, 1871, shall be hereby invalidated or impaired." In plain language this meant that the treaty process—the means by which the federal government and the Indian tribes had interacted and defined their relationships with one another for more than twenty years—was officially over. Now the U.S. government would treat Indians not as foreign nations (as they had been) or as citizens (which, by and large, they had yet to become) but as wards of the state, for whom the government assumed the roles of guardian, banker, and protector. In principle this might have been a good thing, but in reality, the government itself was often the aggressor where Indians were concerned, and negotiated with tribes unfairly and in bad faith. How could Indians rely on American courts and American politicians and American people to champion their interests? Juries and governmental committees seldom included any Indians, let alone a majority. No elected officials were Indians.

With the end of the Plains Indian Wars in the 1880s and the closing of the frontier in 1890, the Office of Indian Affairs became even more important. It handled all Indian claims, adjudications, and assessments. The Office of Indian Affairs' payroll grew from 108 employees in 1852 to almost 2,000 by 1888. Indian agents were expected to distribute treaty rations, dispense annuities, and make sure traders and store owners both served Indians and were paid by them. They hired and trained police (often drawn from tribes) to redress wrongs, keep the peace, and supervise the missions and religious orders empowered by the government to "civilize" the Indians. By 1900 "the Indian agent had, in effect, become the tribal government." So what did that government look like?

A civilian visiting the Indian agency in Anadarko, in Indian Territory, observed, ". . . The [Indian] women gathered in a long line in front of the agent's store to wait their turn for their rations. Each of these had a tag . . . on which was printed the number in each family, and the amount of grain, flour, baking-powder, and soap to which the family was entitled." An Indian agent assigned to the Blackfeet in northwestern Montana reported that the Indians there were in terrible condition: "Their supplies had been limited and many of them were gradually dying of starvation . . . All bore marks of suffering from lack of food, but the little children seemed to have suffered most . . . So great was their destitution that the Indians stripped bark from the saplings that grow along the creeks and ate the inner portions to appease their gnawing hunger." Fifty years earlier, the Blackfeet had millions of bison to feed them; now they had tree bark.

Kevin Washburn ruefully summed it up this way: "Back in the tail end of the nineteenth century, Indians lived in organized communities, but many of them were living, literally, against the walls of federal forts. It was a real low point for tribes. There was a superintendent [called an Indian agent before 1909] for each agency who was viewed as a god. The superintendent had an amazing amount of authority. Consequently, when people talk about the BIA [Bureau of Indian Affairs, formerly the OIA] today there is still a lot of resentment. Back then 'BIA' really did stand for 'Bossing Indians Around.'"

A whole new bureaucracy grew up to support the work of the Indian agent: clerks, stenographers, millers, farmers, carpenters, mechanics, sawyers, stockmen, laborers, freighters, and cops. The commissioner of Indian affairs in 1890 was clear about what the goals were now: "It has become the settled policy of the Government to break up reservations, destroy tribal relations, settle Indians upon their own homesteads, incorporate them into the national life, and deal with them not as nations or tribes or bands, but as individual citizens." Or, as Massachusetts senator Henry Dawes, the chief architect of this new phase, put it: what America wanted was for Indians to "wear civilized clothes . . . cultivate the ground, live in houses, ride in Studebaker wagons, send children to school, drink whiskey [and] own property." The Indian agent, together with the OIA bureau he represented, was the administrative tool to achieve this end. His two greatest weapons were schools and land.

The 1871 Indian Appropriations Act took all the power of the executive branch to negotiate with the tribes and gave it to Congress. Now both houses of Congress, rather than just the Senate and the executive branch, would legislate Indian policy, ensuring that Indian affairs would forever be wrapped up in partisan politics and subject to the local whims of states' rights. This new phase of federal Indian policy was known as assimilation. As bad as the years of warfare and treaty making had been, assimilation would be much worse.

THE BEGINNINGS OF THE INDIAN RIGHTS MOVEMENT

In January 1870, U.S. troops killed 173 Blackfeet Indians, mostly women and children, after being directed to the wrong place by a soldier who wanted to protect his Indian wife and children at another camp. In 1871 four settlers killed thirty Yahi Indians in the Ishi Wilderness near Wild Horse Corral; the entire tribe then only numbered fifteen or so. On December 28, 1872, U.S. troops killed seventy-six Yavapai Indians in the Skeleton Cave Massacre in Arizona. U.S. troops attacked a Nez Perce village in 1877 in Big Hole, Montana, killing as many as ninety Indians before they were driven away by the survivors. After escaping confinement at Nebraska's Fort Robinson in 1879, Northern Cheyenne chief Dull Knife and his band were hunted down and slaughtered; as many as seventy of the Cheyenne perished. Regional coverage of these atrocities by newspapers like the *Portland Standard* and *The Lewiston Teller* was quickly picked up out east.

The struggles of the Nez Perce under Chief Joseph received especially widespread coverage. The tribe had been promised by treaty a reservation in their ancestral lands in Oregon's Wallowa Valley. In 1877, however, the Nez Perce were forcibly removed to a poorer, smaller, and unfamiliar reservation near Lapwai, Idaho. Chief Joseph and his band decided they could not live in this new land, far from the bones of their ancestors, and so they fled, embarking on a twelve-hundred-mile fighting retreat across Idaho, Wyoming, and Montana, on their way to join Sitting Bull's Lakota across the border in Canada. Starving and exhausted, Joseph and his band surrendered to General Nelson A. Miles on October 5, 1877, just forty miles from the Canadian border.

Two years later, Chief Joseph gave a now-famous speech in Washington, D.C., to the government and the public. He opened with a request: "I want the white people to understand my people. Some of you think an Indian is like a wild animal. This is a great mistake. I will tell you all about our people, and then you can judge whether an Indian is a man or not . . . Our fathers gave us many laws, which they had learned from their fathers. These laws were good. They told us to treat all men as they treated us; that we should never be the first to break a bargain; that it was a disgrace to tell a lie; that we should speak only the truth; that it was a shame for one man to take from another his wife, or his property without paying for it. We were taught to believe that the Great Spirit sees and hears everything, and that he never forgets; that hereafter he will give every man a spirit-home according to his deserts: If he has been a good man, he will have a good home; if he has been a bad man, he will have a bad home. This I believe, and all my people believe the same."

Chief Joseph (date unrecorded). His speech in Washington, D.C., was covered in its entirety by the *North American Review*, the first literary magazine in the United States. It generated an incredible amount of sympathy for the Nez Perce specifically, and for Indians more generally.

Chief Joseph told of how the French, the first "men with white faces" the Indians ever met, called the tribe Nez Perce (pierced nose) for ornaments they wore at the time. He describes peaceful encounters with the Lewis and Clark expedition, men who "talked straight." The chief avowed, "It has always been the pride of the Nez Perce that they were the friends of the white men." But his speech continued with never-ending betrayals, illegal or broken treaties, and endless incursions into Nez Perce lands.

Chief Joseph and his band were eventually cheated out of their lands: "White men were many . . . We were like deer. They were like grizzly bears." His powerful, stirring speech ended with a plea for equality and a pronouncement about the future: "I only ask of the Government to be treated as all other men are treated . . . Let me be a free man—free to travel, free to stop, free to work, free to trade where I choose, free to choose my own teachers, free to follow the religion of my fathers, free to think and talk and act for myself—and I will obey every law, or submit to the penalty. Whenever the white man treats the Indian as they treat each other, then we will have no more wars."

Meanwhile, another tragic tale was unfolding out west. The Ponca tribe, under Chief Standing Bear, had decided to walk from their pitiful home in Indian Territory back to their ancestral lands along the Niobrara River near present-day Ponca, Nebraska, on the South Dakota border. The Ponca, never a terribly big tribe, had been decimated by a smallpox epidemic brought by the Lewis and Clark expedition, disrupted by raids from the more numerous Oglala Brulé Lakota and then an influx of white settlers, and displaced, despite several treaties with the U.S. government, the last of which moved the Ponca to Indian Territory in 1877. The Ponca were sent there too late in the year to plant crops and this land proved unsuitable for farming anyhow. They were moved yet again that summer, 150 miles west to the Salt Fork of the Arkansas River. There the Ponca wintered over without supplies. By spring, a third of the tribe had died of starvation.

Among the dead was Chief Standing Bear's eldest son, Bear Shield. Standing Bear had promised his son that he would bury him in their ancestral homelands on the Niobrara River. The chief and a few dozen followers headed north on foot with the body. En route, desperate for food, they were welcomed warmly by the Omaha in what is now Nebraska. But while the Ponca ate and rested, the U.S. government learned of their odyssey; General George Crook was dispatched to arrest them. The Ponca were imprisoned at Fort Omaha. Then a curious thing happened. Crook, a decorated Civil War veteran and a notorious Indian fighter, had a change of heart. A lifetime of fighting seems to have helped him see the true cost of war and the terrible treatment of the Indian combatants. Instead of returning the Ponca to Oklahoma, he let them stay at Fort Omaha. In the meantime, Crook contacted Thomas Tibbles.

Tibbles was a former abolitionist and minister turned journalist with ties to the Omaha. He was now an assistant editor at the *Omaha Daily Herald*. When General Crook asked Tibbles to make some noise on the Ponca's behalf, he was happy to comply. One scathing full-page editorial followed another. Soon two local attorneys offered to represent Standing Bear in court. They filed a writ of habeas corpus in U.S. district court in Omaha, Nebraska. Under the law of habeas corpus, an imprisoned person can sue jailers or captors for unlawful imprisonment. On the last day of the trial, Standing Bear was allowed to address the judge, Elmer Scipio Dundy, one of the first times an Indian had this opportunity in open court:

"I seem to be standing on a high bank of a great river, with my wife and little girl at my side. I cannot cross the river, and impassable cliffs arise behind me. I hear the noise of great waters; I look, and see a flood coming. The waters rise to our feet, and then to our knees . . . In despair I look toward the cliffs behind me, and I seem to see a dim trail that may lead to a way of life.

"I take my child by the hand, and my wife follows after me. Our hands and our feet are torn by the sharp rocks, and our trail is marked by our blood. At last I see a rift in the rocks. A little way beyond there are green prairies. The swift-running water, the Niobrara, pours down between the green hills. There are the graves of my fathers. There again we will pitch our teepee and build our fires. I see the light of the world and of liberty just ahead.

"But in the center of the path there stands a man. Behind him I see soldiers in number like the leaves of the trees. If that man gives me the permission, I may pass on to life and liberty. If he refuses, I must go back and sink beneath the flood.

"You are that man."

On May 12, 1879, Judge Dundy came back with a verdict. His decision ran to eleven pages and was clearly meant to stand as a widely applied precedent in future cases. At the end of his opinion, Dundy set out his ruling carefully, making important points that "an Indian is a 'person' within the meaning of the laws of the United States, and has, therefore, the right to sue . . . where he is restrained of liberty in violation of the constitution or laws of the United States" and that Indians, "have the inalienable right to 'life, liberty, and the pursuit of happiness,' so long as they obey the laws." Standing Bear and his followers were released and were allowed to continue their journey back to their village site on the Niobrara River. They resettled there and lived out their days.

Despite the eloquent speech and the thoroughly reasoned ruling, Indians were not considered Americans. The Fourteenth Amendment, added to the U.S. Constitution in 1868, granted citizenship to everyone born or naturalized in the United States except Indians. Nevertheless, by the 1880s, the struggles of Chief Joseph and Standing Bear and their tribes, the attendant publicity, the abolition of slavery in the wake of the Civil War, and the rise of an eastern protest class and literature forced people to realize that the Indian reservation system was a moral and administrative failure. And with that recognition, an Indian rights movement began to grow.

In 1881, *A Century of Dishonor*, a scathing history of U.S. federal policy, was published. Not content with having written the book, author Helen Hunt Jackson sent a copy to every member of Congress. She included a handwritten note with a quotation from Benjamin Franklin: "Look upon your hands: they are stained with the blood of your relations!" *A Century of Dishonor* was a huge success. It and *Ramona*, Jackson's bestselling romance about a half-Indian, half-Scots girl who suffers discrimination, became founding documents of the emergent Indian rights movement in the late nineteenth century.

Two reformers—moved by their experience in the Indian service, the public lectures of Chief Joseph and Standing Bear, and Helen Hunt Jackson's books—convened a group in Philadelphia and formed the Indian Rights Association (IRA) in 1882. Within two years the IRA opened offices in Washington, D.C., and Boston as well. Many former members of the Indian service began to write books and essays about what they felt was the criminal treatment of American Indians by the United States. Beginning in 1883, these "Friends of the Indian" met annually at a conference held on the estate at Lake Mohonk, near Poughkeepsie, New York. Citizenship was their watchword. The IRA, the Women's National Indian Association (WNIA), and the Lake Mohonk Conference were united in railing against reservations, the corrupt Indian agency system, and the whole treaty-based set of relationships. The solutions seemed clear to the reformers: civilization through citizenship, free enterprise, and private ownership of land. As passionate as the Friends of the Indian were, they did not consider what Indians themselves thought and wanted.

The Friends unofficially audited the Office of Indian Affairs. They monitored the work of agents in the field and wrote reports to the Bureau of Indian Commissioners and to Congress. But the reformers struggled with how Indians would become "ready" for the rights and responsibilities of citizenship. They soon hit upon paths to this end.

THE INDIAN BOARDING SCHOOLS

"Kill the Indian in him, and save the man . . ." That was the plan of military officer turned educator Richard Henry Pratt. Pratt had a lot of experience with Indians. He grew up in Indiana and served in the Union Army infantry during the Civil War. Two years after the war, he rejoined the army and served for eight years on the Plains, fighting Indians in the Washita campaign and the Red River War. At the end of that war in 1875, Pratt interviewed Indian combatants in order to determine how they should be charged. Somehow his sympathies were engaged and he tried to clear as many of them as possible.

Pratt escorted the Indian combatants the government was banishing from their Plains homelands to Fort Marion, Florida. He was only under vague orders, so while he was at the fort, Pratt began experiments in education. He hired teachers to instruct the Indian prisoners in English, art, and mechanical studies. Pratt was so impressed by the Indians' aptitude that he ultimately lobbied Congress for funding for a school dedicated to the "civilization" of American Indians.

In 1879 Pratt opened the Carlisle Indian Industrial School in an abandoned army barracks in Carlisle, Pennsylvania. There were eighty-two Indians in its first class. Most of them were the children of Plains Indian leaders.

Kill the Indian they did at Carlisle. Or tried to. Students were forbidden to speak their native languages, and Pratt condoned corporal punishment to that end. Upon arrival, students were photographed in their traditional garb and then stripped, stuffed into uniforms, and barbered to within an inch of their lives. Luther Standing Bear, son of Chief George Standing Bear, arrived at Carlisle among the first group of students.

"The 'civilizing' process" at Carlisle, he recalled, started "with clothes. Never, no matter what our philosophy or spiritual quality, could we be civilized while wearing the moccasin and blanket . . . Our accustomed dress was taken and replaced with clothing that felt cumbersome and awkward. Against trousers and handkerchiefs we had a distinct feeling—they were unsanitary, and the trousers kept us from breathing well. High collars, stiff-bosomed shirts, and suspenders fully three inches in width were uncomfortable, while leather boots caused actual suffering . . . Of course, our hair was cut . . . In some mysterious way, long hair stood in the path of our development." For the Lakota, moreover, to cut one's hair was a sign of mourning, so when the barber commenced there was loud ritual and heartfelt wailing.

Pratt, being a military man, organized the school along military lines. Students were woken at dawn and marched in regiments out to the yard for morning roll call. Half the school day was devoted to academic subjects, the other half to tradecraft like printing, carpentry, or sewing. There was a military-style court, run by the students themselves, who determined what punishments to dole out for infractions.

Students at Carlisle were punished by having their mouths washed out with lye soap for speaking their native languages, daily beatings, and being locked in an old guardhouse with only bread and water for rations. One former student testified to the intimidations: "We would cower from the abusive disciplinary practices of some superiors, such as the one who yanked my cousin's ear hard enough to tear it. After a nine-year-old girl was raped in her dormitory bed during the night, we girls would be so scared that we would jump into each other's bed as soon as the lights went out. The sustained terror in our hearts further tested our endurance, as it was better to suffer with a full bladder and be safe than to walk through the dark, seemingly endless hallway to the bathroom."

Many Indian leaders seemed to support the schools; they had come to recognize that assimilation was the only hope for the survival of their children. And many Indian children educated there seemed to like the experience and to look back on it fondly. I say "seemed" because it is sometimes hard to look behind the rhetoric of "progress" to recognize the acute pain felt by those who had to say goodbye to their children or parents for years. Even as Carlisle was a stab at equality, it was also a knife in the heart of the Indian family.

Within a decade there were almost twenty boarding schools run by the Office of Indian Affairs, dozens of "agency schools" on or near Indian agencies around the country, and dozens more boarding schools run by religious groups, the majority by the Catholics. Federal expenditures on Indian education rose from seventy-five thousand dollars to about two million dollars by 1894.

Most students had to have money deposited into their personal accounts at school to pay for transportation back to their families during the summer. Most tribal communities were too poor to do this. My grandmother was sent to Tomah Indian Industrial School in Tomah, Wisconsin, in 1930 at age four and did not return home until she was ten.

Conditions back home were often worse, and some parents begged the schools to take their children because they couldn't afford to feed them. The majority of Indian parents, however, didn't want to be separated from their children and resisted putting them in the school system. The Office of Indian Affairs and its agents in the field coerced them. They disempowered Indians in their own communities by stripping them of privileges and position. They held back rations, causing hunger and suffering. Some agents wanted to call the police on the parents.

The boarding schools were evidence of what the U.S. government understood "civilized" to mean. To be culturally Indian and live in one's Indian community was to be a savage. Indian kids went to school to be not-Indian. They also went there to die. Perhaps no other aspect of Indian education during the sixty years of the boarding school era is more tragic than the fact that the grounds at Carlisle and all the other schools include graveyards. (As recently as 2021, a mass grave with the remains of 215 children was discovered at a former Indigenous school in British Columbia, Canada. An estimated forty-one hundred Indian children died in boarding schools in that country. More graves are being discovered in the United States to this day.) The names on the graves are a poignant roll call of Indians from across the continent who never made it back to their tribal homes. The list of the fallen children who died far from the arms of their parents and grandparents, far from the laughter of their siblings and cousins, far from the homelands their ancestors had fought so hard to protect goes on and on. Because of and despite the good intentions of progressives, significant numbers of three entire generations of Indians died in the boarding schools, and countless more were damaged by them.

Wounded Yellow Robe, Timber Yellow Robe, and Henry Standing Bear, members of the Sioux Nation, entering the Carlisle School in 1883–and as they appeared three years later as students.

The full effect of the boarding school system wouldn't be understood until decades later. It was hard for Indian families back in their homelands to know exactly how bad the schools were. Many Indians couldn't read or write English so they couldn't communicate with school officials and teachers. Often children began to forget their own languages, so they couldn't talk easily of what had happened to them. Shame also played a role.

In the late 1920s, the U.S. government decided to conduct its own investigation of Indian administration, health, and education. Over a seven-month period, a team of experts visited ninety-five locations—reservations, hospitals, schools, and agencies—in twenty-two states. The team took another two and a half years to organize and analyze the data they collected. The resulting Meriam Report, released in 1928, was nothing if not thorough. It ran to more than eight hundred pages and included detailed statistical analysis. With facts and data, the Meriam Report argued that federal Indian policy was a disaster. The section on Indian education was particularly alarming. It noted that the boarding schools hired unqualified and underqualified staff and paid them poorly. Turnover was high. In one classroom, ten teachers had passed through in the course of a single semester. Most schools ran largely on Indian child labor. Students milked cows, killed chickens, split wood, mowed fields, whitewashed walls, and cooked the food in the school kitchens. The report cautioned, "It is essential that the pupils be old enough and strong enough to do [the labor]"—which it also noted was often not the case.

The Meriam Report was equally scathing about the schools' teaching and teacher training methods, curriculum, and sensitivity to the individual academic, practical, and emotional needs of Indian children. This disregard for the children as individuals extended even to the uniforms they were forced to wear. In one sad footnote, the writers observed that "there is no individuality in clothes in most schools, and suits are apparently passed on interminably, necessitating repeated repair." A single pair of trousers had been worn, for example, by twelve boys successively.

But the report saved most of its indignation for the health conditions at the schools. In a survey of more than seventy schools, the authors noted insufficient ventilation, rampant overcrowding, frequently broken toilets and sinks, and an almost complete absence of "modern" laundry facilities. In one school very small children were discovered working behind piles of laundry that dwarfed them because the superintendent found they folded more when confronted by big piles. At another, the children were too malnourished to play. Even where they had the energy, children were often required to "maintain a pathetic degree of quietness." Some authorities did not allow them to speak at all. Most schools at the time of the survey included a sort of jail used to discipline children. School buildings in general were decrepit, often to the point of being fire risks; boilers and machinery were out of date and sometimes unsafe. Medical personnel were insufficiently trained, and the children themselves were not offered health education. Nor were they given sufficient milk, and almost nothing in the way of fresh fruits and vegetables. The school day was unusually long, cutting into sleep, and a lack of recreational opportunities provided children with little exercise. According to the Meriam Report, Indian children were six times as likely to die in childhood while at boarding schools than the rest of the children in America.

From 1879 to the late 1930s, when the last compulsory boarding school programs were suspended, tens of thousands of Indian children were torn away from their families, forced to abandon their cultures and religions, and indoctrinated in federally funded religious schools. The effects of this attempt to break a people are still being felt today.

Meanwhile, back in Indian homelands, even worse conditions prevailed as the most crushing form of oppression in America spread across Indian country.

ALLOTMENT

According to reformers, education was only one part of the Indian problem. They also thought the reservation system was holding "the Indian" back.

Herbert Welsh, one of the founding members of the Indian Rights Association, had traveled extensively in the Dakotas, Nebraska, and the Southwest in the early 1880s and expressed his dismay at the

squalid conditions, poverty, and lack of industry that he felt the reservation system encouraged. He was equally dismayed by the greed
and mismanagement of many Indian agents. The only solution, he felt,
was to do away with reservations. Welsh and the IRA had the ear of the
government, which was similarly inclined. Reports from the Office of
Indian Affairs started promoting ideas that the Indian "must be imbued
with the exalting egotism of American civilization so that he will say 'I'
instead of 'We,' and 'This is mine' instead of 'This is ours,'" and that
"We must make the Indian more intelligently selfish . . . By acquiring
property, man puts forth his personality and lays hold of matter by his
own thought and will."

Senator Henry Dawes, a regular attendee of the Lake Mohonk
conferences and a member of the Friends of the Indian, enlisted paid
lobbyists in Washington, D.C., to push forward the General Allotment
Act, which would split up communal, tribal lands into individual
allotments or parcels of land per Indian and then sell the remaining
"surplus." Meanwhile, the National Indian Defense Association (NIDA)
was created in 1885 in an effort to stop the allotment plans of Dawes
and the IRA. NIDA was committed to including Indians' points of view
in policies that affected them. Although they supported private land
ownership, NIDA members foresaw that immediate allotment and
Indians' assumption of private parcels would impede the "civilization"
process. Without tribal governments, and given the abuses rampant
in the U.S. Indian service, Indians would lack the civil structures and
stability necessary to hold on to their land and make something of it.

The IRA and the NIDA debated their views on the General Allotment Act in front of the congressional House Indian Committee in
December 1885. NIDA ultimately argued that the allotment act would
benefit the land-hungry financiers and the railroads more than the
Indians, since the act gave the Indians no choice in what land they
would be "allotted," and that the price the government would pay

for the "surplus" land was criminally low. NIDA's efforts bore fruit in the final edition of the bill, which included clear language stating that tribes would have to agree to allotment beforehand. Additionally, Indians would have twenty-five years before the title of their allotments would revert to them as truly private property; until that time, the land would be held in trust for them by the government. These changes gave the Indians at least some wiggle room (though not enough) in an otherwise disastrous policy.

The General Allotment Act, also known as the Dawes Act, passed in 1887. It transformed the landscape of America and forever altered the ways in which most tribes lived on their homelands. Its key provision stated that Indian reservations that were good for farming and grazing could be broken up and redistributed to individuals, rather than be considered communal land held by the tribe overall. The allotments started with 160 acres for the head of an Indian family, with percentage breakdowns of that for single people and orphans in the tribe. To the reformers, the strengths of the Dawes Act were that it promised to break up the tribe as a social unit, encourage private enterprise and farming, reduce the cost of Indian administration, fund the emerging boarding school system with the sale of "surplus land," and provide a land base for white settlement. For the Indians, it meant that the government stole their land to fund the theft of their children.

By the time of the Wounded Knee Massacre in 1890, allotment was in full swing. Indian agents were busy hiring surveyors, recording deeds, and registering Indian heads of household. Armies of surveyors mapped Indian homelands and marked them off. Clerks worked nonstop copying and recording deeds, although Indians could not buy or sell land. The allotments they "owned" were run by the government in trust.

The General Allotment (Dawes) Act prompted whole new determinations of who was officially Indian. Censuses were taken on reservations across the country. At the time, tribes recognized their members in a variety of ways: residence, descent, marriage, language, etc. Some Indian agents made lists of people they considered Indian for the purpose of distributing annuities and rations. There was no one system.

Compounding the problem, censuses and subsequent tribal enrollment were conducted by white federal employees on the basis of kinship terms that might have no correlation in the Indian cultures in question. The rolls were compiled and kept by outsiders; Indians were not in charge of deciding who was in their own tribe or not. From the outset the process was marked by graft, greed, nepotism, favoritism, and fraud. Indian agents consolidated power by giving good allotments to Indians who supported their policies. In some cases, they excluded especially good allotments entirely so that white people (often business interests who had agents in their pockets) ended up owning vast tracts of the very best land within the boundaries of the reservation. It is no accident that non-Natives own the majority of the shoreline on all the best lakes in Minnesota, or the richest farmland with access to water in Nebraska, Montana, and South Dakota.

The size of the allotments often didn't make much sense. It is one thing to have 160 acres to farm in the Red River Valley or along the Arkansas River. It's another to have 160 acres in the semiarid grasslands and scrub of South Dakota where no crops will grow at all. Where cultivation was impossible, even animal grazing often required more than 160 acres because the land was so poor. Control over the allotted land itself and how it could be transferred between people, even family members, was always subject to the whims of the Indian agent, yet another way for the U.S. government to force Indians to do what they wanted. Indians who were reluctant to adopt this system found their rations came late, diminished, or not at all until they signed allotment papers: starvation is a powerful motivator.

While the first wave of allotments was crashing on Indian shores in the 1890s, the General Allotment Act was amended and supplemented by further acts of Congress.

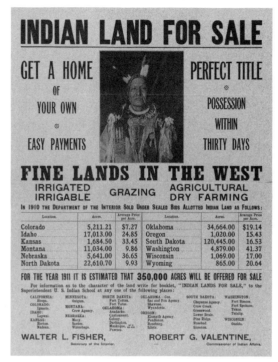

INDIAN LAND FOR SALE

GET A HOME
OF
YOUR OWN
⁂
EASY PAYMENTS

PERFECT TITLE
⁂
POSSESSION
WITHIN
THIRTY DAYS

FINE LANDS IN THE WEST

IRRIGATED IRRIGABLE	GRAZING	AGRICULTURAL DRY FARMING

IN 1910 THE DEPARTMENT OF THE INTERIOR SOLD UNDER SEALED BIDS ALLOTTED INDIAN LAND AS FOLLOWS:

Location.	Acres.	Average Price per Acre.	Location.	Acres.	Average Price per Acre.
Colorado	5,211.21	$7.27	Oklahoma	34,664.00	$19.14
Idaho	17,013.00	24.85	Oregon	1,020.00	15.43
Kansas	1,684.50	33.45	South Dakota	120,445.00	16.53
Montana	11,034.00	9.86	Washington	4,879.00	41.37
Nebraska	5,641.00	36.65	Wisconsin	1,069.00	17.00
North Dakota	22,610.70	9.93	Wyoming	865.00	20.64

FOR THE YEAR 1911 IT IS ESTIMATED THAT **350,000** ACRES WILL BE OFFERED FOR SALE

For information as to the character of the land write for booklet, "INDIAN LANDS FOR SALE," to the Superintendent U. S. Indian School at any one of the following places:

CALIFORNIA: Hoopa.	MINNESOTA: Onigum.	NORTH DAKOTA: Fort Totten.	OKLAHOMA—Con. Sac and Fox Agency.	SOUTH DAKOTA: Cheyenne Agency.	WASHINGTON: Fort Simcoe.
COLORADO: Ignacio.	MONTANA: Crow Agency.	Fort Yates. OKLAHOMA:	Shawnee. Wyandotte.	Crow Creek. Greenwood.	Fort Spokane. Tulalip.
IDAHO: Lapwai.	NEBRASKA: Macy.	Anadarko. Cantonment.	OREGON: Klamath Agency.	Lower Brule. Pine Ridge.	WISCONSIN: Oneida.
KANSAS: Horton. Nadeau.	Santee. Darlington. Winnebago.	Colony. Darlington. Muskogee, Pawnee.	Pendleton. Roseburg. Siletz.	Rosebud. Sisseton.	

WALTER L. FISHER,
Secretary of the Interior.

ROBERT G. VALENTINE,
Commissioner of Indian Affairs.

A 1911 poster from the U.S. Department of the Interior. Pictured is Yanktonai Sioux chief Padani-Kokipa-Sni (Not Afraid of Pawnee), reproduced from a photo taken in 1905.

There were no programs in place to educate Indians on what property taxes were, much less how to deal with them. Without small businesses, steady employment, or the reasonable expectation that their allotment would begin turning a profit (assuming that crops could be grown there in the first place, and that there was transportation and access to markets), thousands of Indians owed back taxes almost immediately. Local and state governments could collect by foreclosing on the land. It did not help that the allotment of so many Indian lands occurred shortly before the Great Depression and the ecological disaster of the Dust Bowl, when so many small farms and farmers were ruined.

And then there was the matter of how to measure the "competence" of people who had never owned land, at least not in the sense of individual allotments. Policy at the time was that Indians who possessed European blood had enough competence—based on their degree of "whiteness"—to buy and sell and pay taxes on land. For the purposes of determining who had European blood, teams of phrenologists were sent to Indian country. Phrenologists believed you could determine mental capacity and character traits by examining the size and shape of the skull. Of course, this pseudoscience determined "scientifically" that Caucasians had the largest brain capacity—1,426 cubic centimeters versus a paltry 1,344 for American Indians and 1,278 for Black people. The phrenologists set about measuring skulls, and on this basis, thousands of Indians were, surprisingly, deemed competent to own land: the better to steal it from them for back taxes owed.

Some people went beyond using political and legal means to deprive Indians of their land—and their lives. In the 1920s, a "Reign of Terror" was launched against the oil-rich Osage in Oklahoma. Wealthy members of the tribe were poisoned, shot, stabbed, beaten, and bombed in a brutal campaign to steal their mineral rights. Twenty-four people, and probably many, many more, died. Among them was Anna Brown (left) and her mother, Lizzie Que (center). William K. Hale, a white settler who had profited from the Oklahoma Land Rush (a direct result of allotment policies) masterminded the plot. He was convicted of only one murder.

The allotment period spanned 1887 to 1934, when the Indian Reorganization Act finally ended the policy. During those forty-seven years, Indian landholdings dropped from 138 million to 48 million acres; Indian homelands had been reduced by two-thirds. What the great process of "civilization" had brought to Indian country was poverty, disenfranchisement, and the breakdown of Indian families. Without steady employment, often homeless on their own reservations, and chronically malnourished, Indians across the country were vulnerable to disease. For some families boarding schools were the sole option: to keep their children with them was to starve them to death. But the "civilizing" assault didn't stop at land and family.

INDIAN OFFENSES

Traditional warrior societies that enforced tribal law and kept the peace, such as the Dog Soldiers among the Lakota and the Bear Clan among the Ojibwe, were in shambles or underground or suppressed. Many tribes who had been traditional enemies were now crowded cheek by jowl on reservations that were entirely too small for all of them. There were shortages of food, clothing, blankets, and shelter. And the very structure of many reservations eroded a people's sense of self. Who are we, a tribe might ask, when we can no longer hunt or fish or gather or travel?

Policy makers and government officials willfully ignored their complicity in creating such an abject state. Instead, they decided that an increased law enforcement presence on reservations was necessary. In 1878 legislation was passed empowering Indian agents to hire police to keep "law and order" on reservations around the country. The legislation included provisions for an Indian-staffed police force. As of 1882, Native police were on reservations, but there were no codes, laws, or policies for them to follow. Nor were there courts in which to try Indians accused of crimes. In 1883 a Court of Indian Offenses was created and funded by Congress. But it was clear that the agents who pushed for the bill and the legislators who drafted it had more than law and order in mind. Here was another assault on Indian cultural selfhood and autonomy.

The Court of Indian Offenses was governed by only nine provisions. The first three concerned its makeup and procedures. The court would be composed of the top three ranking police officers at each agency (although if the local agent questioned their competency, he could appoint the court officers himself); the court had to meet twice a month; and the court would "hear and pass judgment upon all such questions as may be presented to it for consideration by the agent." The other provisions governed what constituted an "Indian" offense and what the punishment should be for conviction of different kinds of offenses. Those participating in the "sun-dance," the "scalp-dance," or the "war-dance," would lose their rations for ten days for a first offense; subsequent offenses meant fifteen to thirty days without rations or thirty days in the agency jail. Any Indians who entered a plural marriage and had more than one spouse would be fined twenty dollars or sentenced to twenty days of hard labor. They would receive no rations as long as they continued in the "unlawful relation." There would also be no rations for any member of the tribe who failed to support his wife and children. Medicine men were deemed "a hindrance to the civilization of a tribe." If he "resorts to any artifice or device to keep the Indians under his influence, or shall adopt any means to prevent the attendance of children at the agency schools, or shall use any of the arts of a conjurer to prevent the Indians from abandoning their heathenish rites and customs" or does anything the court decides is "of an equally anti-progressive nature," the convicted medicine man could be jailed for ten days or until he agrees to abandon his practice. Other rules forbid certain mourning rituals and gift-giving practices.

The codes and offenses now were clear: Indian ceremonial life was to be disrupted by Indian police and tried in the Court of Indian Offenses; adhering to one's traditions would be punished. As with the boarding school system and allotment, the Code of Indian Offenses was designed to destroy Indian culture as a means of making Indians American—but Americans on the bottom rung of the ladder.

Power became more concentrated in the Office of Indian Affairs. The government that appointed itself the guardian of Indian futures instead seemed to be bringing about the "disappearing Indian" that American culture so mythologized. But it was Indians themselves who made sure this didn't come to pass.

THE SEEDS OF TRIBAL RESISTANCE

In 1863 the Red Lake Band and Pembina Band of Ojibwe were induced by the governor of Minnesota to sign a treaty ceding roughly eleven million acres of prime woodlands and prairie on either side of the Red River. The Treaty of Old Crossing promised the Indians considerable annuities and the right to hunt, fish, and travel in the ceded area in exchange for what was described as the "right of passage" for oxcarts and wagon trains headed west.

The wording of the treaty—misrepresented and not adequately translated to the chiefs—was clear enough, as was the intent. The government was after nothing less than extinguishing Ojibwe claim to the whole region, as the next thirty years would prove. The chiefs who signed the treaty saw that their good faith had been misplaced, and they grew deeply suspicious of the government thereafter.

Government representatives returned to Red Lake in 1886, hoping to secure the approval of the tribe to relocate other Ojibwe there, and to prepare the reservation for allotment. The Red Lake leaders were ready for them. Meskokonayed (Red Robed) opened with a salvo of complaints: "We do not know any of our chiefs who have ceded this land; we cannot find the name of a single chief who has ever ceded this land or signed his name on paper."

The chiefs were relentless. They rejected the government's proposals out of hand, and indeed the right of any outsider to put a price on their land. "This property belongs to us, the Red Lake Indians. That is the conclusion we have all arrived at," they said. Then Red Robed and

Medwe-ganoonind (He Who Is Spoken To) began a long recital of ille-gal timber cutting, inroads made by homesteaders, and the past false dealings of the government. He Who Is Spoken To also made clear that "We wish to live alone on our premises; we do not wish any other Indians to come here." The chiefs were resolute: they unanimously opposed allotment.

The Red Lake chiefs were as smart as they were determined: they could read the writing on the wall. Allotment was coming, and they would have to fight it. They used another huge tract of land north of the reservation as a bargaining chip. The chiefs told the government they were willing to cede much of it in exchange for opting out of allotment and as long as the Red Lake Band controlled all the land around both Upper and Lower Red Lake. He Who Is Spoken To also demanded that this sentence appear at the top of the treaty: "It should be premised that the Red Lake Reservation has never been ceded to the United States." (In most cases, during treaties, tribes relinquished title to the land and then portions of it were deeded back to them.)

Another commission was sent to Red Lake in the summer of 1889 to try again for allotment. Once again they were met in force by a united Red Lake leadership.

After days of tense negotiations between the Red Lake leaders and the commissioners, Chief Niigaanakwad (Leading Cloud) declared, "Your mission here is a failure . . . To show you that my assertion is cor-rect, I proclaim it by a rising vote." Two-thirds of the Red Lakers in attendance rose to their feet in support. Another chief, Wewe (Snow Goose), echoed clearly: "I don't want to accept your propositions, I love my reservation very much; I don't want to sell it."

After six days of talks, He Who Is Spoken To spoke for all of Red Lake: "I do not look with favor on the allotment plan. We wish that any land we possess should be not only for our own benefit, but for our posterity, our grandchildren hereafter . . . We think that we should own in common everything that pertains to us." In the end the Red Lake Ojibwe ceded millions of acres of land to the north, but they were never subjected to allotment. The Red Lake chiefs survived and learned a valuable lesson: they needed to maintain strong leadership and a consensus among the general population of the tribe. Only by presenting a united front could they hope to stave off the U.S. government. Other tribes were not so lucky, but they all resisted their own destruction in their own way.

The Chickasaw, Cherokee, Choctaw, Creek, and Seminole charted a different course than Red Lake. The five tribes lost millions of acres due to allotment and were rendered temporarily politically voiceless. Since they didn't have reservations anymore, they essentially borrowed American civic structures to preserve their tribes and their tribal selves. They functioned as citizens and incorporated towns, opened businesses, bought and sold land, levied taxes, founded civic organizations, ran Indian candidates as mayors, aldermen, and city councilmen, and engaged in a frenzy of institution building. The five tribes learned how to adapt in a way that made them relatively strong and able to withstand much of what the U.S. government threw at them.

The Menominee, who had arguably lived in the western Great Lakes longer than any other Algonquian tribe, resisted in their own unique ways. At the time of contact in the seventeenth century, the Menominee had consolidated their territory to an area of about ten million acres in northeastern Wisconsin. They managed to stay there, and to hold on to their land for quite some time. But in the nineteenth century, facing relocation and inroads by white settlers, they began ceding land to the U.S. government. After the last cession in 1856, the Menominee were left with about three hundred thousand acres northwest of Green Bay that were almost entirely given over to old-growth white and red pine forest. As the settlers around them cleared the land and planted crops, the Menominee watched and decided, collectively, not to follow suit. They felt if they could protect the trees, they, in turn, would be protected by them.

Oral history has it that a kind of spiritually based sustainable-yield management system was put into practice shortly after the Menominee reservation was established in 1854. According to a tribal leader, Charlie Frechette, the Menominee invoke this practice as part of many of their ceremonial proceedings: "Start with the rising sun and work toward the setting sun, but take only the mature trees, the sick trees, and the trees that have fallen. When you reach the end of the reservation, turn and cut from the setting sun to the rising sun, and the trees will last forever." The tribe was in a position to use the resources it had left in order to take care of itself and to remain self-sufficient.

The U.S. government, contradicting its own idea of "civilization" (Weren't Indians supposed to learn "I" and not "we," and the value of buying and selling?), quickly put a stop to Menominee logging in 1861 and again in 1876. It competed with the timber barons in Wisconsin, Michigan, and Minnesota who wanted to reap the profit from the forest themselves. When allotment arrived in 1887, the Menominee fought it. They recognized that allotment would forever destroy their sustainable harvest practices and benefit the timber barons. Menominee lands remained unallotted. In 1890 the tribe won a victory in Congress that allowed them to harvest twenty million board feet of their own timber. This, however, did not stop business interests with strong ties to state government from trying to take their wood. Legislation championed by Senator Robert La Follette of Wisconsin allowed the tribe to cut and process timber under the selective cutting system they favored. Still, the tribe had to file suit after suit in court when the "experts" and outside interests continually ignored or violated the terms of the legislation. But because of the La Follette bill, the Menominee kept control of their forest and eventually won damages against businesses and the government. And after 125 years of logging and more than two billion board feet of timber harvested, the Menominee have more board feet of northern hardwoods still standing on their land than they started with.

Four hundred years of contact with Europeans brought rapacious colonization and devastating diseases. But it also showed the supreme adaptability and endurance of Indian tribes across the North American continent. This tough resourcefulness served them well in the years between 1890 and 1934, when the assaults on Indians and Indian homelands were perhaps at their most creative, if not their bloodiest. It was a new kind of Indian war, fought not by the sudden attack of cavalry or by teams of buffalo hunters. These years were more of a siege. The government's weapons were greed and fraud. Indians resisted.

One fascinating side effect of the attempts to crush tribes and tribal solidarity was manifest in homesteading itself. The first Homestead Act, passed in 1862, was meant to pave the way for a new generation of white American farmers to claim "public" land in the western territories and then settle on it and then cultivate it. In 1865 tribes in Wisconsin were allowed to claim homesteads, improve the land, file for an ownership patent after five years, and thereby gain citizenship. Many of them did. The Cherokee and other members of the Five Civilized Tribes were given the same opportunity in the early 1900s. They figured they would fare better if they functioned, politically anyway, as Americans rather than Indians.

Hundreds and eventually thousands of Cherokee, Seminole, Creek, Choctaw, and Chickasaw families fanned out from Oklahoma into Kansas, Nebraska, and Colorado, the first wave of a vast diaspora of Indian families into Indian homelands originally not their own. They put down roots and made lives for themselves as Americans. And they brought their tribal cultures and sense of community with them. The graduates of the Indian boarding schools did much the same: if they returned to their tribes, they brought their experiences of other tribal people back with them, along with the academic and practical skills that would be invaluable in the conflicts ahead.

Kevin Washburn, seemingly tireless on our second lap of the golf course, mused about this resilience. "Someone asked George W. Bush what qualities you needed to be the president. He said, 'You've got to have principles. People have to know what kinds of decisions you're going to make.' I thought, 'That's wrong! You just have to do justice.' But then I became assistant secretary, faced many policy decisions each day, and I realized George Bush was right about something. You do have to have principles. And mine are based in tribal self-determination; tribes know what's best for their tribe and they have the abilities and the experience to make their own decisions." It was so clear walking and talking with him on that sunny spring day in Albuquerque that Washburn was right. Despite the U.S. government's three-pronged assault on Indian communities and people—boarding schools, allotment, and the law—Indian tribes not only clung to the old ways but also found in them a strength that would help them survive decades of crushing control and work to preserve what remained, on their own terms.

FIGHTING LIFE
1914–1945

❖◈❖◈❖◈❖◈❖◈❖

I SAW MANY THINGS AT a mixed martial arts (MMA) event at the Northern Lights Casino on Leech Lake Reservation on March 17, 2012. I saw Tory Nelson defeat my cousin Tony Tibbetts after throwing a dozen illegal elbows, enough so Tony couldn't breathe after the second round. I saw, for the first time, Indians beating up white people in front of a sold-out crowd and I heard the crowd roar. I saw a forty-seven-year-old from the reservation town of Ball Club whose gym was called the Den of Raging Mayhem manage to beat my unbeatable cousin Nate Seelye. I watched my nephew tune out the fights and tune into Skrillex and my mother check her watch to see if she was missing *Law & Order*. I saw two, maybe three, ex-girlfriends; my cousins Nate, Josh, Jason, Delbert, Tammie, and Amber; and my uncles Jerry, Davey, and Lanny. I was part of a sea of baseball caps and braids and Indians and whites and the good people of Leech Lake and Walker, Indian and white, who got up and cheered as we watched the contenders step into the cage and fight.

There were no sponsors and no scouts, no pre-publicity or small prize purses. We were in the middle of the reservation in northern Minnesota and most everyone had a day job or needed one that paid more. Instead of glamour we had hometown boys and girls. It was easy to feel, even if it wasn't true, that little if anything separated us from those in the cage except a willingness to be there. On the reservation, there are plenty of reasons why a person might step into the fighting cage. Oh, I saw a lot at the Northern Lights Casino that night. But what

I didn't see was what I had largely come there to witness: my cousin Sam Cleveland was supposed to fight his last professional fight. But he didn't.

What happened to Sam? Better: What didn't? At the time, Sam was on the far side of fighting age but not over it yet, not by a long shot. "I still got a lot of power, still got a six-pack," he mused as we sat at the Bemidji State University recreation center where Sammy had gone to run and lift weights. He was scheduled to fight the main event in the King of the Cage Winter Warriors Showdown at the casino. His body looked hard and lean. He had strong square hands, wide shoulders, and powerful legs. His face showed not a few scars from years of fighting.

Sam Cleveland is my first cousin. Like me, he grew up at Leech Lake, but, as he put it, much more "in the mix." He is a favorite fighter of many around our reservation and even around the state. He was a star wrestler in high school, as his father had been. Sammy had grown up poor but not destitute. He was popular in high school. Like me, he suffered a particular kind of racism as a red-haired, fair-skinned Indian on the rez.

Sam was, by any standard, a success. He graduated from high school (Native students are more than twice as likely to drop out than whites), and so far, he's avoided a long stint in jail (Indian men are twice as likely to end up there). In Minnesota in 2015, Indians, who made up only 1 percent of the state population, were 7 percent of the jail and 10 percent of the prison populations.

After graduation in 1992, Sammy joined the army and became part of the elite Army Scouts stationed at Schofield Barracks, Hawaii. He loved it. "I really liked the army side of things. It was an elite unit, and that suited me. Always something interesting to do." Back at Leech Lake, the unemployment rate was 46 percent; the median household income was less than twenty thousand dollars a year. Yet Sam missed the reservation and the network of family and friends and the landscape of northern Minnesota, where the boreal forest meets the oak savanna. "I was three years into my tour and I was so far away. And then

Nessa [his sister Vanessa] died the last year of my tour, and it really made me miserable." Nessa grew up scrappy and lippy. She had left a party and driven through two yards and onto Highway 2, where an RV hit her.

Suddenly, all that separated Sam from everyone else (graduation, a job, a life) disappeared. It's one thing to be borne aloft on the wave of the American Dream—safety-netted by college, by working parents, by a backdrop of wealth or entitlement, or even by the illusion that what we do, our work, our effort, counts for something, matters in some way—and another to feel, as many Indians do, totally powerless. That's how Sam felt. He didn't reenlist. Instead, he came back to Leech Lake Reservation. "I got really angry after Nessa died. I drank a lot. I'd fought a little before that. But then, after Nessa died, I wanted to fight every time I went somewhere. I probably got into a couple hundred street fights. Brawls, you know."

I remember seeing Sam during holidays or around town in those years. It seemed like every time I saw him, he had one fewer teeth, or a new cast on his hand, or a new scar. Back when we were kids, he'd had a round, open, cheerful face, and was always laughing. But that boy's face disappeared and in its place was the hard face of a man who liked to fight, who, not to put too fine a point on it, liked hurting people. "Nothing I could do could change anything about Nessa, or my mom, who really fell apart. But I could fight." And that's when Sam became a lot like the rest of our tribemates: he had physical talent and he had mental talent, and none of it mattered. Or none of it felt like it mattered.

Sam was living at Leech Lake Reservation in our village, Bena, at the time. Leech Lake is a big reservation, about forty by forty miles. Within the reservation boundaries, there are a number of towns and villages tucked here and there among the swamps, rivers, lakes, and pine trees. Some of the communities are exclusively Indian, like Inger and Ball Club, some are almost all white, and some, like Bena, are mixed.

Bena was the end of the line during logging days; in the early part of the twentieth century, our village boasted a number of hotels, stores, and restaurants. After most of the virgin white pine and pulp was cut down in northern Minnesota, Bena stayed alive thanks to the growing tourist trade. As roads got better, boats sturdier, and Americans wealthier, they traveled farther and farther north in search of good fishing. Situated on the southern shore of Lake Winnibigoshish, Bena became a fishing destination. But the lake crashed eventually, due to overfishing. Bena got smaller and smaller. Today it has a population of around 118, one gas station, a bar, and a post office.

Despite the seemingly unbreakable bonds the village exerts on those of us whose families are from there, Bena is a place that can encourage destruction and dysfunction. To be from Bena was in some fundamental way to be tough. If people found out they'd be fighting a Bena boy, often they'd take a pass.

I didn't fit the tough Bena mold, but Sam did. He fought at bars. He fought at house parties. He literally fought in the street. Sam also drank a lot. His mother, my aunt Barb, who, like Sam, had done really well for a long time, began to slide after her daughter Vanessa's death. Sober for years, Aunt Barb began drinking and using drugs again. A host of health problems ensued. There was nothing Sam could do except fight, and that's what he did. Fighting and partying led to drugs and crime. This life went on for years. It's a wonder he didn't die. But Sam has always had stamina. Eventually, he was convicted of aggravated assault. "I chose the wrong path, and there I was, sitting in prison. So when I got out, I got out on the right foot. I didn't go back to Bena." Sam went to live with a friend in the Twin Cities (Minneapolis and St. Paul). Around 2000, he was working hard, living away from the reservation, and heard about MMA on the radio. This was, for Sam, a kind of answer. It might, it just might, offer some structure for the fight in him, which was, by this point, as much a part of him as breathing.

Our tribe, the Ojibwe, are not known for being warlike. Until the late seventeenth century we lacked any real sort of tribal identity and didn't engage in much warfare beyond small skirmishes. Loose bands, based on marriage and clan, moved seasonally between beds of wild rice, fishing grounds, and sugar bush. Hunger, more than other men, was the enemy, and battles were small and relatively rare. However, as the demand for furs increased in the East and overseas, the Ojibwe around the Great Lakes acted as middlemen, securing furs from the West and selling them to the East in exchange for guns and ammunition and cloth. They grew powerful in that role. Their land base grew, infant mortality dropped, the standard of living rose, and the small Ojibwe bands joined together into a vast, complicated, calculating tribe that effectively controlled a major part of the fur trade. In an effort to expand their territory and therefore their security, the Ojibwe began battling the Dakota, on and off. Life was war, and anyone who belonged to an enemy band was a legitimate target: men, women, children.

WHAT TO DO WHEN THE FIGHTING IS OVER

After the Ojibwe and our enemies became friends, after open hostilities between the U.S. government and the tribes ended at the close of the Plains Wars, after the reservation period began, the question remained: What to do when the fighting is over? World war provided an answer.

In 1917 tribal authority was being eroded by the Dawes Act and other allotment amendments and the Court and Code of Indian Offenses. Power continued to be stripped from tribes and individual Indians. Indian families endured assault after assault on their autonomy and collectivity. Indian homelands were bled of acreage. And Indian men, in proportions far higher than any other ethnic or racial group, began signing up to serve in the American Expeditionary Forces. The AEF were the U.S. Army troops headed for Europe's western front, the main theater of war in World War I.

Francis Pegahmagabow (Arrives Standing) was Ojibwe from Wasauksing First Nation on Parry Island in Lake Huron. He was drafted at the beginning of World War I. Pegahmagabow served as a scout and excelled as a sniper. He saw action at the Second Battle of Ypres, and at Somme and Passchendaele. By the time of the armistice in 1918, he had been wounded twice and was one of the most decorated Canadian soldiers in history. Pegahmagabow was credited with 378 confirmed kills and the capture of three hundred Germans.

Indians had already been serving in large numbers in Canada (a part of the British Commonwealth) since World War I broke out in 1914. Many Indians from northern tribes in the United States walked or paddled across the U.S.-Canada border and enlisted. But there was no consensus between tribes as they puzzled out how and to what extent they would work with (or against) the American government. When the U.S. government required Indian men to register for the draft in World War I, not a few southern and western tribes bristled. American Indians were not, generally, citizens at the time.

Still, the U.S. War Department estimated that more than seventeen thousand Indian men served in World War I. Sixty-five hundred of them were drafted, the rest volunteered. Some tribes sent very few of their men. Only 1 percent of Diné (Navajo) men served, while more than 40 percent of Osage and Quapaw from Oklahoma joined up.

Meanwhile, many Choctaw Indians, also from Oklahoma, joined the AEF. Nineteen Choctaw transmitted messages about troop movements and dispositions, attacks and counterattacks during the waning days of World War I. They became the first "code talkers." The Germans were unable to decipher the Choctaw language, especially the code talkers' euphemisms and coined words for terms that didn't exist in their language, like "artillery" and "tank." All in all, as much as 30 percent of the adult Indian male population participated in World War I, double the percentage of all adult American men who served.

Within months of the draft in June 1917, Indians—both men and women—could be found in every branch of the U.S. military. (Most of the Ojibwe men from Red Cliff Reservation in Wisconsin served in the military police. Pablo Herrera, a Pueblo student from Carlisle Indian Industrial School, ended up commanding a balloon squadron. Five Osage men from Oklahoma served in an aero squadron as pilots. Fourteen Indian women joined the Army Nurse Corps; two of them worked in hospitals in France.)

Cora Elm, a member of the Oneida Nation of Wisconsin, graduated from a nursing program in Philadelphia, Pennsylvania, in 1916. During World War I, she served with the U.S. Army Nurse Corps in France in 1917 and 1918. As she later noted, "I saw a lot of the horrors of war. I nursed many a soldier with a leg cut off, or an arm."

The Indian boarding schools were a rich source of Indian volunteers. Hampton Institute, Carlisle, Chilocco, Haskell, and Phoenix
Indian Schools all sent hundreds and eventually thousands of students off to World War I. Even many of their underage students were
encouraged to enlist. Since most of the Indian boarding schools were
organized using military principles, their enlistees often had an easier
time adjusting to army life than their white counterparts. They were
often paid more, too: their vocational training in school qualified them
for positions most other draftees and volunteers couldn't fill, such
as carpenters' mates, shipwrights, blacksmiths, electricians, and col-
liers. Most Indians, however, served in the infantry. Most were there to
shoot and get shot at.

After initial clashes in eastern France, the Allied and German forces
repeatedly tried to outflank each other in what became known as the
"race to the sea." Beginning at the First Battle of the Marne in France,
each force jumped north and west in an effort to maneuver around the
other, but they were too evenly matched. By 1915, a mere year after the
outbreak of war, the "war of movement" had devolved into an unbro-
ken line of trench warfare from Lorraine, France, to the Belgian coast.
The scale of the clashes is hard to fathom. In the ten-month Battle of
Verdun (1916), the French and Germans together suffered 975,000
casualties. Farther north at the Somme, the British lost 420,000 men,
the French 200,000, and the Germans 500,000 over a four-month
period.

Indian soldiers descended into this kettle of death, living
belowground in muddy trenches, deprived of light and food, pestered
by rats, and surrounded by the ooze and stench of the rotting
bodies of the combatants who died before them. They suffered from
trench foot and dysentery and were targets of mustard gas attacks,
bombardment, and snipers. Indians fought in the major engagements
of the war. Among them were Sergeant Otis W. Leader, a Choctaw

machine gunner in the Sixteenth Infantry Regiment. Before the war, Leader had been accused of spying for the Germans, and in an effort to clear his name he'd joined the infantry. Leader went on to fight at Soissons, Château-Thierry, Saint-Mihiel, and in the Argonne Forest. Before he was done, he'd been wounded and gassed twice. Sergeant Thomas Rogers (Arikara) and Joe Young Hawk (Lakota) also fought at Soissons. Rogers was an incredible soldier and was cited for bravery after he captured "at night barehanded and alone, many [German] sentinels." During the same battle, Young Hawk was captured by the Germans while on patrol. He turned on his captors and killed three with his bare hands. During the fray he was shot through both legs but nonetheless managed to capture two more Germans and march them back to American lines. During the Allied offensive at Saint-Étienne, Private Joseph Oklahombi of the Choctaw Nation rushed two hundred yards across open ground and captured a German machine gun position. He turned the machine gun on the Germans,

Joseph Oklahombi (center, with two unidentified women), who was also a Choctaw "code talker," was awarded the Silver Star and the Croix de Guerre but was never recommended for the Medal of Honor. In comparison, twenty of the U.S. troopers who opened fire on unarmed Lakota at Wounded Knee had received the Medal of Honor for their efforts twenty-seven years earlier.

killing seventy-nine of them before taking another 171 enemy soldiers captive—and holding them so for four days until reinforcements came to his aid, even while he was wounded and without food or water.

Tales of Indian heroism abounded and fed the stereotype of the "Indian brave" who was inured to death and pain. Firsthand testimony suggests the stereotypes might have been, at least in part, true. Major Tom Riley, the commander of the Third Battalion, 165th Infantry Division, observed, "If a battle was on, and you wanted to find the Indians, you would always find them at the front."

Indian heroism may have had as much to do with army protocol as it did with any cultural or genetic predisposition to bravery. As part of the induction process, recruits were administered "intelligence" tests. The answers to the dubious test questions determined where and in what capacity men served. The army generally attempted to preserve "intelligence" by placing high scorers on the test in less dangerous assignments, while those with lower scores were often assigned to infantry units. As a result, soldiers from inner-city slums, Appalachia, the Deep South, and Indian reservations—men often without access to money, education, or social mobility—wound up in the infantry. For Indians in service, the results were lethal: they disproportionately served as scouts, snipers, patrol leaders, and "you would always find them at the front" because the army put them there. Indians suffered casualty rates five times higher than the American Expeditionary Force as a whole.

Indians served in mixed regiments and battalions, a circumstance that was to ripple out in unforeseen ways through the years. The question of whether to segregate Indians was a fierce ideological battle. Congress declared war on Germany on April 6, 1917. By the end of the month, a congressional bill was introduced that provided citizenship at war's end for Indians who served in the North American Indian Cavalry; their tribal status would not be jeopardized.

Debates about segregated military service and citizenship followed. Wouldn't assimilation of Indians be better achieved by integration into regular regiments? That's what top-ranking military officials felt.

Tribal opinion itself was mixed. Some tribes—the Crow, Lakota, and others—wrote letters urging Congress to allow them to form all-Indian regiments. Others, like Red Cliff Reservation in Wisconsin, were glad that they were able to serve with their white neighbors. In the end, the army won that fight, and while there were some all-Indian regiments, most Indians served alongside white troops.

In the military, as at boarding school, Indians did pick up skills. They became literate and learned trades. They learned how to work within organizational structures, as bookkeepers, secretaries, teamsters, cooks, drivers, and triggermen; they built ships and baked bread and went on patrol. They did this as servicemen and -women and as Indians. And when the war was over, they more often than not came home. They returned changed and they returned to a shock: their homelands had been drastically altered by allotments and leases.

At the end of World War I, fewer than half of Indians were citizens, and even fewer had the right to vote. Not even all the men and women who served in the military gained citizenship. The United States, well on its way to becoming a world power, treated its Indian veterans shamefully and bungled its treaty obligations. For example, Joseph Oklahombi, who returned to Oklahoma the most decorated American Indian hero of the war, remained illiterate and found work loading lumber at a mill and coal company, but that didn't last long. He turned to booze and by 1932 was surviving on his veteran's pension of twelve dollars a month. He was struck and killed by a car while walking along the road on April 13, 1960.

But not all veterans lived—or died—alone. Navajo, Eastern Cherokee in North Carolina, and Lakota on the Rosebud Reservation in South Dakota established American Legion posts that provided a supportive community for former armed service members. Other Indians quietly parlayed their war experience into spiritual and political leadership positions within their tribes.

The men and women who returned from World War I were the first generation of Indian people who could begin to see the United States from outside both the American and the Indian lens. They had been to Brest, Paris, London, Lille. Now faced with acculturation at the bottom or forging a new Indian political identity where they had a say in what happened to them, the choice must have been clear. So it was not surprising that at the close of the First World War, Indian men and women began building new kinds of Indian communities and governments. And for the first time, they were armed with the tools of the modern nation-state. And something else was happening, too, something that escaped notice at the time. By 1917, for the first time in more than a hundred years, American Indian births outstripped Indian deaths. Our population was on the rise.

There was a push after World War I to extend citizenship to all Indians born in the United States. Once again, the push came from everyone except Indians themselves. The Friends of the Indian and the Indian Rights Association lobbied heavily. Reformers, increasingly disturbed by the degree of corruption and malfeasance in the Indian service, found a receptive audience in Congress. Surely the nation was capable of treating the most disenfranchised people within its borders less poorly. Citizenship for Indians, in other words, was meant to curb abuses by non-Indians. It arrived on June 2, 1924, without much fanfare. Passed by Congress, Public Law 68-175 read:

"Be it enacted by the Senate and House of Representatives of the United States of America in Congress assembled, That all non-citizen Indians born within the territorial limits of the United States be, and they are hereby, declared to be citizens of the United States: Provided, That the granting of such citizenship shall not in any manner impair or otherwise affect the right of any Indian to tribal or other property."

All of a sudden, the three hundred thousand Indians alive in 1924 in the United States became American citizens and remained tribal citizens. What this meant was profound: Indians could vote, own property, have wrongs redressed in court, and claim every other right of a U.S. citizen. And at the same time, all the treaties not yet voided, all the rights to communal and tribal ownership of land, all the basic building blocks of tribal sovereignty were left in place.

Many Indians, however, didn't gain suffrage, as states often used what power they had to limit Indians' access to the ballot. These states argued that Indians shouldn't be allowed to vote because it wasn't right for them to participate in both tribal and U.S. elections, or because they didn't pay taxes on real estate, or because many of them lived on land held in federal trusteeship. In the Southwest, depriving Indians of the right to vote was a clear attempt to block their influence in local and state elections. Because there were so many Indians in that region,

Native men and women register to vote for the first time in New Mexico, circa 1948.

their participation would likely skew elections away from desired Anglo outcomes. As of 1938, seven states hadn't extended suffrage to Indians. It wasn't until 1948—after thousands of Pueblo, Navajo, Hopi, and Apache had served in World War II—that Arizona and New Mexico, the two states with the largest proportion of Indians in the population, bent to court rulings and finally allowed Indians to vote.

EMERGENCE OF TRIBAL GOVERNMENTS

As early as 1918, Indian tribes began to organize themselves formally despite the control exerted by the Office of Indian Affairs and the federal government. At Red Lake Reservation, they formed the Red Lake General Council Red Lake Band of Chippewa Indians. ("Chippewa" was the older mispronunciation of "Ojibwe" but was in common usage among the Ojibwe.) This was, arguably, the first and only tribal representative body in the United States at the time.

White people outnumbered the Red Lakers on their own reservation. They had made inroads as timber crews, homesteaders, tourists, and fishermen. The U.S. government also wasn't content to let the reservation alone. They kept trying to allot it. The new General Council combined centuries-old hereditary Ojibwe chieftain positions with voting representatives they appointed. This new/old Red Lake government wed ancestral modes of government to modern democratic rule. It became the force that governed the reservation. Though it didn't happen overnight, gradually the General Council was able to erode the power of the Indian agents and expel all of the white people living at Red Lake reservation. But even as Red Lake took control of its destiny, things changed yet again. Once again, that change came to Indians all across the country from the top down, dreamed up by a few white officials and imposed uniformly in diverse communities, regardless of their needs.

President Franklin Delano Roosevelt's New Deal reached Indian country as the Indian Reorganization Act, passed in 1934. The IRA, or Wheeler-Howard Act, was revolutionary. It stopped allotment, created processes by which some of the Indian land already lost could be reclaimed, and provided means by which new lands could be incorporated. It also brought constitutions and governments to Indian communities that had suffered under the lazy but energetically corrupt hand of the Office of Indian Affairs. The kicker of the act was that tribes did not have to agree to the models of government proposed in the IRA, or even be reorganized along the lines drawn in it. Indians could vote on what worked best for their tribe.

This was a far cry from the punishing way legislation had generally been forced down the throats of Indian communities. Still, more subtle pressure nevertheless ensued. It was intimated that it would be difficult if not impossible for tribes to receive federal grants and assistance for public projects, livestock and grazing, roads, hospitals, and schools without a government in place that the U.S. federal government recognized. Moreover, the voting process was murky. Who was eligible to vote if tribes set up these recognized governments? By 1934 many non-Indians lived within the boundaries of Indian reservations as a result of allotment. Could they vote? And what about absentees? Many thousands of Indians didn't live in their homelands or on their reservations. It was decided that absentees counted as votes for the new government.

It seems clear that the U.S. government imagined a very specific kind of Indian government. The IRA provided sample constitutions for a governing body of five to nine people, election cycles, rights and responsibilities such as entering into contracts, acquiring and disposing of land, administering and collecting funds, hiring and firing, and enrollment. No wonder the majority of the tribal constitutions adopted between 1934 and 1938 as a result of the Indian Reorganization Act created governments like those in small towns across America.

That kind of government might work for the Pueblo, who lived in village-centered communities. But the Pine Ridge Reservation or the Blackfeet Nation or the Wind River Shoshone and Arapaho were nothing like villages at all. They were large, diverse nations, defined by treaties. They had been sedentary for only fifty years, and each comprised many villages and family groups, not to mention bands. And they were still contending with the predation of outsiders. As the years began to show, IRA constitutions were grossly inadequate for the enormous job of policing large tracts of land, making education truly "local," resolving disputes not just between Indians of the same tribe but between Indians of different tribes and between Indians and their non-Indian neighbors.

Indians fought the government plan after plan, policy after policy, legislative act after legislative act. They continued to fight to remain Indian and be Americans on their own terms. Only now, in the early twenty-first century, are tribes radically rethinking their constitutions and redrafting founding documents in ways that fit their culture, land, history, and sense of self as peoples.

WAR AND MIGRATION

After the Japanese attacked Pearl Harbor, Hawaii, on December 7, 1941, the United States officially declared war on the Axis powers. Just as they had in 1917, Indians too went to war.

By 1944 more than a third of the Indian adult male population had served in World War II. They were in every branch of the military and fought in every theater. Many were drafted (though some, in states where they still didn't have the right to vote, resisted), and many more volunteered for service. Indians were integrated into regular units. Back home, Indian women, like many other American women, joined the workforce as factory laborers and took over the majority of the harvest. My mother's mother worked in a plant near Austin, Minnesota.

It is tempting to see the exodus of Indians into the workforce and the fighting forces as the first massive migration of Indians in America. It wasn't. Indians, as we have seen, had been moving and shifting, migrating, forming and re-forming as far back as the archaeological record can show.

Among the most noted group of American Indians to serve in World War II were the Marine Corps' Navajo code talkers. Like the Choctaw of World War I, these Diné soldiers used their own language to create and memorize a complicated and unbreakable code to confound the enemy. The Navajo code talkers served in the intense fighting in the Pacific.

Perhaps the most famous Indian to serve in World War II was Ira Hayes. Hayes was a Pima Indian from Sacaton, Arizona. He enlisted in the Marine Corps in late August 1942 and volunteered for the paratrooper program. He had already seen battle action in the Pacific by February 19, 1945, when he landed with the Marines on the Japanese island of Iwo Jima. After four days of fierce fighting, Marines from Third Platoon Easy Company captured the summit of Mount Suribachi and raised a small American flag there.

The next day, Sergeant Michael Strank was ordered to pick three men from his platoon and to fly a bigger flag from the summit after they had dropped off supplies there. He took Harlon Block, Franklin Sousley, and Ira Hayes. Rene Gagnon, a battalion runner, brought the larger flag. After they scavenged a bigger flagpole, the five of them, along with Harold Schultz, raised the flag over Iwo Jima.

Hayes spent another month and a half fighting the Japanese who remained on the island. By the time he left with his unit at the end of March, he was one of only five surviving Marines out of a platoon of forty-five. The flag-raising photo made Hayes famous. In the spring of

The flag-raising on Iwo Jima, February 23, 1945. Ira Hayes is the soldier farthest to the left. Joe Rosenthal of the Associated Press won a Pulitzer Prize for what became the most famous photo of World War II.

1945, he toured the United States, raising money for war bonds. Then he rejoined his unit and was sent back to the Pacific, where he was part of the occupying force in Japan until he was honorably discharged in December 1945.

The after-war years must have been confusing and complicated for Hayes. He was arrested fifty-two times for public drunkenness. He was unable to hold down a steady job. He once said, "I was sick . . . I guess I was about to crack up thinking about all my good buddies. They were better men than me and they're not coming back." That was about as close as he came to naming his ghosts. Later, in 1954, at the dedication of the Marine Corps War Memorial, a reporter asked him how he liked all the "pomp and circumstance." All Hayes said was, "I don't." He was found dead near his home in Arizona on January 24, 1955. Cause of death: exposure and alcohol poisoning.

Hayes's life became symbolic for many Americans of the "plight" of modern Indians. They tried to read the entire history of American Indians into it: proud peoples who had been mistreated by a government they nevertheless protected and served as warriors, only to return to reservations where they and their service were forgotten by everyone except the warriors themselves, who couldn't forget.

Who knows? Most servicemen and -women fell somewhere in between the experiences of the code talkers and soldiers like Ira Hayes. My grandfather, for instance.

Eugene W. Seelye spent his entire life in the village where he grew up on the Leech Lake Reservation in northern Minnesota—with the exception of the two years and eight months he spent in the United States Army. Fifteen months of that, he spent overseas, in England, France, Belgium, and Germany. Growing up, I didn't know any of that. I didn't know about World War II or my grandfather's part in it, or what he thought and felt about it. He was, at least to me, frightening, angry, and sharp-tongued. By the time I was born in 1970 he spent most of his time in his easy chair by the window smoking Pall Malls, nursing a kind of acidic rage.

My grandfather didn't talk about World War II, though hanging from a knickknack shelf in the corner were ribbons on which were stitched the words "Normandy" and "France." His uniform, with the Indianhead star of the Second Infantry Division, hung in the closet behind his chair. I got up the courage to ask him about the war, once, when I was in high school. All he said was, "The worst time of my life. Wouldn't wish it on anyone."

In 1998 I went to France to promote my first novel. On my return, I stopped in at Teal's Super Valu in Cass Lake, the seat of our reservation. I saw my grandfather standing at the deli counter ordering pork chops and potato salad. *Hey, Gramps,* I said. *Hey, boy,* he said in that way of his. *Where you been?* I told him I had been in France, in Paris and Saint-Malo. I explained that Saint-Malo was in Brittany, but he interrupted me to say he knew exactly where that was.

That was the beginning of a shift, some kind of recalibration I didn't understand. I said, *So you were in Normandy. You bet, boy,* he said.

June seventh, I imagine. Maybe later? I asked. *June 6, 1944,* he said vehemently. I said, *Maybe we should go to my mom's house, cook up those pork chops.* And, to my surprise, he agreed.

My mother sized up the situation quickly. She stood at the counter prepping dinner, standing purposely outside the conversation, as if anything she might say would end it. It was as if someone had cast a spell of volubility over her father. On he went about Belgium. The trees, the countryside. The ways the peasants (in his words) cleaned the forests of sticks and trees felled by wind and how the whole forest felt manicured, unlike the tangle of our northern pine and poplar forest. How he had his shoes resoled in Vielsalm. How, while bivouacked in the same village, he befriended a red-haired kid. How he carved his name in a tree near the château where they were camped. How he was wounded near Aachen, just over the border with Germany. My grandfather stayed long into the evening, even though his eyes bothered him and it was hard for him to drive after dark. He wondered, with real longing, if the tree where he carved his name was still standing. I told him I would go back to France and find my way to Belgium, find Vielsalm, find the château, find the tree. I don't think he believed me. But months later I did go back, with the map of the village he'd drawn from memory.

Vielsalm is a Belgian village on the Salm River in the Ardennes region near the German border. The Allies and the Germans traded the town back and forth a few times before the Germans were pushed back in January 1945. The Ardennes is wild country—steep wooded ravines, small fast-flowing streams and rivers. The land is folded, crumpled in on itself. I imagined there would be one château in Vielsalm. There were at least a dozen. With the help of the man who owned the motel where I was staying, I found a likely place. But I returned home, not sure I'd seen anything other than beautiful country. My grandfather called me the day I returned; when my photographs were developed, he came over without even calling first. He sat at my table and paged through the photos. He pointed to one. *That's it. That's the one.* I thought maybe he was simply hoping, that there was a pleasant lie in the act of stabbing his finger into the frame. *When you face the building, there was a door on the right, in kind of a tower thing,* he said. *That's the door I used.* My heart fell. There had been no door. No tower. Nothing like that. He was wrong. Or more like: he wanted to recognize the place more than he wanted to be right. He flipped two more pictures. *See, boy. See? There's that door.* I looked, and sure enough: covered by ivy, obscured by some hedges, there was a round stone outcropping on the building, and set in the stone was a small green door.

I was almost thirty when I went to France. But it was as though I'd just become my grandfather's grandson then.

We became close. I wasn't the only one in the family curious about him, or the war, or even just his time on earth. My cousins were. His children were, too. But maybe it was just that I had walked where he fought. I had slept where he'd been sleepless. I'd seen that other place. He shared his war stories.

My grandfather didn't talk at all about Normandy except to say that he saw guys drowning and he would rather get shot than drown. And that nothing saved him except luck. About the Ardennes he said only that they learned to hug trees because the Germans would fire shells aimed at treetop level, sending splinters down in all directions. The safest place to avoid those was directly under a tree. He did say that he hadn't been shot. Rather, while he was on patrol, just over the German border, one of the men in his patrol stepped on a mine. It blew off the man's legs and sent a shard of shrapnel through my grandfather's shoulder. He remarked how surprised he was to see this man, last name Van Winkle, in a hospital near Seattle after the war. He mentioned how he was attached to the 101st Airborne during the Battle of the Bulge. But mostly he talked about the land and the weather and the buildings and the forests and the people. He mentioned how the army had wanted him to be a sniper but he was too scared to be tied into a tree. How he was assigned to be a truck driver but never once got a truck to drive and so he walked and fought the whole way through France and Belgium. These were the stories he told until he shot himself in the head in 2007, just after his eighty-third birthday.

My grandmother asked me to clean up the room where my grandfather shot himself, and I did. He died without giving me the answers I thought I needed. And his death was also some kind of question. That day, however, I took the time to look for his discharge papers, his service record, some kind of record of his life as a soldier. As though whatever paper he kept after the war could tell me something he couldn't. I didn't find anything.

Five years after my grandfather's death, I petitioned the National Personnel Records Center, and after a few months, they sent me his file. Eugene W. Seelye was inducted at Fort Snelling, Minnesota, on January 21, 1943, a month before his nineteenth birthday. At the time of his induction, he was healthy. He stood five-foot-ten and weighed 155 pounds. He listed his race as white. He had attended eight years of grammar school and one year of high school. He received "morality and sex education training" and immunizations. He received desert training near Yuma, Arizona, and reached the rank of T/5, or corporal, before he shipped out, but by the time he embarked for the European theater of operations he was once again a private. Most of his file is taken up with medical documents concerning his shoulder injury. But it's hard to tell when and how the injury occurred. One physician notes that according to my grandfather he hurt it throwing a rope over a truck while logging with his father in 1941. In other documents he states he hurt it while boxing in Yuma, or "roughhousing" with another soldier. Nowhere does it say he received his wound in combat. According to hospital records he was not in Normandy on June 6, 1944. He was in Indiana, where he received an operation on his shoulder on June 16.

I didn't know what to make of any of this. According to government records, my grandfather left for Europe on September 4, 1944. He was in France by September 15. He entered Belgium on October 24. By December 27, 1944, he was in England and had shoulder surgery again. He was returned to duty and entered Germany on March 6, 1945, five days after his twentieth birthday. He was awarded a good conduct ribbon, and one battle star for the campaign in Belgium, but not a Purple Heart.

After he got back to the states, he went AWOL twice. They confined him to the military base and docked his pay. As of September 8, 1945, my grandfather was honorably discharged. There wasn't much to learn from his service record. Paper lies. So do people. And there is no way to crack open some other truth, some greater truth, as though buried there waiting to be found by me. I told my father—who served in the same war, in the Pacific—about what I found out about his father-in-law, my grandfather. *Look, Dave,* he said, *it's enough to know he was there. He was in it. He was a part of that.* It will remain something I don't understand. Except that the war stories my grandfather told were of the beauty of the land, the look and feel of it. That and how miserable and scared he was. How much he hated his war. The Second World War was transformative in raising Indians' visibility in the American landscape. But it also transformed the personal mental and emotional landscape of those who served in it; it shaped us as Indians and Americans in ways that are still being felt.

ENTERING THE CAGE

I was sitting around one night listening to the radio," says my cousin Sam. "And this advertisement came on, 'Local fighters wanted,' and there was a number to call and so I called the number. I went down there to talk to the guy on Thursday and I fought my first fight on Saturday. I didn't know anything. I just showed up with a nut cup and a mouth guard. I was scared. [It] was just this little underground place and they threw a cage up in the middle of it and packed a few hundred people in there and then put two guys in the cage and let 'em go. Didn't even matter if they were matched up good or even the same size or anything. It was pretty wild."

Sam quit his job and moved down to Moline, Illinois. He trained at an MMA gym there for two months and learned the basics. He won five fights over the next year. Everything was looking up until his mother's death in the summer of 2005.

When Sam's mom, Barb, died, we all wondered what would happen to Sam. Would he bottom out again as he had when his sister Nessa died? "When Mom died I had a job, and a family," Sam muses. "I was living in South Dakota by then. I had people I was responsible for, maybe that helped." Sam stayed in control and he kept his job and he didn't drift back into the violence that had marked his life for most of his twenties. "When I fight, right before I step into the cage, I kind of visualize my opponent as a sickness I've got to beat—not that I am hating on the guy or anything, just that I'm not fighting him, I'm fighting some disease. I leave all the rage and anger I've got for that."

Maybe he does. Maybe he does leave it all there. But if he does, Sam brings something away from the cage as well. "It feels good to win at something you've worked hard at, and put your time in at, to win at something you want real bad." More than anything, that's what Sam and maybe a lot of the other Indian fighters bring to fighting in the cage: the desire to be good at something and to have a chance to win. It may sound like a small thing. Or it may sound like the very idea that America is built on. But it is a huge thing for an Indian man to want, a very huge and noble thing to dare to hope that hard work and talent will actually win the day.

In the end, Sam didn't get to fight at the Northern Lights Casino on March 17, 2012; his opponent failed to make weight. But earlier, in December, I had gotten to see him fight there. He had won against a much larger opponent in the first two minutes of the first round in his trademark style: he took him down, wrapped him up, and then submitted him with strikes. God, how Sam could hit. How could a man like him lose? It was unimaginable. I didn't have the words for it then, what it felt like to watch my cousin, whom I love and whose worries are our worries and whose pain is our pain, manage to be so good at something, to triumph so completely. What I felt—what I saw—were Indian men and boys doing precisely what we've always been taught not to do. I was seeing them plainly, desperately, expertly wanting to be seen for their talents and their hard work, whether they lost or won.

That old feeling familiar to so many Indians—that we can't change anything; can't change Columbus or Custer, smallpox or massacres, can't change the Gatling gun or the legislative act; can't change the loss of our loved ones or the birth of new troubles; can't change a thing about the shape and texture of our lives—fell away. I think the same could be said for Sam: he might not have been able to change his sister's fate or his mother's or even, for a while, his own. But when he stepped in the cage he was doing battle with a disease. The disease was the feeling of powerlessness that takes hold of even the most powerful Indian men. That disease is more potent than most people imagine: that feeling that we've lost, that we've always lost, that we've already lost—our land, our cultures, our communities, ourselves. This disease is the story told about us and the one we so often tell about ourselves. But it's one we've managed to beat again and again by insisting on our own Indian existence and struggling to exist in our Indian homelands on our own terms. For some this meant joining the U.S. military. For others it meant accepting the responsibility to govern and lead. For others still, it meant stepping into a metal cage to beat or be beaten. For my cousin Sam, for three rounds of five minutes he gets to prove he can determine the outcome of a finite struggle, under the bright, artificial lights that make the firmament at the Northern Lights Casino on the Leech Lake Reservation.

MOVING ON UP
1945-1970

❖❖❖❖❖❖❖❖❖❖❖

THE THREE DECADES FROM 1945 to 1975, sandwiched between World War II and the rise and quick fall of the American Indian Movement, have been treated as something of a blank spot on the map of Indian experience. The days of tribal warfare were over. The federal assault on Indians, Indian life, and Indian homelands was over, too. Reservations had been established as nothing more or less than basins of eternal suffering. I wanted to know what the postwar years looked like on the Plains, so in the fall of 2014, I drove from Rapid City, South Dakota, to Browning, Montana, home of the Blackfeet Nation.

The first leg took me from Rapid City up to Williston, North Dakota. It was the right season for the drive: the crisp, dry, golden time of fall on the Plains when the aspen leaves rattle across the road with a hiss and the wheat stubble catches the light. It was some of the most beautiful land I have ever seen, shamelessly beautiful. North of Sturgis, South Dakota, I passed Bear Butte—Mato Paha to the Lakota, Noaha-vose to the Cheyenne. The sacred mountain sits off by itself on the plain, the northernmost outpost of the Black Hills. After that the land flattens out into grassy plains that roll on until they're broken by a limestone shelf near the North Dakota border.

As soon as I crossed into North Dakota I was buffeted by trucks and heavy equipment. The roads were cracked, the fencing was gone, and great gashes in the turf opened up on both sides of the road. Sidings like those next to rail lines began to appear along the highway. The Bakken oil fields loomed to the north. By the time I reached Williston, oil was all I saw: oil rigs, cleared and graded land, flames off-gassing the methane in the wells. All along the roads there were staging areas for heavy equipment, stacks of pipe, metal fittings, and oil rigs. The Russian olive, willow, and poplar trees planted as windbreaks toward the end of the Dust Bowl era had been ripped out and burned. The truck stops were full of trucks.

I turned west toward Montana on U.S. Highway 2. The highway passed through ghost town after ghost town. Here and there, abandoned farmhouses showed sky and range through their broken windows and even through their roofs. Most of the towns were empty of people, too, as were the roads.

I drove through Fort Peck and then Fort Belknap; here things were different. Indians walked down the road. Indian kids played in the yards. Near Wolf Point, I saw Indian kids who looked like they were floating in the air until I realized that they were launching themselves from a trampoline over the roofline of their house. By nightfall the next day I made it near Browning, the capital, if you will, of the Blackfeet Nation.

The Blackfeet shouldn't really be called the Blackfeet. They are the Southern Piikuni, the southernmost band of a confederation of bands and the only Piikuni in the United States. No one seems to know how this misnomer happened.

Primarily bison hunters, the Blackfeet weren't quite as nomadic as other Plains tribes, but they cycled between different seasonal camps. Adopting the horse, around 1730, greatly increased their range. The tribal culture began to grow, in particular the ability and desire to make war on basically everyone. The Blackfeet won and became known as the "Lords of the Plains." Despite their capacity for making enemies and waging war, the Blackfeet largely stayed out of the conflicts that erupted across the Plains in the nineteenth century. But America made war against them all the same, by hiring buffalo hunters to eradicate the herds as a means of subduing the Lakota and other Plains tribes. The Blackfeet could not maintain their way of life without the bison. Weakened by disease and warfare and starvation, they had little recourse when the U.S. government illegally modified and ratified new treaties with the southern bands of the tribe, stealing millions of acres. By 1900 there were fewer than two thousand Blackfeet left, according to the report of the commissioner of Indian affairs, though tribal members put the number at half that. And yet the embers of this proud people burned on. Over time, their numbers grew back. What remained of their culture and language was reconstituted. What remained of their land base was consolidated and protected.

I had never been to Browning and I didn't really know any Blackfeet except by reputation, but I had asked a Facebook friend, Sterling HolyWhiteMountain, if he'd set me up with some people to talk to and show me around. Tall, thick, and affable, with short hair and an indecisive beard, Sterling has a fondness for loud, brightly patterned button-down shirts. We shook hands when we met up at the local casino and then headed to Sterling's house in the reservation border town of East Glacier. The house he shares with a sister, her husband, and their kid is the one he grew up in. His mother lives across the yard in a newer house, and another sister lives across the street. The family seemed raucous and vibrant and testy. We ate dinner and then started talking. The talking didn't stop that night, nor the next day, or the next: the whole week was spent shifting from one talker to another. The morning after that first night, I found myself in a back room behind the convenience store/gas station on the outskirts of Browning owned by Sterling's father, Pat Schildt. Seated across from me was Red Hall, a weathered old-timer, who was there because Sterling and his father had asked him to come.

Red Hall is one of the old people we call elders. He had lived through three wars and the forgotten years from 1930 to 1960, when Indian communities emerged from the dark days after the fall of tribal government into a period of constitutional, representative Indian government.

Red spoke with a gruff sharpness. His voice was clear and crisp. He had the clipped tones of the High Plains along with a kind of "Don't mess with me" cadence that I always think of as "elderly Indian voice." He was born here in 1931; Red and his family survived on rations and cows. "I worked around stock my whole life. That's why we got so many bronc riders. World champions." He goes back to an earlier time. "But you see—they starved us to death here. Gave us smallpox, we was hanging in all the trees." The old stories don't feel old at all coming from Red: he's talking about seeing bodies "buried" on scaffolds in the trees according to the traditional Blackfeet death rites. As a young boy Red saw bodies that had been placed there in the winter of 1883–1884, when many of the tribe died during that "Starvation Winter."

Red talked in that way particular to Indians of a certain age, where the telling isn't quite a linear narrative. Instead, what Red remembered ran, stilled, and then bottomed out in the lowlands of his memory, pooling there around ancestors and horses and stock and fiddle playing and the railroad. These were the defining features of his landscape. He was not nostalgic in the slightest. For Red, and for Indians in a lot of places, life got better as time went on, and it got a lot better with FDR's New Deal. "I remember when they used to give out rations here. Roosevelt was the guy who really helped the people. Before that it was the Dust Bowl and all that went on. We was part of it. Back then there was a jail and a post office in the front of it, and rations were given around the back. I remember first time I ever seen a grapefruit . . . They give 'em out. People didn't know how to eat 'em. Or peel 'em. People didn't like 'em, they were too bitter. I was about seven."

Red had eleven siblings and grew up in a log house on a ranch by a river. The family weren't all in the house at the same time, as some of the children were in boarding schools. Red attended a local school to about the eighth grade. As a kid, he'd seen people putting up teepees each year. "I got two now. I saw 'em putting up teepees for the Sun Dance. Special occasions. More and more people are going back into their reality. College helps. That's one of the best things that helped here. The college. Before, we made fun of our language. We had to sneak and talk in schools. They might learn a little bit at school, but they get home and there is no one to talk to. You lose the language, well, that's losing your culture."

As Red tells it, in his circular way, things got better in the 1940s and 1950s. "I worked around and worked for the railroad for a long time. I was in the army too. Roosevelt made a big change here. We had it good once he was in charge. The New Deal was a big deal here. That's when we got commodities and rations. WPA, CCC, ECW—a dollar a day." You can still see the work done on the reservation by the Civilian Conservation Corps (CCC). "These ditches were built. Canals. They were built by Indians. They built them with horses and plows. They'd do it all summer. Go live out there in tents. Teams. Some of them guys went all the way to Yakima [Washington state]. They had a boxing team, basketball team, cooks. They lived good! Baseball teams! There were guys who'd kill to earn a dollar a day. Soup lines. People were starving on the streets."

No matter how Red tells it, life on the reservation changed and improved during the forties and fifties. The Blackfeet tribal constitution, adopted in 1935, gave them a government—flawed and inadequate, but still a government—and a process by which the tribe could control at least some of the leases for timber and cattle. New Deal jobs programs were a boon to Indians across the region, and their numbers increased. Indian lives didn't change in spite of what was going on in the rest of America. Rather, Indian lives changed in step with the rest of the country.

MIGRATION

When the sun rose on America after World War II, it rose on a vastly different country. The United States alone had emerged stronger from the war. It sought to bind the struggling European countries to itself and American interests through aid, loans, and protection. It invested in advantageous trade relationships, and its agricultural sector was strong. The U.S. population grew, and the standard of living rose. In 1945 a third of the country was without running water, two-fifths lacked flush toilets, and three-fifths had no central heating. More than half of those who lived on farms didn't have electricity. This would soon change. As more than $185.7 million in war bonds matured, nearly eight million WWII veterans were able to go to college or training schools under the GI Bill. Labor unions ensured that working-class Americans would make high enough wages to admit them to the middle class. A new interstate highway system facilitated movement and trade across all regions of the country.

The Great Migration, which had started in 1916, brought African Americans from the South to the North, and from rural areas to urban ones, in search of better employment opportunities and an escape from racism and the constant violent threat of lynchings and beatings. In 1910, 90 percent of all African Americans in the United States lived in fourteen states, and only 20 percent of them lived in cities. Thirty years later, a million African Americans had moved to the North and half of them lived in urban areas. By 1970 six million African Americans had migrated from the South, more than 50 percent of all African Americans lived in the North, and more than 80 percent of African Americans lived in cities across the country. Urban populations swelled, with not only migrating African Americans but Anglo Americans and Native Americans as well.

In 1943 the federal government conducted a new "survey of Indian conditions." Even though it was less thorough and less impartial than the 1928 Meriam Report, the survey told roughly the same story: Indian life was bad. It was hard, Indians were poor. Reservations were rife with disease and deplorable living conditions. The Office of Indian Affairs and its successor, the Bureau of Indian Affairs, were doing a horrible job administering to Indian communities and more often than not made things worse. Despite the similarity of the findings, however, the 1943 survey reached a radically different conclusion. The upshot of the Meriam Report had been that Indians could better administer to their own needs and affairs and that tribal governments should be empowered in Indian communities. The 1943 report, however, led the U.S. government in the opposite direction.

The Indian Reorganization Act had only been passed in 1934, so it is hard to know what the legislators and commissioners thought would be radically different in the space of only nine years of "self-determination." In any event, the Senate Committee on Indian Affairs, again confronted with the "Indian problem," again reversed itself. It instituted the fifth new policy meant to "help" Indians. After enduring the policies of treaty/reservation, allotment, relocation, and assimilation, they were about to enter the era of termination.

TERMINATION

After the Second World War, the newly powerful United States saw its own civil, social, and political institutions as the only effective models in the world. The United States was deeply suspicious of anything communal or collective—such as tribes—because of the rising threat of Communism. And tribes were communal if nothing else. Nonetheless, termination, like previous Indian policies, required some degree of participation by the tribes themselves.

By the 1940s, tribes across the country were filing more claims against the U.S. government for wrongful taking of land through force, coercion, or removal than ever before. Tribal citizens were getting better at understanding their rights, and tribal governments were getting better at advocating for them. By 1946 more than two hundred claims had been filed in the United States Court of Claims, mostly for damages for unlawful land seizure or for criminally low prices paid for land taken legally, violations of both treaty rights and human rights. Only twenty-nine claims had been addressed by the court. The majority of the rest had been dismissed, largely on technicalities. Still, the roles and numbers of Indians who served in World War II, and the important nature of their service, had resulted in some sense of obligation to Indians on the part of the federal government. The government needed a process by which to hear their claims, but it also wanted a process that would put an end to them, once and for all. The Indian Claims Commission Act of 1946 was the result, and "finality" was its watchword.

The Indian Claims Commission expanded the grounds for a lawsuit to include five categories of "wrongs": claims based on the Constitution, laws, treaties of the United States, and executive orders of the president; claims that would have been brought if it was possible to sue the United States itself; claims related to treaties or other agreements that the United States had revised due to fraud, pressure, or misunderstanding; claims that were the result of land seized by treaty or cession and not paid for fairly and with consent; and claims not governed by existing rule of law or equity even if the deal had been "fair and honorable."

The Claims Commission intended to address all the wrongs done to Indians by monetizing those damages. And there was a finish line in sight: all claims were supposed to be filed within five years of passage of the act. As it turned out, the date would be extended by another five years as tribes—understaffed and often without legal teams—limped toward the deadline. The Claims Commission wouldn't finish dealing with the claims, which numbered in the hundreds, until the 1970s. The commission was extended from 1976 to 1978, after which point, the claims were transferred to the U.S. Court of Claims. The last claim on the docket wasn't finalized until 2006.

While the Indian Claims Commission Act represented a "broad waiver of the United States' sovereign immunity" and was remedial in nature, it was also coercive. Cash-strapped tribes with crushing unemployment and chronic poverty and no infrastructure or tax base needed the claims money for sure (even if most of it would take years, if not decades, to arrive). But it was a mistake to think that the magnitude and kinds of loss Indians had suffered could be monetized. It required a very narrow sense of reparations to think that the loss of land, which was at the heart of the Claims Commission mission, only had economic impact and could be adequately addressed by cash payments. The loss of Indian land had resulted in a loss of Indian life and culture, a loss of a people's ability to be a people in the manner it understood itself. Many tribes—particularly tribes in the Southwest—had ceremonial lives that revolved around sacred sites that had irrevocably passed into private ownership. Tribes were left on small islands holding cash they couldn't use to reconstitute their cultures, their ceremonies, and their homelands.

To make matters worse, the Indian Claims Commission was used as a lever to move tribes into the next phase of federal policy. The broad demographic shifts brought about by World War II—the Great Migration, the shift from farming to manufacturing, the trend away from FDR's New Deal toward private enterprise under presidents Truman and Eisenhower—solidified the belief in majority rule. Democracy, understood as the supremacy of the individual on one hand and market capitalism on the other, was seen as not just the best way but the *only* way. The federal government's relationship with tribes followed this trend.

As in the period from the 1890s through the 1930s, it became federal policy to try to absorb Indians into the mainstream, whether they wanted to be absorbed or not. Instead of "encouraging" Indians to become American via the boarding schools and allotments, now official thinking held that institutions like the tribes themselves, as well as the BIA and the Indian Health Service, were blocking Indians from assimilation into the larger current of American life. Utah Senator Arthur

Watkins, a devout Mormon, lawyer, and successful rancher, felt what was needed was "the freeing of the Indian from wardship status." Watkins pushed through legislation in 1953 that became known as the Termination Act. It proposed to fix the Indian problem once and for all by making Indians—legally, culturally, and economically—no longer Indians. It does not seem to have occurred to Watkins and others like him that the "Indian problem" was and had always been a "federal government problem." Be that as it may, the Termination Act of 1953—actually House Concurrent Resolution 108—passed concurrently with Public Law 280: a dry pair of names for exceptionally bloody acts.

The Termination Act changed the ways tribes would relate to the U.S. government to this day. Up until 1953—with the exception of piecemeal legislation—federally recognized Indian tribes were "domestic dependent nations." The tribes had sovereignty, or something approaching it, which meant they related to the federal government on a government-to-government basis. Public Law 280 dealt a serious blow to this status.

When it came to most crimes, Indians lived in a kind of legal gray area. Some crimes were prosecuted in federal court, some were tried in the Court of Indian Offenses, some were tried in tribal court. The legal process wasn't clear. Public Law 280 was intended as a law-and-order act to end all that. It spelled out how to address the wrongs committed by Indians against other Indians and gave Indians equal access to protection under the law in criminal and civil disputes. The law granted six states the right, ability, and responsibility to prosecute all criminal offenses and civil disputes within its borders: Minnesota (except for Red Lake Reservation), Wisconsin (except for the Menominee Reservation), California, Washington, Oregon (except for Warm Springs Reservation), and Alaska (upon statehood). Tribes in states not covered by Public Law 280 continued to administer civil and criminal matters in tribal and federal courts.

Tribes within the six states covered by the law were not offered any chance to vote on, amend, or ultimately reject the legislation. Other states had the option of adopting the provisions of the law, with some limited input from the tribes. Nevada, South Dakota, Florida, Idaho, Montana, North Dakota, Arizona, Iowa, and Utah ultimately followed along and adopted some of the provisions of Public Law 280. Even narrowly defined and implemented, the law put most tribes under state control and state oversight. Public Law 280 had been put forward as a piece of law-and-order legislation, but states almost universally interpreted it as giving them new regulatory powers. States now levied taxes on the Indians, administered their schools, and stepped into health care and licensing, even on reservations. States curtailed treaty rights by extending the jurisdiction of game wardens and overseeing licensing for harvesting game, edibles, and the like. This illegal overstepping would not be rectified until a Supreme Court ruling in 1976. Tribes are still in the process of defining and limiting the excesses of Public Law 280.

Just as that law was transferring legal power over Indians to states across the country, the Termination Act of 1953 ended Indians' status as wards of the federal government. Individual Indians became "subject to the same laws and entitled to the same privileges and responsibilities as are applicable to other citizens of the United States . . . and should assume their full responsibilities as American citizens." As for tribes, the Termination Act lived up to its title. Tribes were terminated as sovereign nations. They were no longer eligible for government aid. Their Indian lands in trust were no longer federally protected. States would have jurisdiction over crimes on reservations without tribal consent.

Even as this disastrous legislation was being passed, it was possible to know what might result. There were tribes that had, in effect, lived under termination long before it became federal Indian policy. The Little Shell Band of Ojibwe provided one such cautionary tale.

The Little Shell and other Pembina Ojibwe clustered around the Turtle Mountains in the northern part of what became North Dakota, on the Canadian border. The Turtle Mountains were a great place to settle: almost completely forested, they provided timber, game, and shelter from the ravages of Plains weather. Wild rice grew in the rivers, creeks, and sloughs.

Even though the Old Crossing Treaty was signed in 1863, it took Congress until the 1880s to officially create the Turtle Mountain Reservation. The boundaries of Turtle Mountain weren't established until 1882. Then the federal government did what the federal government always did. In 1884, without consulting the Indians there, it reduced the size of the Turtle Mountain Reservation. The 460,800-acre reservation shrank overnight to a tenth its original size: a mere 46,800 acres. Tribal leader Esens would not negotiate and would not cede his claim to the millions of acres that rightly belonged to the Little Shell. So the federal government arbitrarily chose thirty-two Pembina "chiefs" and brought them to the treaty table. Never mind that they had no authority to sign on anyone's behalf and didn't represent any constituency. They signed the McCumber Agreement in 1892, which formally ceded all of Little Shell's land for the pittance of about ten cents an acre. Esens was off hunting in Montana, on the western frontier of Pembina territory. When he returned to Turtle Mountain with his people, he found that not only had the other so-called leaders sold his land out from under his feet but also, he had no official standing at Turtle Mountain. Overnight Little Shell and his band were written out of existence by a stroke of the treaty pen.

"We're called the 'landless Indians of Montana,'" Sierra Fredrickson tells me wryly. We are sitting in a brewpub in Williston, North Dakota. Sierra is Little Shell Ojibwe. "You call us landless and at the same time you ask where we're from. How's that supposed to work?" Sierra is young and brilliant, a writer and a teacher at the community college here, passionately committed to advancing the cause of her band however she can.

Sierra is talking about the aftermath of the McCumber Agreement. "It was kind of a power grab by other bands around Turtle Mountain," she says. "There were only a certain amount of people who could enroll in the new [tribal] rolls. A lot of Little Shell's people were Métis, or half-blood, so they didn't get on the rolls and got pushed off [the land]. Some of the Little Shell people had left the reservation before the agreement was signed. Others didn't go and they were rounded up and put on boxcars and brought to the Hi-Line [U.S. Highway 2] in Montana and just dropped off." From there the Little Shell Band endured a hellish diaspora, wandering in their own former territory. They settled in small groups in Le Havre, Lewiston, and Great Falls, Montana, and then splintered into even smaller groups as they chased work. Some other reservation communities took them in. Sierra's own grandparents grew up on the Chippewa-Cree Rocky Boy Reservation. The Little Shell lost more of their sense of themselves with each split and each move. Without community, without place, without land, a people lose the safety net that shared language, experience, lifeway, and place can provide. Sierra's life story bears some of these scars.

"I was born in Great Falls, Montana, but grew up in Bridger. My parents got divorced then. My dad was in and out of treatment a lot." The atmosphere at home was pretty violent. "We moved to get away from all of that. The population of the town [Bridger] is about seven hundred. We're probably the only Indian family in town. There wasn't a lot of racism that I noticed. People would say things in class and there were no other Natives there except me, so I would say things and they would say things back."

It's difficult enough to pick up the pieces of a life, of a community if there is a place of return, some remnant of a homeland. But Sierra's tribe of the "landless Indians of Montana" didn't even have that.

Some Little Shell lived in tent encampments into the 1950s and 1960s. Without a land base, without some kind of center—no matter how corrupted or reduced it might be—there was not much the Little Shell people could do except hold on somehow. Their religion was in jeopardy, their ceremonies lost and forgotten. "I don't know what their [her ancestors'] religion was when they left Turtle Mountain. My grandma would probably know those things more. They had dances, but it was sort of a mix. It was a mix of fiddling with Native dancing. She's told me about going to those dances.

"I'm away from where most of our people are. There's no real getting together and talking with other Little Shell people. We have no place to gather. But social media is how we do it. The tribe's Facebook page has been really great for us."

A few years after Sierra Fredrickson and I met in the brewpub—and almost 130 years after the Little Shell were made landless—the tribe finally had their day in court. Their century-old petition for legal, federal recognition as a tribe was affirmed. In December 2019, Congress passed a law officially acknowledging the Little Shell tribe. Its approximately fifty-three hundred members will now have access to federally funded health care and BIA services, and educational opportunities. "I was stunned when it actually happened," Sierra told me. Or rather: she narrated on a Facebook Messenger audio clip recorded while she was driving. "We've been working on this so long and to have it happen during the Trump presidency was even more shocking. For me it's felt like some sort of validation. I wish that it didn't but it does. I've always felt connected to my culture, but now it feels like we're Native people to the rest of the world and it's brought more strength to our community and it's been a uniting force, which is something amazing to see. Day to day it doesn't change a whole lot for us. But long term? It changes everything. We're building a medical facility and we're looking at land. None of that would have been possible without federal recognition. It's life-saving for some of us. Yeah—it's hard to believe. My brothers and I joke with each other and say, 'Hey, guess what? We're finally real Indians!' It makes me happy for Grandma. She never thought this would happen during her lifetime. But it did. And *that's* amazing."

Even though reservations have been characterized by Indians and non-Indians alike as places where hope goes to die, as a kind of final resting place for Indian lives and cultures, they are clearly much more than that. They have functioned as a home base for Indians and have preserved, in both positive and negative ways, a kind of together-ness vital to the continued existence of Native people. All of this was painfully obvious in the 1940s and 1950s, but the federal government chose not to see it. Instead, they plowed ahead with the Termination Act as the best plan for Indian people. And at the top of its list of those to terminate were the Menominee of Wisconsin.

As they prepared for Wisconsin statehood in the 1840s, the fed-eral government tried to relocate the tribe to points much farther west. But as we saw earlier, the Menominee would not be moved. They resisted allotment, settled on a small reservation, and developed their very successful, sustainable timber industry. They filed a suit against the federal government in 1934 for damages resulting from illegal cutting by white timber companies and damage caused by the U.S. Forest Service's decision to clear-cut the reservation after a big wind-storm in 1905. It took twenty years for the suit to be settled, but the tribe was eventually awarded $8.5 million in federal court. By then, the Menominee logging operation employed several hundred predomi-nantly Indian workers, funded a school and hospital, and paid the sala-ries of two doctors, eight nurses, and an orthodontist, as well as four policemen, six night watchmen, a truant officer, a game warden, and a welfare administrator. It also supported a tribal loan fund of nearly five hundred thousand dollars and paid a yearly stumpage (timber price) dividend to each of the twenty-nine hundred tribal members. By any measure, the Menominee were everything the government said it wanted them to be, with the exception that they did everything their own way: in common. Hence, in the anti-Communist, post–World War II era, they were at the very top of the list for termination.

In 1953, shortly after the Termination Act was passed, Senator Arthur Watkins visited the Menominee personally, since one of the stipulations of the act was that tribes had to buy into it. He told the Menominee that if they wanted to see the $8.5 million settlement they had won, they would have to agree to termination. He recast a legal settlement that was recompense for abuse of treaty rights as a reward that could be withheld for insubordination.

The Menominee were not interested in termination. However, controlling the $8.5 million settlement was crucial to their well-being. Rather than lose the money, the tribe agreed to undergo termination, with a grace period of four years to get their affairs in order, a deadline that was extended for two more years. In 1961 the Menominee Reservation and the Menominee tribe ceased to officially exist. All reservation lands and tribal property were transferred to Menominee Enterprises, Inc. (MEI), a private business. Four Indians sat on the MEI board of trustees, along with three non-Indians. What had been the reservation was converted into Menominee County.

There was trouble from the start. Menominee County, since most of it was corporate-owned now, lacked a tax base. Basic services such as police, waste management, firefighting, and road construction ate up the tribe's savings. The sawmill needed renovations, and MEI couldn't afford them. The hospital funded in part by the Menominee and in part by the federal government had to close for lack of funds. Schools, utilities, and other services either closed or were cut to the bone. When Congress passed the Menominee Termination Act in 1954, the Menominee had cash assets of more than ten million dollars, *not* counting the settlement. By 1964 they had only three hundred thousand dollars. The tribe was so cash-strapped that the white-controlled MEI board voted to sell lake lots for summer homes rather than log the land in an effort to increase the tax base. Tribal members, told simply that they were voting on an "economic plan," voted for the development; when it had been approved, MEI created a huge artificial lake and sold thousands of lake lots, diminishing what land and small amount of tribal control remained.

There was a silver lining, however. The process of termination took so long that those tribes slated for it witnessed what happened to the Menominee. Termination was, clearly, a disaster. Other tribes watched and learned and fought. And after years of struggle, the Menominee themselves were reconstituted, termination was undone, and they got their reservation back in the 1970s. But this was decades away. For now, termination rolled on.

On April 22, 1975, reservation status was restored to the Menominee's tribal land in Wisconsin. Tribal elder Ernest Niconish (center) received the deed.

RELOCATION

Solutions for the "Indian problem" seem only to have generated more problems for the government, not to mention for Indian people themselves. When termination became the face of federal policy, the question became: What to do with the Indians? In 1940, 56 percent of Americans lived in cities, but only 6 percent of American Indians did. The next move seemed clear to the federal government: termination was set to take care of reservations, but Indians needed an extra push to get them to leave their disappearing homelands and move into cities. So in the 1950s, there was another flurry of legislation.

The Navajo-Hopi Law funded a jobs-training program for Navajo and Hopi Indians of New Mexico and Arizona and provided money to relocate them to Denver, Salt Lake, and Los Angeles. The program was expanded by the Department of the Interior in 1951 to include other tribes and other cities in Oklahoma, Arizona, and New Mexico. It expanded again in the years to come to get more Indians into more cities: Cleveland, San Francisco, St. Louis, San Jose, Seattle, Tulsa, and Minneapolis. The piecemeal legislation, budget lines, and policies coalesced into Public Law 959, passed in 1956, which authorized a national program of vocational training and relocation for Indians.

Indian agents on reservations across the country hawked the benefits of urban living. Flyers and posters were distributed. Attractive brochures were handed out. And many Indians signed up. One of the families whom agents reached was that of Sterling HolyWhiteMountain's uncle David Schildt, Red Hall's cousin.

"I'm from Birch Creek, Montana, on the Blackfeet Reservation," David tells me at a Starbucks in San Rafael, California. "We barely survived the Birch Creek flood. We missed that water by about thirty seconds." He smiles but it's not a real smile. David is handsome in that way Indian men who've put on a lot of miles are handsome. He's generous and kind, and yet there is a hardness and a diffuse pain that hovers over him like a sound that just won't die. "June 8, 1964. That was when that flood broke. Swift Dam Reservoir, Birch Creek, Montana. Our neighbors who lived upstream, hell, maybe three hundred yards—three of them died. Practically everyone below us died."

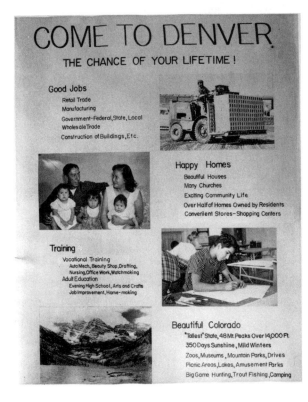

Bureau of Indian Affairs relocation brochure distributed to Native Americans, 1950s. Although some Native Americans chose to move off reservations to urban areas, 50 percent returned home to their families and reservations within five years because of a lack of job opportunities, education, and social services.

The flood David can't get out of his mind was the worst in Montana history. Higher than average, heavy snow piled up in the mountains all winter; a cool spring followed, so much of the snow had not melted as of early summer. Then in early June it began to rain, warm, heavy rain. For several days, the rain fell, at a rate of one inch an hour. All that water was too much for the earthen dam on Birch Creek above the Schildt homestead. David's grandmother told him to go down to the creek to have a look. A rock they used to jump from, normally ten feet above the water, was now so far submerged you couldn't even see it. "She's like, 'Grab your coat and we gonna walk up to the top of the hill and sit up there for a while.'" The "hill" was more of a cut bank about 150 to 200 feet high. "We's walking toward the hill and then my uncle come running through the brush. 'The dam broke!' . . . So we took off . . . And just when we got up there the water came." A wall of water at least forty feet high came barreling down the creek bottom. "We saw the earth chewed up before our eyes."

Their home destroyed, David and his brothers and sisters and other surviving relatives climbed in a truck and headed for another village on the reservation on higher ground. "The water was blasting over the bridge. It was usually a little creek but now it was a river. There were seven or eight kids hanging on the back of the truck. We made it. Barely. We went to my uncle Dave's house. There must have been twenty or thirty people stranded at his house. People crying and sobbing about people in their families that had drowned. We were cut off. The navy flew in medical supplies and food in a helicopter."

Even before the flood, life had been hard for David Schildt and his family. Their house on Birch Creek didn't have electricity or running water. Their father—a tank commander in the Korean War and a recipient of three Bronze Stars, a United Nations Peacekeepers Medal, a National Defense Service Medal, and the Korean Service Medal—was maniacally hard on his family. David wonders if it was the war or the life or both that made his father into what he was. "He practically raised himself. He was kind of booted out of his house by his stepfather. I don't think he ever got over that." Sometimes after he'd been drinking, David's father made the children stand at attention "and listen to his war stories till he went to sleep or got laid out. Sometimes it'd be daylight. We'd have to stand at attention till he was done. It was a hard life."

Whether it was the flood that took their home and their neighbors or the rage of their father that swept comfort and care away in its own torrent, life for the Schildt family was a precarious thing. So when the opportunity came for them to move to Los Angeles as part of the government's relocation program, the family enrolled. David's father was admitted to a vocational program that would teach him to be a diesel mechanic. In 1968, David, his parents, and ten other siblings piled into two cars and headed down to California.

Upon their arrival in Los Angeles, the relocation program housed them in a fenced-in motel near the freeway in Compton, a small, rough city slightly south. Next, the relocation program found a place for the Schildts in Burbank, another small city near Los Angeles. "I didn't know a soul when I got there," David recalls. After his one-room schoolhouse back in Montana, he says, "I was in the blind, socially and academically. We had a real limited education in Los Angeles. I flunked everything. But they still let me play basketball and track and field because they probably felt sorry for me. I had to learn to adjust, learn how to interact with other people. Learn to communicate with people who couldn't understand me."

The Schildts lasted a year. "My dad couldn't do nothing down there. The only background he had was he was a tank commander. He could kill people. That was his only skill." The family was headed back to Montana. David, sixteen, asked if he could go to Flandreau Indian School in Flandreau, South Dakota.

"It was the safest place I'd ever lived. Flandreau Indian boarding school. Three squares [meals] a day. A roof over my head. School. Coaches. I had everything I needed to be secure. And I excelled. I was in the rodeo club. I had a great time in sports. Athlete of the year. Set records. Triple jump. Went to state in pole vault. Big handful of medals." But eventually Flandreau came to an end: he couldn't stay there forever.

It's hard, sometimes, to understand a life, to narrate it, when it doesn't have a through line. David's life feels this way to me. It has stops and starts, changes of altitude, different scenes come in and out of focus. "I went from Flandreau, being very happy, to moving back to the rez and being very, very sad. It was a different world, and I had to survive somehow. I remember being basically on welfare. I didn't have anyone I could lean on for a job." He started to drink. "I remember once I got drunk, stayed drunk for seven days straight. I remember that one day just shaking, I was just so . . . saturated. And I thought, 'I gotta get out of here. I've got to get out of here or I'll die.' So I started trying to make plans to get out of there somehow. I got into the rodeo business." Life on the rez was so unsafe that climbing atop a one-ton bull was better than living it out at Birch Creek.

David spent the better part of the 1970s and 1980s hanging on the backs of bulls and later broncos. When he talks about riding his eyes come alive and he smiles, really smiles. "I've broken so many things. Fourteen breaks in my arms. Collarbones. I didn't quit riding bareback horses till I was in my forties. I finally got thrown in Palm Springs in 1990. I landed on my back and neck and couldn't feel my legs. I'm fourteen hundred miles from home and I am lying in the dirt and I can't move. I could hear the [rodeo] clown saying, 'Are you all right?' And I'm thinking, 'This is enough. This is enough.'"

So David went to Billings, Montana. His girlfriend was managing a horse ranch, and she let him work with the quarter horse colts and mares. He stacked hay and helped with the fencing, irrigating, and basic ranch work. "When you're in a state of survival, which I've been in most of my life, it changes every day. You go from a profession to a day job. Back and forth."

Back and forth, up and down, holding on for dear life, getting bucked off but climbing back on: riding bulls and broncs was a bit like riding life for David. But he wasn't alone. Or rather, he was alone but in good company. Termination and relocation meant more and more Indians were being pulled away from their communities on reservations that disappeared from underneath them. By the time David was a teenager in Los Angeles, more than a hundred reservations—most of them in California and Oregon—had been terminated and the Indians who had belonged to them were, technically, Indians no longer. People who had been in America before America existed, whose homeland had once been the whole wide country, were now homeless immigrants. They ran into many of the same difficulties as other immigrants: segregation in crowded ghettos or enclaves, poor education options, and lack of access to capital and mortgages that would admit Indians to the middle class.

Termination was, by the 1960s, clearly a catastrophe. The gains tribes had made under the Indian Reorganization Act were wiped away. The IRA was flawed and the tribal constitutions were inadequate tools for tribal governance, but they had created structural changes in the right direction. The circumstances of hundreds of thousands of Indians in the form of tribal employment, housing, education, and hospitals were slowly improving. But no more. Under termination and relocation, unemployment skyrocketed and so did the number of Indians falling below the poverty line. By 1970, when termination officially ended, half of all Indians lived in urban areas, the single largest demographic and cultural shift in Indian country in a century. A total of 1,365,801 acres of Indian land were removed from trust status during the termination and relocation period, and twelve thousand Indians lost their tribal affiliation.

Many tribes waged long, hard legal battles to regain their federal recognition and to have their lands returned to tribal ownership. Some, like the Menominee, successfully sued to be reincorporated and have their treaty rights restored. Other tribes are still fighting.

Nonetheless, many Indians found new life in cities. They endured the poor housing and the distance from their homelands. They learned to be Indians *of* America rather than simply Indians *in* America. And, as with David Schildt's extended family, relocation wasn't necessarily a one-way street: Indians moved to the city and moved back to the reservation, or their children did. And while they were in cities they mixed not only with other races but with other tribes as well. Red Hall noted that the old tribal warfare, and the intertribal bigotry that marked tribal relations in the nineteenth century, faded away as Indians from vastly different tribes found themselves living as neighbors in the city. They discovered they had much more in common with one another:

a shared historical experience if not shared cultures, the same class values, the same struggles. Networks among tribes—forged through marriage, school, city living, and service in the armed forces—were strengthened from 1940 to 1970.

Even David found this to be true, despite all the loss he'd experienced. "I'm a relocated Indian. I see myself as a classic example of what the government wants. The government wants you separated from your family, your home, your kids, your spiritual belief system, and they got you in the city, in white America." He still has most of his medals and buckles and spurs—proof of a life lived. And he has a kind of peace. "All I want to do is work, pay my bills, and go home and be happy. I don't want anything else."

And yet—behind the cowboy songs and the belt buckles and the stories of mischief—there is a kind of sorrow in David. I can feel it. Part of it may be that he still hears the floodwaters of Birch Creek. Or the stream of cars in Compton in 1968, or his father's voice telling him to stand at attention. Or part of it could be that David—together with many, many other Indians—still feels the effects of termination and relocation in his body and in his mind. Federal policy isn't abstract unless you're rich. If you're not, it's something that affects your life, your blood, your bones.

BECOMING INDIAN
1970–1980

◆◇◆◇◆◇◆◇◆◇◆

"WELCOME TO MY OFFICE!" BOB Matthews shouts with a smile, his arms raised to include the white spruce towering over our heads near Rabideau Lake just off the Leech Lake Indian Reservation in northern Minnesota. It's late August and the pinecones are coming in. We are each carrying a five-gallon bucket, a shallow white Tupperware tray, leather gloves with the fingers cut off, and a tube of Goop. We are looking for white spruce cones.

The northern Minnesota woods, once virgin white pine with an understory of spruce and birch, have been logged many times since the timber boom of the late nineteenth century. In place of the lonely majesty of old growth is a wild patchwork of poplar, spruce, jack pine, birch, and Norway pine in the uplands and ironwood, sugar maple, tag alder, basswood, ash, and elm in the lowlands. The whole region is scrubby, dense, at times impenetrable, united by vast swamps and slow-draining creeks, rivers, and lakes. The land is desolate in the winter and indescribably uncomfortable and nigh impassable in the summer. The spruce grow together and block out the sun. The forest floor is dun colored and the roots stick up out of the soil. I, for one, love our woods. I love the complications, the puzzle of it.

Once Bobby finds the green, gummy, crescent-shaped white spruce cones we came for, he drops to his knees and begins picking them off the ground and putting them on his tray with astonishing speed. "Here—take a bucket, a tray, and the Goop. The Goop's so the cones won't stick to your fingers and slow you down. That tray there, that's for speed, too. That way you don't have to lift your arm so high every time you get two or three cones in your hand. Just fill up the tray and then dump it in." Bobby picks fast. Then he dumps his full tray of inch-long cones into his bucket. They rattle as they fall in. To me it is a pleasant sound. To Bobby it sounds like money. (The seeds are sold to nurseries and the empty cones are sold to craft supply chains.)

The Indian hunter-gatherer, who was supposed to have died out in North America along with the buffalo, continues to live on—just not as in the romantic Anglo fantasy. Wanting to know what that looks like, I'd come back to the Leech Lake reservation to find my uncle Bobby Matthews. You'd hear Bobby's name whispered a lot when I was growing up. Who had the best rice? Bobby Matthews. Who had the *most* rice? Bobby Matthews. Who knew where the best boughs were for picking? Bobby Matthews. Who was the damnedest trapper in northern Minnesota? Bobby Matthews. At funerals and picnics and feasts and Memorial Day services at the cemetery—wherever you went on Leech Lake Reservation and even across northern Minnesota—when talk would turn to hunting or trapping or general woodsiness, his was the name always mentioned.

Bobby is not that tall—maybe five feet eight—but he has the arms and shoulders of a much larger man. His hair is thinning and gray and pulled back in a ponytail. He shaves once a year, on his birthday. His eyes are powerful, deep set, searching. His voice, calm in one moment, will rise to a shout in the next. Bobby is excited and excitable, and he laughs a lot. There is, under all his energy and excitement, the persistent threat of violence. Not directed at me or even at any other person, necessarily. It is the deep violence of the tribe—ready to erupt if necessary but usually held in check. Whatever happens, Bobby's going to go all the way. He has the aspect of the wild animals he's spent his life pursuing. But there is something else in there, too, something finer—a profound and ultimately beautiful curiosity about the environment he inhabits. Bobby is plagued by wonder.

He has spent much of his life on the question of how nature fits together and how it can serve him. He speaks rapidly and has the rare habit of always using your name. "I begin each day like this, Dave. I get up at four thirty and I turn on the coffee. I sit in my chair and drink my coffee and look at my books, Dave, going back five, ten, fifteen years. I keep notes on everything I see. The temperature. The barometric pressure. Where is the wind coming from? What little flowers are in bloom and how many leaves are on the trees. I keep track of all this stuff, Dave. So I can know the patterns. So I can compare one year to the next. No one sees my books, Dave. No one. Not ever. I told Julie [his wife] that when I die all my books go with me or she can burn 'em."

Bobby's life follows a rigid seasonal cycle. And the cycle revolves around money: he collects, harvests, and traps, and sells what he gets for profit. In the spring and early summer, he catches leeches for bait. Late summer, he begins picking pinecones and at harvest time, collects wild rice. When the wild rice harvest is done, he goes back to pinecones. After cones comes hunting, trapping, and more hunting. When the ground is frozen hard, he goes out in the swamps to cut cranberry bark, which will be sold as a natural remedy for menstrual cramps. By the time that's all done, he starts leeching again. When the zombie apocalypse comes, I am certain that I want to be with Uncle Bobby. I am in awe of him.

Bob Matthews was born in the 1940s and grew up in Bena. Like my mother, he is an Indian baby boomer, though they and their siblings and cousins and friends did not, as a rule, enjoy the economic benefits of America's baby boomer years the way their mainstream peers did. Still, some of America's success trickled down. Thousands of Indians who served in World War II and Korea made use of the GI Bill and went to college. Cars became more plentiful. Because of the boarding schools, war, and termination and relocation, many Indians now had family and kinship ties across ever greater distances. When they moved to cities, they often lived in almost exclusively Indian enclaves, but those enclaves were composed of members of many tribes. Termination and relocation allowed Indians to understand themselves as part of a much larger historical process. They pooled their knowledge and brought it with them wherever they went.

Even the disastrous land grabs that occurred as a result of allotment had their collateral benefits. While many millions of acres passed out of Indian control and into the hands of white farmers, homesteaders, businesses, and developers, Indians learned (the hard way) how landownership worked in the context of American capitalism: individual legal title to and control of property, real estate taxes, land values, leases, rents, mortgages, liens. They needed this knowledge when new tribal governments were formed in the 1930s. And they needed it again when the U.S. government tried to shove termination down their throats; it helped Indians fight the policy long enough that it died before their communities did. Allotment also meant that Indians suddenly had a lot of white neighbors, and many millions of Americans had Indian neighbors, too. They met and married and mingled and went to the same schools and, when there were jobs, worked at the same places. Contact with white people changed Indian culture, but contact with Indians and Indian cultures changed the white people who came to live among them as well.

By the time Bobby Matthews was a teenager in the 1960s, half of all Indians lived in cities and towns, and they were in close and constant contact with the other half that remained on reservations. Although Bobby was around the same age as the Indian activists who came up in the 1960s and 1970s, he didn't have much to do with them or their movements. Yet, at least to me, Bobby has a similar kind of wildness, a similar intensity. And to my mind he took his own path toward the activists' goals of becoming Indian—not through protest and politics, but through learning to live a life on the land, an Indian life.

THE RISE OF RED POWER

In the 1960s and 1970s, Indians grew in numbers and in strength. The Civil Rights Movement that was beginning to rock the country in the 1960s had a counterpart that rocked Indian communities and would grow, by the 1970s, to capture the attention of the entire country.

The rise of Red Power, and on its heels the American Indian Movement, reflected both federal Indian policy and larger demographic shifts. After World War II, many African American veterans and ordinary citizens looked at what the fight for world freedom had given them and found America wanting: they saw a considerable gap between how America saw itself and the policies it practiced.

The National Association for the Advancement of Colored People (NAACP), founded in 1909, stood true to its mission to "ensure the political, educational, social, and economic equality of rights of all persons and to eliminate racial hatred and racial discrimination." But progress through lobbying, publicity, and lawsuits was piecemeal and slow. The NAACP and other organizations like it continued their steady work, but many citizens began to take part in civil rights boycotts, sit-ins, marches, public demonstrations, and other forms of civil disobedience, often in coordination with other social justice organizations.

American Indians had been organizing similarly. In 1944 scores of delegates from fifty tribes met in Denver, Colorado, to form the National Congress of American Indians (NCAI). Their goal was to unite in force to stop the federal policy of termination, resist bad federal policy, and strengthen the ties between tribal governments. The Denver congress was led largely by men who had worked in the federal Office of Indian Affairs. By the second NCAI congress a year later, many delegates were women, and people who worked directly for the federal government were deemed ineligible for leadership positions because of possible conflicts of interest.

Founding members of the National Congress of American Indians included men and women. They passed eighteen resolutions focused on "sovereignty, civil rights, and recognition for all Indians."

The NAACP and other African American organizations and movements had a clear common goal of equal rights under the law, but as members of sovereign nations Indians had a somewhat different stance. The NCAI therefore fought for equal rights and equal protection, but it also lobbied for the restoration of treaty rights, the reclamation of land, and respect for cultural and tribal religious practices. It was, and is, a very effective organization. Among other victories, NCAI's efforts helped overcome federal job discrimination against Indians, stopped a ban on reservations in the founding documents for Alaskan statehood, limited state jurisdiction over Indian civil and criminal cases, and effectively addressed broad issues of health care, employment, and education. However, the NCAI had a strict policy against the kind of direct action that was proving so effective in the Civil Rights Movement. Unlike the NAACP, which initially urged students and others not to protest but then joined them, the NCAI made no such common cause with Indian groups engaged in direct action. The organization was criticized for this and their slower-paced approaches.

Most change in the first half of the twentieth century had been imposed on Indian communities from the top down with every switch in federal Indian policy. But now change was coming from within Indian communities, too. The NCAI tried to work within the system through the 1950s and 1960s (until its more conservative members were purged in the 1960s). Meanwhile, another organization sprang up in the 1950s, with a different philosophy and outlook: the National Indian Youth Council. NIYC was led by Clyde Warrior, a Ponca from Oklahoma who was a magnetic powwow dancer and truly a man of his people. Warrior had attended seminars and summer programs administered by the Southwest Regional Indian Youth Council meant to educate a new generation of Indian leaders on Indian history, federal policy, and the like. He had learned from them, but he wanted more. In the late 1950s, Warrior wrote that the "white man tends to rate the Indian as being lazy and worthless . . . The Indian seems to make it a point to act and be exactly as he's rated." This was part of the problem. The other part of the problem was that programming meant to help Indians—national housing initiatives, health care, educational opportunities, and leadership training programs—was run by non-Indians. The two parts of the problem came together in such a way as to prevent Indian people from charting their own destiny.

Warrior ran for the presidency of the Southwest Regional Indian Youth Council in 1960. Rather than prepare a speech or outline a policy position, he mounted the stage, pushed back his cowboy hat, rolled up his sleeves, and exposed his brown forearms. "This is all I have to offer," Warrior told the attendees. "The sewage of Europe does not flow through these veins." He won. His message was beginning to win, too: being Indian was good, maintaining Indian culture and tradition was good, and Indians were up to the task of being Indian in the twentieth century and beyond. This doesn't sound so radical in our age of identity politics, but it was radical then, especially among Indians. Hundreds of years of being missionized, colonized, reservationized, mainstreamed, marginalized, and criminalized had had a damaging effect on Indian self-regard.

Under Warrior, the youth group met on reservations instead of in city hotels, as the NCAI did. Every meeting concluded with drumming and singing, often led by Warrior himself. By 1966, under his leadership, the NIYC was involved in direct action. Indians from around the country participated in "fish-ins" to protest the abrogation of treaty rights in the Pacific Northwest. The NIYC was doing what other organizations weren't: pursuing tribal sovereignty by engaging in direct conflict with the U.S. government. Its members embraced Indianness as the most potent weapon in their arsenal, rather than settling for the weapons given to them by a government they were trying to change.

Stillaguamish chief Frank Allen and Esther Ruth Ross plan a "fish-in" in 1968 to protest loss of their fishing rights on traditional tribal lands. Civil disobedience in these "fish wars" resulted in a federal court's Boldt decision (1974), which affirmed Indian treaty fishing rights.

By government design and necessity, Indians had become "American," but for the most part, they had become Americans at the bottom. Their life expectancy was between fifty and sixty-five years, compared with seventy and over for whites. Indian infant mortality was one and a half times that of white babies. Even as late as 1988, Indians age fifteen to twenty-five were twice as likely to die in vehicular accidents and three times as likely to commit suicide. Middle-aged Indians committed suicide twice as often as whites, had incidents of liver disease nearly six times higher, died in car wrecks three times as often, and were three times more likely to be murdered. And there were more than four times as many deaths due to diabetes among Indians aged forty-five to sixty-four as among whites of the same age. Some Indians—like Clyde Warrior—turned their dissatisfaction into informed and passionate protest. Other Indians did violence to their loved ones and themselves in the form of assault, domestic abuse, rape, child abuse, drinking, drugs, and suicide. But for all the grim statistics, there were corresponding shifts in the direction of Indian lives.

Even as many Indians moved to cities, they looked back over their shoulders. Perhaps the good old days before the coming of the white man had actually been good after all. That idea offered more than pleasurable nostalgia. Indians began turning to themselves—to their cultures and religions and lifeway—to sustain them. The long hair, big belt buckles, beadwork aesthetic promoted by some Indian activist leaders spoke of something deeper: a profound sense that if America wasn't going to serve Indian people, the personal and cultural dignity vested in Indian practices might. This didn't mean dismissing all the skills and opportunities their American experience had afforded them, at great cost. Indians were figuring out how to be Indian and American simultaneously. Yet they did so with growing impatience with gradual systematic change. As the 1960s drew to a close, Indian activists looking for a model of resistance turned away from the NAACP and to the Black Panthers.

Direct action protestors and the steady work of the NAACP had done much to reduce the structures of racism in the South and in federal law. But these combined efforts had done not quite as much to address the conditions of urban Blacks in other parts of the country who encountered new forms of poverty and of racism. As white flight to the suburbs increased, African Americans found themselves concentrated in decaying city centers with few job prospects, substandard housing, failing schools, and overtly racist, non-Black police forces. (In Oakland, California, a mere sixteen of the city's 661 police officers were Black in 1966.) In response to this dilemma, activists Huey Newton and Bobby Seale, both of whom had worked extensively in community clinics and organizations in Oakland, formed the Black Panther Party for Self-Defense in 1966. The killing of a Black teen by police in Oakland and the subsequent riots across the city prompted Newton and Seale to make good on their ideas to harness Black urban rage and bend it toward the fight for political power. And so they set up the Panthers as a self-consciously militant force.

The Panthers' first big action was to make use of California's lax open-carry gun laws. Members armed with shotguns and rifles followed Oakland police around the city. They set themselves up as watchdogs on a police force notorious for its excesses. Less than a year later, more than thirty Black Panthers showed up, nineteen of them armed, at the California statehouse, where the party promoted a ten-point plan for freedom, employment, housing, education, jury by peer group from the Black community, and an immediate end to police brutality. This political wish list was published in the Black Panthers' newspaper in November 1967.

Beyond the violence and theatrics for which most people remember the Black Panthers, their mission had a strong community-action component. The Panthers organized citizen patrols, health clinics, day-care facilities, and schools. They disseminated information and registered voters. The party itself eventually crumbled due to power-hungry Panther leadership, excesses of violence, and undermining by the FBI. By the 1980s, the Black Panthers had ceased to exist as a viable political force in the American landscape. But while it was, urban Indians in Minneapolis, San Francisco, and other American cities had been watching. And they liked what they saw.

THE RISE OF THE AMERICAN INDIAN MOVEMENT

The early founders of the American Indian Movement (AIM) were mostly Ojibwe in Minneapolis, Minnesota. They looked around at their South Minneapolis neighborhood and asked themselves what the Indian Reorganization Act, the Indian Claims Commission, termination, and relocation had done for them. Indians in Minneapolis endured, as African Americans endured, high unemployment and poverty rates, racist policing, redlining of residential districts, a lack of adequate schools, and terrible housing—the worst in the state. A particular grievance, according to Dennis Banks, one of the founders of AIM, were the frequent Friday night police raids. Officers would burst into one of the neighborhood Indian bars and arrest everyone for drunk and disorderly conduct. They'd exploit the detainees for free labor over the weekend, then release them on Monday morning.

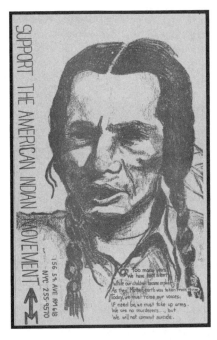

A poster created between 1968 and 1980 to help raise funds for the American Indian Movement (AIM).

Dennis Banks, along with brothers Clyde and Vernon Bellecourt, George Mitchell, and Harold Powless (Oneida), founded the American Indian Movement in July 1968. Their first act was to form AIM Patrols that, modeled on the Panthers, followed police around their neighborhood and documented instances of police brutality. Meanwhile, other Indian organizations—the National Indian Youth Council and the Red

Power Movement—were planning other militant actions, with a view to the impact they'd make on TV.

In November 1969, students and activists in the San Francisco–Oakland Bay Area took over Alcatraz Island. The takeover was, initially at least, the brainchild of Red Power and student activists, but it would become part of the mythology of AIM. The Bay Area had become one of the urban power intersections for Indians beginning in the 1950s. Some Indians had migrated there on their own from tribes across the country; others had been moved there during termination and relocation, and still others had been drawn to the liberal admissions policies of the University of California system.

Alcatraz sits in San Francisco Bay, a little more than a mile offshore from the city. It was the site of an infamous federal prison closed in 1963 because of rising maintenance costs and crumbling structures. Indian activists' interest in Alcatraz had been brewing since the closure. They were motivated by a clause in a treaty with the Lakota that said that they had the right to occupy any abandoned federal buildings for their own use. Alcatraz was far from the Lakota homeland, but it was federal and it was abandoned. On March 8, 1964, some forty Indians—among them two welders, a housepainter, and a Lakota navy shipyard worker named Walter Means and his twenty-six-year-old son, Russell—took boats out to the island and claimed it on behalf of America's first peoples. The occupiers offered to pay the federal government forty-seven cents an acre, the going rate for unsettled one-hundred-year-old Indian land claims in California. The protesters were surprised by the degree and intensity of public support. The coverage eventually died out and the lawsuits fizzled, but the Indians hoped that their publicity stunt would spark a movement. Five years later, it did.

Among those inspired by the early Alcatraz protest was Adam Nordwall, an Ojibwe business leader who owned a pest control company and had moved to the Bay Area from the Red Lake Reservation in the 1950s. Another was Richard Oakes, a charismatic young Mohawk steelworker who pulled up stakes in Rhode Island and drove to the Bay Area.

Nordwall and Oakes each wanted something more for Indians in the Bay Area. The men dreamed their separate dreams; then the San Francisco American Indian Center burned to the ground in October 1969. Nordwall and Oakes had a place on which to pin their hopes for Indians: Alcatraz could be the site of an expanded new Indian center.

The spirit of the idea was laudable, but the logistics were something else: Alcatraz was accessible only by boat; even the federal government couldn't afford to maintain the place; and the proposed Indian center was meant to serve a population so poor and so scattered that most would have a hard time getting to Alcatraz. Nevertheless, plans for the takeover moved quickly. Oakes met with students, Nordwall met with other Indian leaders, and the two met each other, at a Halloween party thrown by a local reporter. They joined forces. The activists announced the opening of the center for November 9. Boats were arranged, reporters were notified. At the appointed time, everyone gathered at the wharf—except the boats weren't there. Finally, Oakes sweet-talked the owner of a three-masted schooner, the *Monte Cristo*, into ferrying them across. When they neared the island, Oakes and some others stripped off their shirts and jumped into the bay to swim the last leg. The Indians returned to the wharf via the schooner an hour later, alive with the possibility of a real takeover.

On November 20, 1969, Oakes and seventy-seven other Indians, mostly students, arrived on Alcatraz Island with plans to stay. The occupation was fraught from the beginning. Many of the Indians hadn't brought clothing, basic supplies, warm jackets, or bedrolls. Many of them, however, had brought a lot of pot.

In the egalitarian and anarchic spirit of the sixties, the activists initially avoided a leadership structure; they soon had to accept that that didn't work, so they formed a leadership council. Richard Oakes was tagged as spokesman for the occupation, but he and Adam Nordwall quarreled from the start. (Jockeying for power and position became a recurring melody in the song of American Indian social movements, beginning with Alcatraz.) Sometimes, the occupiers scrounged to

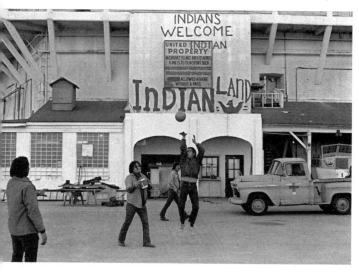

The 1969 AIM takeover of Alcatraz. In the end, no Indian educational or cultural center was built there and the island became part of the U.S. National Park Service. NPS acknowledges the historical importance of the takeover on its Alcatraz website and has preserved some of the graffiti from the time.

feed themselves; at other times, donated food and other supplies threatened to sink the island. On Thanksgiving, for example, Alcatraz was littered with frozen turkeys. In the news, the Alcatraz occupation sounded great, but on the ground it was a mess.

The takeover leaders met with representatives from the state of California, but the negotiations floundered. But nothing hurt the effort more than the infighting between the group's leaders. Oakes was accused of keeping donations and money for himself. Then in early January 1970, his twelve-year-old daughter, Yvonne, fell from a structure on the island; she died five days later. Oakes and the rest of his family left Alcatraz, though he continued to fight for Indian rights until he was shot to death in an altercation with a YMCA camp man-ager in 1972. (The shooter claimed self-defense; Oakes was unarmed, however.)

Conditions on Alcatraz worsened. Communication to the mainland was cut and the death of Yvonne Oakes soured many occupiers and supporters on the whole takeover. People were living in squalor, violence spiked. Public support waxed, then waned. Nordwall went back to the mainland and drifted away. With Oakes and Nordwall gone, new leaders tried to continue negotiations to turn Alcatraz into a cultural center, but talks with the National Council on Indian Opportunity died. Fires destroyed several buildings. The federal government then began the process of transferring the island to the National Park Service. On June 11, 1971, the remaining fifteen protesters were forcibly removed. After nineteen months, the occupation was over.

The Alcatraz takeover had a deep and lasting impact, however. It was hugely influential in President Richard Nixon's decision to formally end the termination period. And it inspired the American Indian Movement to organize bigger actions. In 1970 AIM occupied an abandoned property at a naval air station in Minneapolis to draw attention to Indian educational needs. That same year, the organization took over a dam on the Lac Courte Oreilles Reservation in Wisconsin to secure reparations for the largely illegal flooding of much of the reservation. (The damage claims from the dams were eventually settled, though it would be a stretch to suggest that AIM's involvement led directly to the settlement.) In 1971 AIM also briefly occupied the Bureau of Indian Affairs headquarters in Washington, D.C., to protest BIA policies and paternalism. Twenty-four AIM members were arrested for trespassing. Although there were no concessions, at a BIA meeting convened after the protesters were removed, BIA commissioner Louis Bruce showed his AIM membership card.

In 1972 AIM embarked on its boldest protest yet. In the summer, Robert Burnette, chairman of the Rosebud Reservation in South Dakota, proposed a caravan that would travel from reservation to reservation across the country, drawing media attention to the struggles of Indians and to the federal government's failure to address them or to meet its treaty obligations to sovereign Indian nations. Burnette dubbed the procession the "Trail of Broken Treaties." AIM, sensing an opportunity, jumped on board and began organizing in cities across the country. They were emboldened by the support of tribal leadership on the reservations, including the blessing of traditional elders, and spurred on by the controversial murder of Richard Oakes in September. George Mitchell and other AIM leaders in Minneapolis drafted a twenty-point list of demands. In October a caravan of cars, vans, and buses started off from the West Coast, gathering momentum as it moved east.

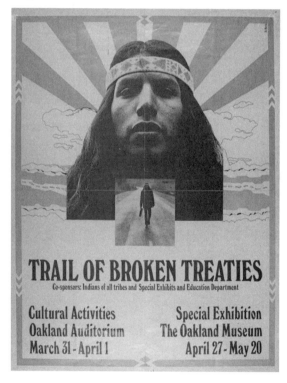

This poster is for a commemorative exhibition in the Oakland Museum of California, held in 1973, a year after the Trail of Broken Treaties caravan rolled into Washington, D.C.

AIM was a relatively new organization in 1972. The caravan showed them that coalitions matter, that allies matter, that methods matter. The Trail of Broken Treaties was widely supported by Indian citizens. Material, administrative, social, and political support for the action was offered by the Native American Rights Fund, the National Indian

Youth Council, the National Indian Leadership Training Program, the American Indian Committee on Alcohol and Drug Abuse, the National American Indian Council, the National Council on Indian Opportunity, and even the National Indian Brotherhood, a Canadian organization. But the resulting standoff with the U.S. government would be AIM's show.

The caravan, a few hundred Indians strong, arrived in Washington, D.C., on November 1, 1972, a week before the presidential election. As at Alcatraz, they arrived with no food and no place to stay. The permits they had applied for to protest near the Washington Monument had been denied, and government officials had quietly shut down any places where the Indians could protest, hold press conferences, or even stay. They found refuge in the basement of St. Stephen and the Incarnation Episcopal Church at Sixteenth and Newton in the northwest quadrant of the city, a predominantly Black area. Police convened at the church and refused to leave when the pastor told them to get lost. Meanwhile, the congregation was confused, the kitchen staff was overwhelmed, and there was no space for the youth activities the church normally sponsored. The situation was obviously untenable.

On November 3, the Indians headed to the Bureau of Indian Affairs: if the White House was going to shut them out of D.C., they would go to the agency tasked with helping Indians. Late in the morning, they entered the BIA with their bedrolls and belongings and gathered in the auditorium. The caravan leaders crowded into the offices of Harrison Loesch, assistant secretary for public land management, and John Crow of the BIA. Loesch, alarmed that the Indians intended to stay, complained that they had been let into the building only for a meeting. Everything went south from there. At an AIM press conference on the BIA office steps, activist Russell Means channeled the legitimate grievances that had brought the caravan to D.C., and its frustration at the government's failure to engage with them, into what would be his characteristic tendency toward violence. Means warned the crowd: "You can see the frustration here, in the young people and even in the old. Our full-bloods, the chiefs of our tribes, are saying it's time to pick up guns."

Almost immediately, the government scrambled to find accommodations for the protesters—more to keep the machinery of Washington running smoothly before the election than because they were seriously worried about armed resistance by the Indians. But sensing a shift in power, the Indians not only refused to leave the BIA office but also demanded a meeting with one of Nixon's representatives. It was scheduled, initially for three in the afternoon. But then the government postponed the meeting till eight that night. In the meantime, police began to mass outside the BIA office. The occupiers got nervous, and around five p.m. they took over the building and barricaded the doors. Panic ensued. BIA workers escaped out of windows and down fire escapes. One pro-Indian lawyer was lowered to the ground out of a window by AIM leader Clyde Bellecourt.

Protesters met inside the occupied Bureau of Indian Affairs office. An American flag upside down signals distress. Outside the BIA building, a teepee was set up with a sign that read NATIVE AMERICAN EMBASSY—just the sort of photo op AIM wanted.

On Friday, November 3, there were resolutions, meetings, countermeetings, and then more resolutions inside the BIA building. Security forces were ready to forcibly evict the protesters but received instructions from Nixon not to. The president preferred to stall through court orders and negotiations rather than risk confrontations so close to the election. Some agreements were reached and the occupiers were set to leave when, suddenly distrustful, they reconsidered.

Late on Friday, more than a hundred protesters armed with broomsticks and makeshift clubs faced off with U.S. marshals in front of the BIA. The marshals didn't engage them and the situation deescalated. By Saturday, the battle had moved to the courts after a judge issued an order for the arrest of the protesters. The occupiers were still restive. Means and others painted their faces, again fanning the flames of violence. "War paint traditionally means that the Indian who is going into battle is prepared to die," he told reporters. "If federal officers are ordered to evict us, we know there will be Indian deaths." But why? And over what exactly?

The occupiers finally released the twenty-point memo they'd drafted back in Minneapolis. Its provisions included, among others: New Indian commissions to make treaties and review treaty violations and reparations; new protections for Indians' religious freedom and cultures; a congressional committee on Indian relations; the abolition of the Bureau of Indian Affairs by 1976; and health, housing, employment, economic development, and education.

Many of the demands were sensible and might have been enacted with little difficulty. Other demands, however, were plainly out of the realm of possibility: giving 110 million acres back to the Indians, reopening the treaty-making process, removing the U.S. Congress from the government-to-government relationship between tribes and the federal government. The AIM leadership demanded a meeting with President Nixon. Nixon refused. The caravan-protest "leadership," after all, had not been elected or otherwise officially appointed, so they were hardly in a position to reaffirm a government-to-government relationship between tribes and the federal government.

By Monday, whatever goodwill had existed within the U.S. government had evaporated. Election day was twenty-four hours away. Government officials were behind a court order for the eviction and arrest of the protesters. Upon hearing this, the protesters erupted into an orgy of violence. They made a big show of ripping open cabinets, burning files and desks, and tearing out fixtures. By the time they were done, they had caused more than two million dollars' worth of damage to the BIA offices. Frank Carlucci, a midlevel CIA agent, was chosen by the Nixon administration to try one last round of meetings with the protestors. He seemed perfect for the job—stable, dark, sneaky, and sensitive to the place where power and desire overlapped. Carlucci immediately engaged the AIM leaders in negotiations, and by the next day, the government had agreed to give them $66,650 to help the caravan return home. The money was transferred in cash to Vernon Bellecourt in the presence of AIM leaders and officials from the NCAI, the Office of Economic Opportunity, and the White House. It is unclear what happened to the money after that, but most of the caravan had to find their own way back to their communities. The occupation was over, with little accomplished. Never again would AIM receive such broad support, especially after violence seeped into its character in the way it did.

AIM had begun to forge its image, however: that of the proud Plains warrior fighting the overwhelming forces of whiteness that sought to erase him. And it was a "him"—women were often forced to march in the back of a protest or asked not to march at all, as were lighter-skinned Indians. AIM leaders were obsessed with image and given to grandstanding. Yet in the midst of the counterculture movement that co-opted so much Indian aesthetic and culture, AIMsters (as members of the group were called) were doing one thing right: they showed they were proud of being Indian and did so in the most uncomfortable ways possible for the mainstream. My uncle Bobby Matthews was of that generation. AIM came up when he came up, though violence, tradition, and being Indian were combined differently in him.

When Bobby and his brother got home from school they'd go out to the woods and help peel and stack the logs their father had cut by hand. In the summer the family traveled to Ray, Minnesota, near the Canadian border, to pick blueberries. They got paid twenty-five cents a quart. In the fall, Bobby's dad took his kids out of school and they went ricing as a family. They sold some and they kept some for themselves. "We were raised on rice and rabbits and meat and potatoes. We got to trap and fish and net and camp. We got to know the woods."

When Bobby was eighteen, he and his cousins broke into summer cabins, mostly for the whiskey and beer. At one cabin, Bobby grabbed an old shotgun on his way out. He was caught and got four years' probation. Then Bobby fell in with his uncle Billy. "I started in robbing banks and liquor stores and things like that. I used to be able to open a safe pretty fast. An exciting life."

Bobby's run in the safecracking business lasted seven and a half months. By then he'd had enough. He got work as a concrete finisher, more work as a carpenter. He moved to Alaska and worked as a roofer. "Got in a car crash in Alaska and came back to Minneapolis in the early 1980s. At the time I was selling weed . . . And I quit all of it and started leeching."

There are probably no more than a few hundred Indians who spend most of their time living off the land, and only a very proud few like Bobby Matthews who do it exclusively. "You know, Dave," Bobby tells me, "the Creator or God or whatever you call it made the universe and all the beings in it and put this tree here and that bush there and he made the beavers and the deer and the plants that are good to eat and the ones that are good for medicine. He made all of it and it is beautiful! And I look out over that creation and sometimes I don't see it like other people do. I look out at all of it and what I see is money. And by God I am going to find a way to liberate it out of there." Uncle Bobby and AIM leaders were of the same era, but with different approaches to what would liberate them as Indians.

AIM AT PINE RIDGE

In the winter of 1972, an Oglala Sioux named Raymond Yellow Thunder was murdered in Gordon, Nebraska. Yellow Thunder dropped out of school to work as a ranch hand: fencing, breaking horses, hauling hay, mucking out stalls. He worked hard during the week and spent the weekends binge drinking in Gordon. On weekends when he didn't drink, he'd stock up on groceries and make the rounds among his siblings, distributing food along with gifts for his nephews and nieces. Often, when very drunk, Yellow Thunder would bring himself to the police station in Gordon and ask for a cot, and the cops would oblige him. He never fought and he wasn't belligerent. He was a hard worker and a hard drinker but a gentle, mellow man.

On February 12, 1972, Yellow Thunder was drinking in Gordon. At some point he crossed paths with Leslie and Melvin Hare and their friends Bernard Lutter and Robert Bayliss. They had been drinking, too. According to court documents, while joyriding around Gordon, they saw Yellow Thunder enter a used-car lot. They "found him in an old pickup truck and opened the door, causing Yellow Thunder to fall to the ground." They hit and kicked him while he was on the ground. Leslie, wearing heavy work boots, grabbed the stock rail of the pickup and jumped up and down on Yellow Thunder as he lay on the ground. The men then took off Yellow Thunder's pants and shoved him in the trunk of their car and drove him around for forty-five minutes before stopping at the American Legion Club. There they shoved Raymond Yellow Thunder into the hall and allegedly told him to do some Indian dances for everyone. Some of the patrons came to his aid, and the bartender asked if he needed any help, but Raymond waved them away. Naked from the waist down, he staggered into the frigid winter night. The temperature was twenty-two degrees. Later the men found him again. They picked him up, drove back to the used car lot, and retrieved his clothes. The men kidnapped him again and left him at a laundromat. They threw his pants inside and then left.

The next day a Lakota boy saw Yellow Thunder and asked what had happened. Yellow Thunder said he'd been jumped by some white guys. That was the last time anyone saw him alive. Eight days later Yellow Thunder was found frozen to death in the cab of the truck in the lot where his attackers had first found him. An autopsy showed he had died of a subdural hematoma caused by blunt-force trauma above his right eye. The Hares, Bayliss, and Lutter were picked up quickly: many people had seen them with Yellow Thunder that night. They were charged with manslaughter and false imprisonment.

Yellow Thunder's nephew thought AIM could help. He took up a collection from friends to finance a drive to Omaha, where AIM was meeting. He told them about what had happened to Yellow Thunder. AIM mobilized their membership. By the end of the week, more than fourteen hundred Indians from over eighty different tribes descended on Gordon, Nebraska, in a righteous rage. AIM organized protests and a boycott of city businesses and assembled a tribunal that it said would deliver real justice if the authorities failed to. The Pine Ridge Reservation began transferring its program monies out of Gordon banks to other holding companies. The pressure worked, after a fashion. City officials agreed to convene a human rights commission. A police officer notorious for mistreating Indians in the Gordon jail was suspended. The Nebraska state legislature instructed the state's attorney general to conduct an inquiry, and the governor sent a representative to meet with the protesters. The Hares, Bayliss, Lutter, and one other man were charged with manslaughter and released on fairly low bail. The county attorney called the incident a "cruel practical joke" that had gotten out of hand.

Yellow Thunder's family was outraged by the insufficiency of the charges and the dismissiveness of the response. The undeniable truth was that an innocent Indian man had been killed because of white drinking, white bigotry, and white violence. In the end Leslie and Melvin Hare were found guilty of manslaughter. Leslie was sentenced to six years and Melvin to two; Leslie was paroled after two years, Melvin after nine months. Raymond Yellow Thunder died in a truck in a used-car lot at age fifty-one from a traumatic injury. One of his assailants, Bernard Lutter, died at age seventy-seven from natural causes.

AIM's involvement in the quest for social justice in an off-reservation town known for exploiting Indians was exhilarating. Perhaps a little too exhilarating: on their way out of Gordon, a few hundred AIM-sters stopped at the Wounded Knee Trading Post in the heart of Pine Ridge. The "trading post" epitomized the exploitation of Indians for outsiders' gain. A tourist attraction owned by James Czywczynski, a non-Indian, the trading post stood on the site of the 1890 massacre at Wounded Knee Creek and sold moccasins and plastic bows and postcards showing Chief Big Foot's twisted, frozen corpse. It also lent money at supposedly exorbitant rates. And recently, Czywczynski had been accused of choking an Indian boy. The AIMsters trashed the place, stealing merchandise and smashing windows, while threatening and humiliating Czywczynski.

While AIM had continued to grow, it lacked a solid base of support on the reservations. The movement, which had been born in the city, was essentially urban-oriented, geared to do battle with white aggression and injustice through symbolic occupations and agitprop. AIM's agenda did include reclaiming Indian pride by way of Indian cultures and ceremonies, but reservation communities were not entirely sold on the organization. And even if some portion of the community might be sympathetic, tribal leadership often was not. This was the case at Pine Ridge in the early 1970s.

At that time the South Dakota reservation was led—some might say controlled—by Dick Wilson. Wilson came from the village of Pine Ridge, which was the seat of the reservation. Pine Ridge held the clinic, the best schools, the municipal buildings, and the few businesses that catered to the reservation. Its residents were somewhat better off and more racially mixed than the Indians from smaller villages around the reservation.

Wilson entered politics in the late 1960s, when he won a seat as a district representative. Almost immediately his detractors accused him of nepotism, favoritism, and mismanagement. It was said that he diverted funds for public projects into his own coffers and hired a private security force to intimidate his opponents. Nonetheless, in 1972 Wilson was elected chairman of the Oglala Sioux of the Pine Ridge Reservation. It was a narrow contest and most of his support came from the village of Pine Ridge.

Chairman Wilson set up a housing authority on the reservation, the first of its kind to deal with the epidemic of substandard housing. But he also continued firing reservation employees and replacing them with family members. He stopped consulting with the large tribal council and met only with the more easily controlled four-member executive council. He awarded cheap grazing leases on tribal land to white interests and proposed opening up large portions of the reservation to mining. All of that might have been regarded as reservation politics as usual: six previous tribal chairmen had been through impeachment proceedings, and only one had served more than one term. But Wilson went further.

At the outset of his tenure, the Indian Claims Commission had been ready to award the Lakota damages for ongoing land claims dating back to the 1870s, when Custer and his Seventh Cavalry broke open the Great Sioux Reservation after the discovery of gold in the Black Hills. On July 31, 1979, the Sioux were awarded $17.5 million; with 5 percent interest (calculated from the original claims) that came to $105 million. Tribal members were split over the proposed settlement. More traditional Indians from outlying areas strongly rejected it. The Indians residing in the Black Hills feared the notion that if they accepted the award, their land would be officially sold. This led many Sioux to believe that they would lose their land, culture, and identity. Progressives wanted the cash because Pine Ridge was (and still is) crushingly poor. Wilson wanted the cash. As unrest grew, so too did his reliance on his ever-growing private security force, who were aided and advised by President Nixon's domestic commando force, the Special Operations Group, an illegal domestic CIA intelligence outfit. Pine Ridgers referred to the security force as goons. Wilson's thugs proudly appropriated the name: they began calling themselves GOONs, Guardians of the Oglala Nation.

AIM had not had a significant presence at Pine Ridge, but now it waded into the fray at the behest of traditional Pine Ridge residents. Russell Means was Oglala, and he called the leader of his tribe a dictator, a liar, and a drunk. Wilson responded that if Means came to Pine Ridge, he'd cut off the activist's braids. The tribal chairman dismissed AIM as a bunch of "bums trying to get their braids and mugs in the press."

In February 1973 there was enough of a backlash against Dick Wilson to spark impeachment proceedings. He was not impeached, because of technicalities. More and more AIM members came to Pine Ridge. Wilson remained in office, and the village of Pine Ridge became increasingly militarized, packed with GOONs, Special Operations Group forces, U.S. marshals, and FBI agents. Tribal headquarters were sandbagged and crowned with a .50-caliber machine gun. It was under these circumstances that Russell Means did in fact come to Pine Ridge, along with much of the rest of AIM's membership, including Dennis Banks, Carter Camp, and Vernon and Clyde Bellecourt. Two GOONs jumped Means in a convenience store parking lot and beat him up. Undeterred, he continued to a meeting convened by traditional people in nearby Calico to discuss what to do now that the effort to impeach Wilson had failed. On the advice of spiritual leaders, AIM caravanned from Calico to the village of Wounded Knee. They held a ceremony at the gravesite of the victims of the 1890 massacre. While that was going on, AIM militants attacked the village and were able to control it almost immediately. Federal, state, and tribal law enforcement, already at Pine Ridge because of the political situations of the past year, blocked the roads and surrounded Wounded Knee. The militants were surprised when it became obvious that the government was neither going to storm the village nor disappear. A siege was on. The protesters would remain in Wounded Knee for seventy-one days.

March 1973: armed AIM activists at a roadblock near Wounded Knee, South Dakota.

Almost immediately AIMsters exchanged gunfire with federal and state agents. Backup forces and supplies arrived. Somehow the activists were able to deliver a list of demands to federal negotiators in the first days of the siege. Among the AIM demands were that Senator William Fulbright convene the Foreign Relations Committee to hold hearings on Indian treaties, that Senator Edward Kennedy convene a subcommittee to investigate public wrongdoing at the Bureau of Indian Affairs, and that Senator James Abourezk investigate "all Sioux reservations in South Dakota." Over the next few days the list of demands grew to include the immediate removal of Dick Wilson from office.

By this point, the U.S. government had some experience dealing with Indian militants. Alcatraz was behind them, as was the takeover of the BIA. This time the occupiers were armed, however, and they held eleven hostages from the village of Wounded Knee, most of them elderly non-Native residents of the village. Russell Means, always good for a sound bite, said he wasn't afraid to die, and if he did, the hostages would die, too. The government decided to wait out the protestors, who hadn't planned on a long occupation. The occupiers quickly organized themselves, but they lacked food—the town's grocery store had been looted clean on the first night of the takeover. Meanwhile, Dick Wilson's GOONs set up roadblocks in every direction for fifteen miles surrounding Wounded Knee. No one was allowed through.

After ten days a cease-fire between the government and the protesters was arranged. The feds got Wilson to disperse his GOONs. But when the roadblocks were lifted, more activists and supporters flooded in, bringing with them guns and supplies. The AIM leadership declared Wounded Knee the "Independent Oglala Nation" and said that as a sovereign nation it now would negotiate directly only with Secretary of State Henry Kissinger.

On March 1, George McGovern and James Abourezk, South Dakota's two Democratic senators, came to Pine Ridge to see what could be done. They spoke to the eleven hostages and were surprised to learn that they had always been free to go. One of them, Wilbur Reigert, told reporters, "The fact is, we as a group of hostages decided to stay to save AIM and our own property. Had we not, those troops would have come down here and killed all of these people." The militants traded gunfire with federal agents regularly, but no serious injuries were incurred, at least at first. AIMsters had an odd assortment of shotguns and deer rifles, and most of their arms couldn't even reach the federal troops in their bunkers. The feds, however, escalated. Americans across the country were shocked to see armored vehicles, machine guns, helicopters, and federal troops on U.S. soil. It was as if America itself had become a war zone.

The 1878 Posse Comitatus Act forbids using the U.S. military against American citizens. Still, General Alexander Haig authorized the use of armored vehicles and the U.S. Air Force at Pine Ridge before the siege even began on February 27. The agents who manned the roadblocks were FBI agents and U.S. marshals; military personnel wore civilian clothes rather than uniforms to disguise their presence. The military was there, illegally, and everyone knew it. Early negotiations with the U.S. attorney general's office were laughably unproductive. The attorney general's office then abruptly disbanded the National Guard and withdrew. The government hoped that without a military standoff everyone would lose interest. AIM's leader Dennis Banks declared victory. Journalists reported that the siege was over. Instead, more protesters flooded in with more weapons and more food.

On March 11, federal postal inspectors arrived at Wounded Knee to, as they claimed, investigate mail tampering. In reality they were trying to get a sense of what was happening in the village. With journalists observing, Russell Means ordered the postal workers held at gunpoint and said, "If any foreign official representing any foreign power—specifically the United States—comes in here it will be treated as an act of war and dealt with accordingly." A couple of hours later there was a gunfight between AIM militants and federal agents. One of the agents was wounded. And the real siege was on again, as armored personnel carriers, tanks, and agents moved back into place.

A couple of weeks after the siege began, Harlington Wood Jr. arrived to negotiate. Wood was a World War II veteran, noted legal expert, historian of Abraham Lincoln, and an assistant attorney general with the Civil Rights Division who had negotiated with Indian activists during the Alcatraz takeover. He was the first unescorted, nonmilitary official to enter Wounded Knee. Wood met and talked with AIM leaders for days and brought the Indians' demands to the U.S. government. They were still fighting for the recognition of earlier treaties and for some way to deal with the corruption and violence of Dick Wilson's regime. Wood did his best but failed. After he left, one of the most intense gunfights erupted, with federal agents firing on the village with M16s and a .50-caliber heavy machine gun. The cycle—violence, demands, negotiation, breakdown, more violence—continued.

The next negotiator was not so sympathetic or as effective as Wood had been. A month into the siege of Wounded Knee, Kent Frizzell was sent by the Department of Justice to end it. He cut off power and water to the village in an attempt to starve out the protesters. Food and fuel continued to arrive as Indians with backpacks hiked in over the hills. The gunfire continued. In late March, firefights were so frequent that government agents told reporters they could no longer guarantee their safety. Many journalists left. Those who remained were unable to report directly about the siege and so Wounded Knee began to drop from the daily coverage on TV and in newspapers.

Demands, meetings, breakdown, violence, repeat. April came around, though it didn't feel like spring in Wounded Knee. The federal government, getting nowhere, removed the BIA and the Interior Department from the negotiations and this helped: Means and other AIM leaders saw this as a move to more formal government-to-government relations.

In early April an agreement was reached: the Oglalas would have their grievances heard by the White House, and the Justice Department would investigate criminal activity on Pine Ridge. Another stipulation was that Russell Means would turn himself in and face the charges against him. A helicopter landed to pick up Means, who was applauded and cheered by his people. Before jail, however, Means was to appear in Washington, D.C., at a meeting to conclude the terms of the agreement. Misunderstandings arose immediately. The government said that Means had to order the evacuation of Wounded Knee before the meeting commenced. Means said he wouldn't do so until after. Means held a press conference and then left on a national speaking tour. He never returned to the Wounded Knee siege. On April 15, 1973, an AIM supporter and pilot from Boston dropped supplies by parachute over the village. When the militants came out to collect the supplies, government agents opened fire. Firefights grew in intensity and duration after that until, nine days later, Buddy Lamont was shot by a government sniper. Unlike Clearwater, Lamont was from Pine Ridge. He was a Vietnam veteran, well liked and low key. Everyone knew Buddy. He wasn't a zealot. He had worked for the Pine Ridge tribal police until he was fired for criticizing Dick Wilson. After his death the Oglala who had invited AIM to come and help them get rid of Dick Wilson and bring fairness, due process, and clean politics to the reservation ended the siege. They'd had enough. The AIM leaders—not from Pine Ridge—wanted to continue, but the rank and file didn't support them. A hasty agreement was drawn up and the siege ended. Banks and Means were charged with conspiracy and assault; they both got off because of a technicality.

Wounded Knee was both the high-water mark and a deeply disappointing action for AIM. The siege successfully drew national attention to many of the issues that had plagued Indian country for some time. The government never really felt the AIM occupation was more than a sideshow. It had been, in the words of a reporter, "war games without a war." Dick Wilson remained in office. Dissidents and Pine Ridge tribal members continued to be killed at an astonishing rate on the reservation. Violence continued to plague AIM. Before the siege was even over, an African American activist named Ray Robinson, an avowed pacifist who had marched on Washington with Martin Luther King Jr.

in 1963, disappeared from Wounded Knee a week after his arrival. AIM leadership claimed not to have met him or even to know who he was, which seems unlikely.

Despite the destructive behavior of its leadership, which hurt a great many people and arguably accomplished little, the American Indian Movement did make changes in Indian country, thanks mostly to its rank and file. Energized by the ideas of AIM's leadership, AIM-sters embraced the radical idea that simply "being Indian"—*choosing* to be Indian—constituted a social good.

Overall, the group was never very well organized. Still, AIM members helped open new schools in Saint Paul and Minneapolis, Minnesota. Despite the empty promises of relocation, many families who had moved to the Twin Cities from their reservation homelands had stayed in the city. High dropout rates and poor academic performance were two of the greatest issues these families faced. (Even now, Indians don't complete high school at a rate more than twice the national average.) Part of the problem, as community members saw it, was the ways in which education had been used against Indians for as long as anyone could remember. Boarding schools weren't far in the past. In the 1970s the conventional curriculum and the teachers who taught it still did not take Indian experiences into account. Instruction about Columbus's "discovery" of America, Thanksgiving, and the "opening" of the Western frontier presented Indians as inferiors or impediments to progress. Indian parents in the Twin Cities decided they wanted a school for Indians, managed and staffed by Indians, one that taught the usual subjects as well as classes on American Indian culture, ceremony, and life. They wanted a school for *their* kids.

The Red School House, an Indian-controlled community-based charter school, opened in Saint Paul. Other schools—the Heart of the Earth Survival School in Minneapolis and the Indian Community School—soon followed. When the government abruptly pulled grant

Students at the Red School House in the Frogtown neighborhood of St. Paul, Minnesota, an Indian-controlled accredited community school founded in 1972 by Native parents.

funding from Indian schools following AIM's takeover of the BIA in 1972, community members successfully lobbied to get the grants restored. By 1975 there were sixteen Indian-run schools across the United States and Canada with culturally specific curricula designed to suit the needs of their Indian students. More schools across the country would open in the decades to come.

Urban Indians sought to improve their position in other ways as well. In Minneapolis, Indian community members and AIMsters worked together to launch the Little Earth housing project in 1973. Little Earth, in the center of Minneapolis's Southside, provided homes for low-income Indians along with on-site day care and health care and Indian-centric cultural programming. At its inception, Little Earth was the only HUD-funded Section 8 assistance-based housing project in the country that gave preference to Indians. It still is and still serves the Indians of South Minneapolis.

Although AIM had a national presence, the depth of leadership and community buy-in were especially strong in Minnesota. In 1978, AIM members threw their weight behind Indian education in prison. Indian educators and spiritual leaders led classes and ceremonies at

Minnesota Correctional Facility–Stillwater and in St. Cloud, a program that continues to this day. The following year, AIM created the American Indian Opportunities Industrialization Center in Minneapolis, which was meant to fulfill another empty promise that the U.S. government had made back in the 1950s. Over the past four decades the center has helped train more than twenty thousand Indians for entry into clerical, construction, plumbing, and other occupations. But the growth of such opportunities through the 1970s wasn't only the product of grassroots activism.

WAR ON POVERTY

On January 8, 1964, President Lyndon Johnson declared "war on poverty" in an impassioned State of the Union address. Speaking before a joint session of Congress, he told the assembled lawmakers:

". . . Whatever the cause, our joint Federal-local effort must pursue poverty, pursue it wherever it exists—in city slums and small towns, in sharecropper shacks or in migrant worker camps, on Indian Reservations, among whites as well as Negroes, among the young as well as the aged, in the boom towns and in the depressed areas. Our aim is not only to relieve the symptom of poverty, but to cure it and, above all, to prevent it."

Johnson's remarks were the first time that Indians had been mentioned in a State of the Union address not as belligerent enemies of the state, or a special, bedeviling "problem," but as American citizens who deserved and needed the help of their government. In 1964 more than 19 percent of the population lived below poverty level. Lack of access to day care, employment, job training, adequate housing, and schools was not just an Indian problem: it was an American problem. Eight months after Johnson's speech, the Economic Opportunity Act was signed into law. It contained eleven broad measures meant to alleviate poverty and create programs that would help eradicate it. A new

Office of Economic Opportunity (OEO) was tasked with implement-
ing the War on Poverty legislation. One of the OEO directives was to
bypass federal and state bureaucracies and work as closely as possible
with poor people themselves, on a local level. It had the unintended
side effect of empowering Indian tribes to seek and secure funding
without the intervention of the Bureau of Indian Affairs.

On Leech Lake Reservation in Minnesota, this meant that a
young, handsome, energetic, idealistic Jewish Holocaust survivor,
World War II veteran, labor union organizer, and erstwhile BIA
employee could do what he did best—put power in the hands of
people who, until then, didn't have any. In 1965 my father, Robert
Treuer, began working as a local coordinator for a Community Action
Program (CAP) administered by the OEO. At the Red Lake and Leech
Lake and White Earth reservations, he met with tribal councils and
district representatives and organized meetings for tribe members
in small villages and larger towns. At these meetings he did what few
white people ever did when meeting with Indian people: my father

My family in the
1980s: my parents,
Robert Treuer and
Margaret Seelye Treur;
my brother, Anton
(left), and me (right).

asked them what they needed and what they were willing to do to get it. The lists were long: School lunches. Community centers. Job training. Elder assistance. Credit unions. An ambulance (Red Lake Reservation had none). One of his colleagues at CAP was Margaret Seelye, a young Indian woman from Leech Lake, fresh out of nursing school. They began to date, and eventually they married.

The Office of Equal Opportunity evolved an unofficial partnership with the National Congress of American Indians, another marriage of sorts, and together they were able to provide real services to Indian people, such as ambulances, housing, and reservation-based credit unions. The OEO was the beginning of the end of the top-down control that had been exercised on Indian people from the beginning of contact with white people. President Nixon did his best to undercut it and President Ronald Reagan finally dismantled the OEO in 1981. But the effects of its seventeen years of existence are still being felt in Indian country and across America.

THE INDIAN EDUCATION ACT AND THE INDIAN RELIGIOUS FREEDOM ACTS

Change was coming from other directions as well, perhaps nowhere more so than in the passage of two acts that were to have far-reaching results: the Indian Education Act of 1972 (IEA) and the American Indian Religious Freedom Act of 1978 (AIRFA).

The Indian Education Act mandated that local educational agencies (LEAs) with more than ten Indian students or more than 50 percent Indian enrollment develop curricular materials and support services to meet the needs of that population. For the first time, legislation treated Indian education as an American concern, not just the purview of the BIA or tribally run schools. It also required LEAs applying for funding to "use the best available talents, including people from the Indian community," and to develop their programs "in open consultation with Indian parents, teachers, and where applicable, secondary school students." At the same time, the scope of the IEA legislation was broad enough to deal with many issues that extended beyond cultural differences and curricular sensitivity. For example: transportation and nutrition, and providing eyeglasses and dental work. (It's hard to pay attention in class when you can't see properly, haven't eaten, or your teeth hurt.) For the first time, school districts, tribal governments, and parent groups could apply for grants to fund programs in public schools that facilitated Indian education. Public schools—and the vast majority of Indian students attended public schools—started to become something more than an ordeal.

By the 1980s, most high schools in Indian country had Indian education programs and a dedicated staff of Indian counselors who advised students about everything from home life to drug and alcohol addiction to college. Some schools had begun to offer instruction on subjects that emerged from the lives of their students: tribal languages, customs, history, and culture. For me, as a freshman entering the doors of Bemidji High School off the Leech Lake Reservation, it meant something to see my fellow Indians in the roles of teachers and counselors. When my older brother was a freshman, the school guidance counselor put him in shop, small engine repair, and welding classes because he was Indian, and so the best he could hope for was work in a trade—simultaneously insulting Native people and tradespeople. By the time I was a senior, there were Native guidance counselors in that school to make sure that never happened again.

Tribes also began to implement significant changes in Indian college education. The first tribal college in the nation, Navajo Community College, had been established on the Navajo Nation in 1968 and was accredited in 1976. Early on, it faced a dilemma: whether to emphasize "Western" curricula and adhere to the same standards and procedures as non-Indian colleges, or to tailor its offerings, even its whole educational approach, to the needs of the community. The school weathered the dilemma and, now as Diné College, offers a vibrant bouquet of programs, from the technical to the artistic.

In the 1980s, other tribes, recognizing that many Indian high school students—despite the best efforts of some high schools and teachers—were not prepared for college, established two-year accredited tribal colleges. Facing the same curricular questions the Diné had, most committed educators responded similarly: Why not both? By this time, research showed that culture-based bilingual programs greatly increased students' performance and competence in all subjects. The tribal colleges set up programs that prepared some Indian students for trades like engine repair, computer technology, and construction and others for the rigors of four-year colleges and universities. All in all, in this period, Indian educational institutions, for so long part of the process of indoctrination and eradication, became places *for* Indians. In 2013 Montana became the first state to have a fully accredited tribal college attached to or administered by every reservation within its borders.

In 1999 Montana passed the Indian Education for All Act, which mandated that Indian culture and history had to be taught to all Montanans, from preschool through high school. The legislation recognized that a history of the region, if not the country as a whole, was not complete unless it seriously considered the presence of Indians. Such a transformation in curriculum was facilitated by Congress passing the American Indian Religious Freedom Act (AIRFA), which was signed into law by President Jimmy Carter in 1978.

Until 1978 it was, technically at least, illegal for Indians to practice their various and varied religions. But if Indians weren't prosecuted for religious practice per se, they were often charged with possession of illegal objects and substances, which included eagle feathers, eagle bone whistles, and peyote. In this sense they still lacked one of the most basic of civil rights: the freedom of religion. And because for many tribes religion is tied to place, losing many sacred places to the reservation system, allotment, and subsequent private ownership also meant Indians could not practice their religion legally.

The effect of the American Indian Religious Freedom Act was profound. Ceremonies that had migrated underground and persisted only in what were, in effect, secret societies were now performed in the open. Younger and urban Indians had a chance to discover and participate in traditions that had been lost to them. Within a decade, tribes in Northern California—the Yurok, Tolowa, and Karok—used the provisions of the act to file a lawsuit against the U.S. Forest Service to prevent various bridge and road construction projects from destroying sacred sites. The tribes lost the case and other tribes lost similar lawsuits as well. The failure of these cases established that the AIRFA was too limited to protect the geographical expression of religion.

In 1971 an old cemetery had been discovered in the path of a new road being constructed near Glenwood, Iowa. Twenty-six Christian burials were found. Forensics revealed that two of the skeletons belonged to an Indian woman and her child (though they, like the rest of the dead, had been buried as and presumably were Christians). The remains of the Anglo Christians were reburied with ceremony nearby, while those of the Indian woman and her child were boxed up and sent to a museum in Iowa. Maria Pearson (Running Moccasins), a Yankton Sioux woman living in Iowa with her family, was incensed. Why should the Indian woman and her child be treated as artifacts while the bodies of the dead white people were treated with the respect they deserved? Dressed in ceremonial regalia, Pearson waited outside the Iowa governor's office until he emerged and asked her what he could do for her. She replied that he could "give me back my people's bones" and "quit digging them up." Pearson continued to lobby against the state, museum culture, and academic mindset that saw Indian remains as a scientific opportunity rather than as human remains. In Iowa, Pearson's work culminated in the passage of the Iowa Burials Protection Act of 1976, the first legislation in the country that sought to protect Indian remains and artifacts from exploitation. Wide-scale looting of burial mounds in Illinois and Kentucky where skeletons were tossed aside as looters tried to secure burial objects, and subsequent protests, added visibility to the issue. Momentum built through the 1980s, and in 1990 the Native American Graves Protection and Repatriation Act was passed.

Maria Pearson was Iowa governor Robert Ray's liaison for Indian affairs. She served for two decades under Ray and his successor.

NAGPRA was, like a lot of legislation, meant to right historical wrongs and to curtail those ongoing. It initiated an official process for the return of Indian remains and funerary, non-funerary, and religious objects held at state and federal institutions and in any museum or collection that received federal funds or grants. It also established procedures for the treatment of Indian remains and objects discovered during construction on state and federal land. Last, it made the trafficking of Indian remains a federal offense (though possession of remains is still legal). Although imperfect, NAGPRA has had a profound effect on tribes themselves and on their relationship with the federal government. As of 2018, the remains of more than 189,415 Indian people, 1,670,000 associated funerary objects, about 245,000 unassociated funerary objects, and nearly 15,000 sacred objects have been repatriated, in what continues to be a powerful and significant homecoming for tribes across the country.

FIREFIGHT AT PINE RIDGE

By the mid-1970s, AIM had been largely dismantled as a force for change. It still existed (as it does to this day), but the organization had been done in largely by infighting, violence, FBI meddling, and perhaps by its own insistence on "warrior affect." AIM emitted one last violent gasp heard around the world in 1975, when AIMsters got in a firefight with FBI agents. One Indian and two agents were left dead in a pasture near the Jumping Bull compound at the Pine Ridge Reservation.

It's hard to say how the fight started, much less what, exactly, happened. But in the summer of 1975, things at Pine Ridge were as bad as, if not worse, than they had been before and during the occupation of Wounded Knee two years earlier. Dick Wilson's GOONs were still terrorizing the reservation. Between 1973 and 1976 there were more than fifty homicides at Pine Ridge, many never investigated.

One of the murders on the reservation that the FBI did investigate, if only cursorily, was the assassination of Jeannette Bissonette, a Native woman and AIM supporter whose brother-in-law was a leader of the Wounded Knee occupation. In March 1975, Bissonette and a friend were parked in an empty field when someone opened fire on her car. She was struck in the back and bled to death before her friend was able to get her to the hospital. The FBI found shell casings nearby that matched a rare gun that was easy to trace to a ranch in the area. When the FBI showed up at the Lame Ranch, they were met by a number of Indian men, AIMsters, who were in the process of digging a trench, as though in preparation for a standoff. The FBI left, and shortly thereafter the AIMsters left, too: they were going to attend the annual AIM conference held that year in Farmington, New Mexico. Among them was Leonard Peltier, who had been on the FBI's radar for years.

Peltier was Métis (mixed Indian-Euro-American ancestry) from the Turtle Mountain Reservation in North Dakota. He had dropped out of high school at age fourteen and moved around out west before his drifting pulled him into AIM's orbit. On the West Coast, Leonard had met Dennis Banks, who took him on as a bodyguard. On the night of November 22, 1972—just a week or so after AIM activists had trashed the BIA headquarters in D.C.—Peltier got into a fistfight with two off-duty police officers at a bar in Milwaukee, Wisconsin. The police said that Peltier had a gun and drew it on them. He was arrested and charged with attempted murder.

That's where paths begin to fork in the way Peltier's story is told. Those who see him as a hero say that the police officers bragged about helping the FBI "get a big one" who had been targeted for his politics, even though in 1972 Peltier hadn't done anything much more political than accompanying Banks to Washington, D.C. Those few who don't see Peltier as a cultural hero tend to shrug as if to say that he grew up violent, engaged in violence, and was, in fact, violent, and whatever reasons the cops had for arresting him were probably very real. The only thing clear from this first full-throated encounter with the law was that Peltier was dangerous. He sat in jail for a number of months before making bail. When he did, he skipped the state. So in addition to being wanted for attempted murder, he was now a federal fugitive.

On October 21, 1973, Peltier was spotted in Pine Ridge by two BIA agents who were monitoring the funeral of Pedro Bissonette, Jeannette's brother-in-law, from their car. Someone in another car opened fire on the agents. They managed to get the license plate number and determined that the car was registered to Peltier. After that, he was arrested on a weapons charge in Washington state, and he jumped bail there, too. So by the age of thirty, Peltier was wanted in connection with three crimes: attempted murder in Wisconsin, the attempted murder at Pine Ridge, and a weapons charge in Washington state, plus two federal fugitive charges for skipping out on bail.

In 1975 Peltier and his cousin Bob Robideau, who had served time for burglary and was wanted for violating parole in Oregon, along with Darrell "Dino" Butler, a prison buddy of Robideau's, set up camp at the Jumping Bull compound. It was unclear what they intended to do. Peltier later claimed that he and his fellow warriors were called to Pine Ridge by traditionalist residents to help combat Wilson's GOONs, a scourge that certainly needed to be checked. But it's hard not to wonder if men like Peltier weren't simply drawn there by their own long association with violence.

On June 25, 1975, FBI agents Jack Coler and Ron Williams were driving nearby, looking for a red and white International Scout belonging to a man named Jimmy Eagle, who was wanted in connection with the torture and robbery of two white ranchers near Pine Ridge. The agents had heard that a vehicle matching that description was seen near the Jumping Bull compound. The agents were very interested in what was going on at Jumping Bull, not only because of Jimmy Eagle but also because of the ongoing investigation into Jeannette Bissonette's murder.

On June 26, Agents Coler and Williams were again patrolling Highway 18 separately near Jumping Bull when they spotted a vehicle matching the description of Jimmy Eagle's Scout. It seems to have been Peltier's van (though a Scout, built like a Jeep, is hard to confuse with a van). At 11:50 a.m., FBI agents listening to Coler and Williams's radio communications heard them say that the van was full of Indian men with rifles. Williams radioed that the men were getting out of the car. Then: "It looks like they're going to shoot at us." After that, intense gunfire could be heard over the radio. Forensic reports and testimony later heard at Peltier's trial suggest that the agents had followed the van onto the Jumping Bull property. They didn't make it farther than the middle of a ten-acre pasture before the Indians ahead of them took position on higher ground and fired more than 125 rounds into the agents' cars. The two men, seriously wounded, huddled behind one of their cars until someone (or perhaps more than one person—this is unknown) walked down from the ridge above the pasture and executed them. The Indians scattered to the hills.

When the authorities combed the compound, they found bullet casings matching the gun that had killed Jeannette Bissonette. Peltier, Robideau, and Dino Butler separated. Butler and Robideau were apprehended and stood trial in federal court in Cedar Rapids, Iowa. They pled self-defense and were acquitted. Peltier fled to Canada, where he was apprehended by Canadian Mounties. After a long and not entirely legal extradition process, during which the U.S. federal government supplied the Canadians with some very sketchy evidence, Peltier was returned to the United States. The prosecution proved that Peltier had motive to kill the agents, considering his previous warrants and charges. And they proved Peltier was the only one who carried and used an AR-15 assault rifle during the firefight; a casing from that gun had been found in the trunk of the agents' car, and ballistics also showed that the men had been executed with that kind of rifle. Peltier received two consecutive life sentences. He is still serving time.

MURDER TRAIL

Not long after the final fatal shootout at the Jumping Bull compound in 1975, a rancher in South Dakota was checking on his fence line when he saw a body in the ditch. It was the battered and partly decomposed corpse of a young woman in a ski jacket and jeans. The coroner later determined she had been raped repeatedly and shot in the back of the head at close range. The victim was identified as Anna Mae Aquash, a young Mi'kmaq loner from Canada. Inspired by AIM, she had left her two daughters with her sister in Boston, Massachusetts, and headed west to join the militants. She wrote her sister saying, "These white people think this country belongs to them . . . The whole country changed with only a handful of raggedy-ass pilgrims that came over here in the 1500s. And it can take a handful of raggedy-ass Indians to do the same, and I intend to be one of those raggedy-ass Indians." On her first night at Wounded Knee, Dennis Banks ordered her and some other women to perform kitchen duty. Anna Mae responded that she wasn't there to do dishes: "I came here to fight." Shortly thereafter she began a long affair with Banks.

Despite Aquash's fervor for the cause, sometime around the Wounded Knee siege AIMsters began whispering that she was an FBI informant. AIM was paranoid about turncoats and informants. Not without cause: COINTELPRO (the counterintelligence program run by the FBI to disrupt and discredit domestic political organizations) had indeed infiltrated AIM, the Black Panthers, and other political dissident and protest groups. However, there was no evidence (then or later) that Aquash was anything other than what she appeared to be: a dreamy, fierce, committed Indian woman. After the siege was over Dennis Banks went into hiding. Aquash drifted along with AIM, still wearing the "bad jacket" (the phrase used to describe someone who had been semipublicly accused of being an informant). In early June 1975, during the AIM conference in Farmington, New Mexico, Aquash was questioned by Leonard Peltier, who at the time still functioned as security for AIM. Allegedly, she was taken to a nearby mesa and asked by Peltier at gunpoint if she was an informant for the FBI.

After the Jumping Bull shootout, AIM leadership was on the run.

Banks was still in hiding, shifting from house to house in the West. Both Aquash and Darlene Nichols (with whom Banks eventually had four children) joined him at various times, sometimes at the same time. Eventually Banks, along with Peltier, showed up at Marlon Brando's house in Los Angeles. The famed actor lent them his RV, gave them ten thousand dollars in cash, and the two Indians continued on their way. In November, as Banks, Peltier, Aquash, and Nichols were driving through Oregon, they were stopped by police and a gunfight ensued. Peltier bailed out of the RV and ran for the trees. He was shot in the back but got away. Banks stayed in the RV and tried to drive away, later jumping from the vehicle to elude capture. I don't know what it says that the two men fled, leaving the women behind to face charges. Nichols and Aquash were taken to jail, where they initially shared a cell. According to Nichols, Aquash was scared for her life because back in the RV before their capture, Peltier had confessed to the women that he had killed the FBI agents at the Jumping Bull compound. He told them that one of the agents was "begging for his life, but I shot him anyway." Aquash—already suspected of being an FBI informant—was worried that she was going to be killed.

After her release on bail, Aquash fled the jurisdiction and failed to show up in court. Instead she went to Denver to meet Banks at a safe house. Aquash waited for over a week for Banks to show up, but he never did. There were, however, many other AIMsters, principally women, drifting in and out of the safe house. Anna Mae wrote letters home and looked after children in the house until, after about a week, she got into a red Pinto with three other AIM members and was never seen alive again.

Years after the siege at Wounded Knee, in the process of securing testimony and convictions for Anna Mae Aquash's murder, federal authorities leaned on and got help from Darlene Nichols. Nichols also uncovered more about the murder of Ray Robinson at the Wounded Knee siege. In 2001 Nichols showed up at Dennis Banks's house on the Leech Lake Reservation ostensibly to visit their daughter Tiopa; really she was there to probe Banks about Aquash's death. Nichols was nervous and failed to get Banks to talk about Aquash. But he did end up talking about Robinson's death. According to *The New York Times*, Banks said that Robinson had been shot by another AIM member during the siege. Banks recounted how he saw the corpse "shortly afterward and puzzled what to do." Banks told Nichols that eventually he found someone to "bury him where no one will know." Prosecutors thought they could use this to roll up witnesses from one case (Robinson) and use them on the other (Aquash), but that went nowhere. Robinson's murder is still unsolved and his body still hidden. But with Nichols's help, AIM member Arlo Looking Cloud confessed to murdering Aquash with John Graham, another AIMster. Both men were convicted and imprisoned. (Looking Cloud was released in November 2020; Graham is still serving a life sentence.) Prosecutors are not content with the convictions: they are certain that the two men were acting on orders, but they have not been able to walk testimony up to the top.

Many Indians muttered under their breath that AIM really stood for "Assholes in Moccasins." I am ambivalent. AIM did some good things but it is hard for me to separate their violence, and especially violence against women, from their cause. Nevertheless, a kind of cult worship, largely by white people, grew up around the AIM leadership. Also, partly as a result of Peter Matthiessen's book *In the Spirit of Crazy Horse*, Leonard Peltier was transformed into a sympathetic warrior whose only crime was defending himself against a tyrannical government. Russell Means, who was charged with domestic abuse by his Navajo wife (and who also allegedly beat his father-in-law), refused to appear in Navajo Nation court on the grounds that it didn't have jurisdiction over him. He went on to write a book, *Where White Men Fear to Tread*, and to play Pocahontas's father in the Disney movie and Chingachgook in the film *The Last of the Mohicans*. Dennis Banks continued to work as an activist and published a memoir, *Ojibwa Warrior: Dennis Banks and the Rise of the American Indian Movement*. Shortly before his death from pneumonia in 2017, at age eighty, Banks was asked by a reporter about whether he ever advocated for killing someone he "knew for certain" was a traitor to AIM. He said, "I don't know if I would participate in some sort of getting-rid-of-the-person. But I would say, 'Take care of this.' Or, 'Take the guy out, and I don't want to see him again.'" The reporter followed up and asked specifically about Ray Robinson's murder. Banks said nothing. Then the reporter asked about Anna Mae Aquash, someone Banks claimed to have loved and who, in turn, loved him. His response: "If there's a burning house, no one gives an order to put out the fire. Someone just goes and does it. It was people who fell into an idea."

The Jumping Bull incident was largely the end of AIM's efficacy as a prod to the nation's conscience. Strong Indians empowered by their Indianness was one thing; criminals who killed people because they didn't want to face the consequences of their own violent crimes was quite another. Increasingly, traditionalist Indians stood up to AIM's authority.

Yet much of the work that AIM members had accomplished in schools and job-training programs and housing carried on. And by the time the 1980s drew to a close, Indian life had become Indian again, due in no small part to the activism begun in the 1960s.

◈

It is March, and winter is bone-deep in the Northwoods. It seems like forever ago that there was anything green and giving in this world. As brutal and bitter as the winters are in the northern reaches of the Ojibwe homelands, there is a kind of peace that falls over the land in February and March. Or if not a peace exactly, a kind of watchful waiting: April and May will erupt with their usual vernal violence soon enough. But for now the snow isn't deep at all, and the swamps and lowlands are frozen solid, so you can walk wherever you need to go. Bobby Matthews and I are driving along an abandoned railroad grade on the south edge of Leech Lake Reservation, looking for cranberry bark. Typically, my uncle Bobby has gone all-in on this new revenue stream. So in addition to cutting and selling his own bark, Bobby now buys from other pickers. "I want people to know they can do this, David. They can live off the land, just like I do. What could be better than spending the day in the woods, getting exercise, and getting paid for it? It's what we've done for centuries. And we can still do this. But we have to change our thinking. We have to work together and we got to want it. I just wish our people wanted it more."

I think people do want it, increasingly so. Our people spent the better part of the 1960s and 1970s figuring out how to be both Americans and Indians: how to move forward into the future in such a way as to not leave the past behind; to once and forever destroy the idea that to live one kind of life meant shedding the other one; and to find some productive balance between growth and violence, between destruction and regeneration. This balance eluded the leaders of AIM. It eluded Leonard Peltier. But it did not elude the many thousands of Indians who worked together to build schools and clinics and jobs programs, who went to college and went to powwows, who, like my mother, practiced the law as a way of perfecting it while carrying herself with the kind of fierce dignity that characterizes our Ojibwe tribe. As the 1970s wound down, so did the public and private violence that gave rise to, and was added to by, AIM. The effects of that violence—done to us and caused by us—will surely be felt for years. But we shuffled into the Reagan years with a kind of collective sigh, ready for some peace and quiet for a change.

THE SOVEREIGNTY SURGE
1980-2015

❖❖❖❖❖❖❖❖❖

AT EVERY TURN, EDITORIALS, INVESTIGATIVE pieces, and popular culture reinforce the idea that reservations are where Indians go to suffer and die. Many Indians and non-Indians see them as little more than prisons or concentration camps, not as expressions of tribal survival, however twisted or flawed. But reservations are not stagnant places. They are home not only to traditional ways of living but to modern tribal business: the casino. Its arrival in Indian country about fifty years ago had as defining an effect on the social and economic lives of Indians as the mass migration of Indians to American cities.

As soon as the subject of casinos comes up with outsiders, the same questions always arise. I present them here to dispense with them up front. They get in the way of our actually understanding the effect casinos have had on Indian life.

Q: Have casinos made Indians rich?

A: Some. Of the 574 federally recognized Indian tribes in the United States (at this writing), fewer than half (245 tribes) own and run gaming operations. For instance, in 2019, 12 percent of tribes earned more than 65 percent of all Indian gaming revenue. So some tribes do very well with gaming, others so-so, and the majority not so well at all.

Q: Do Indians get money from casinos directly?

A: Some. Some small tribes pay per capita payments to tribal members from their casino profits. The smaller the tribe and the bigger the casino, the bigger the payment. The St. Croix

Chippewa Indians of Wisconsin have roughly one thousand enrolled tribal members. The tribe owns and operates three casinos. Tribal members receive per capita payments of between five thousand dollars and eight thousand dollars annually. By comparison, the Pechanga Band of Luiseño Indians, who own Pechanga Resort and Casino in Temecula, California, with the same number of tribal members, distributed $360,000 annually to each of them as of 2012. Most gaming tribes, however, do not distribute per capita payments at all; revenues, such as they are, are used for roads, schools, eldercare, and so on.

Q: How come Indians don't have to pay taxes on any of this?

A: They do. Most Indians don't pay state tax if they work and live on their home reservations, but all pay federal income tax and property tax on land they own outright. Tribal casinos don't pay corporate taxes, but they do payroll taxes, etc., just like any other business operating in the United States. And the gaming compacts signed between tribes and states often include provisions that redirect some casino profits to states and state organizations.

Q: Why did the government give casinos to Indians?

A: The government didn't "give" us casinos. Gambling is (among many other things) a civil matter and a right we've reserved or retained. The freedom to gamble for money is a right we had long before white people showed up in the New World.

Q: Isn't it sad to go into casinos and see Indians gambling? I mean, they have all sorts of other addictions to contend with.

A: Ha ha. When I walk into casinos I see way more white and Asian people gambling than Indians.

Q: Have casinos destroyed Indian culture?

A: That's a stupid question. Has commerce destroyed American/Chinese/German/French culture?

Indian casinos owe their existence to a $148 tax bill on a trailer in the village of Squaw Lake on the remote north end of Leech Lake Reservation. In the spring of 1972, Helen Bryan and her husband, Russell, were sitting at their kitchen table drinking coffee when they saw a pickup truck pull into the yard. They watched, curious, as a man got out of the truck and began measuring their trailer. Once he was done measuring, he took pictures. Then he got back in his truck and drove away, never having introduced himself or asked the Bryans' permission to step onto their property.

The trailer was a modest two-bedroom affair, but it was home to Helen and Russell and their six kids. They had heat, running water, and electricity at a time when having all three at once, in a home of one's own, was something of a rarity on the reservation. Helen worked at the Leech Lake Head Start for minimum wage, and Russell didn't work at all, but even on their meager income they could cover the trailer's ninety-two dollars a month mortgage. A few weeks after the arrival of the mysterious visitor, however, Helen received a tax bill of $29.85 for the remainder of 1971. She was confused: Why would she have to pay taxes? Her trailer was on tribal land. "I said it was wrong," remembers Helen. "And how was I going to pay for taxes and feed my kids and make house payments?" She ignored the bill. But like all tax bills everywhere, it didn't go away. The bill for 1972 was $118.10, bringing her total to $147.95. Helen didn't know what to do. Things were so tight for her family that even a small bill mattered a great deal. And then there's Helen's nature: she might be a poor young mother from a remote reservation, without access to lawyers and help, but she knew that the tax bill was wrong. It was just wrong. And she wasn't going to pay it.

Helen remembered that a legal program had been started on the reservation a few years back. The Leech Lake Reservation Legal Services Project was founded in 1967 under the auspices of the Office of Economic Opportunity. It was the first independent Indian legal-services project in the country. Helen called them up and explained her situation to Jerry Seck, who thought she had a good case and agreed to take it on. Helen mailed the tax notice to the legal services office, and over the ensuing months, their lawyers called occasionally. Seck promised Helen he'd buy her a beer if they won.

The social genius of legal-services organizations is that they can take good cases and argue them in broad and interesting ways that can then become legal precedent. Helen's case could have been argued narrowly: the Bryans' trailer was attached (annexed) to Indian land. As such, it was considered tribal property and exempt from state taxes in the same way that state, county, and federal lands and buildings are not taxed by states. The broader and bigger argument was that the state didn't have the authority to assess personal property tax on Indians living on Indian lands. The idealistic young attorneys at the Leech Lake Reservation Legal Services Project opted for this harder path. They lost. The Bryans' lawyers appealed to the Minnesota State Supreme Court. They lost again. That beer, and relief from the taxes, had begun to seem very unlikely. But then the U.S. Supreme Court agreed to hear Helen's case.

By now, many of the lawyers who had started on the case had left the legal-services team. A new lawyer stepped in. Bernie Becker, from New York, was portly, brilliant, and personable; a great ally. He argued that Public Law 280, which transferred some criminal and civil jurisdiction from the federal government to the states in 1953, had been meant as "law-and-order" legislation, and only that. If the government had intended PL 280 to grant all civil actions like taxation to the states, it would have said so. And if it had been written with that intent, it would have, in effect, been "termination" legislation.

Itasca County's lawyer argued that PL 280 was indeed intended as an "integration and assimilation" initiative. Becker was ready for him.

True, the government had wanted to terminate tribes. It had passed legislation that did just that. But those laws were very clear, whereas PL 280 had no such language. And that was because it had been passed to help tribes, not demolish them. Becker further argued that tribes had not consented to PL 280. On June 14, 1976, the Supreme Court ruled unanimously for the claimants. In the opinion of the court, there was nothing in PL 280 "remotely resembling an intention to confer general state regulatory control over Indian reservations." Jerry Seck called Helen with the news. "I was really happy," she says. "That was $147 off my mind. And I didn't get no more tax notices."

For Helen Bryan and her family, life didn't change much. She was still poor, and she remained poor. "I never got nothing from nobody," she told me in that quiet, fierce way of hers. "I supported all eight of us my whole life. But when Russell died the tribe offered to pay for his funeral and for his headstone, but only if they could choose the wording for it. I said sure. So they put RUSSELL BRYAN VS. ITASCA COUNTY—VICTORY right on the headstone."

FROM COURT TO CASINOS

Helen may not have gotten much from standing her ground, but tribes got a lot from Helen. The Supreme Court decision opened many doors the government and most Indians had considered closed. Regulatory control over commerce, banking, gaming, liquor, tobacco, and a host of other things is a tremendous kind of power. Within a year or two after the Supreme Court's ruling, tribes across the country began testing its limits.

After the Bryans won their case, the Seminole tribal chairman saw a big window of opportunity. In 1979 the tribe built a high-stakes bingo parlor. At that time, Florida state law only allowed nonprofit organizations like the Catholic Church to operate bingo games, no more than two times a week, with jackpots no higher than a hundred dollars. The Seminole advertised that they would be open six days a week and their jackpots would be much bigger. The sheriff threatened the tribe with arrest even though many local non-Indian residents were supportive of the enterprise. The tribe promptly sued. They won in the U.S. Fifth Circuit Court of Appeals, which ruled that states have no power to abrogate or regulate treaty rights. So the Seminole didn't just open their bingo hall, they made it bigger.

Meanwhile, in Southern California, the Cabazon Band of Mission Indians opened a poker room and bingo hall. As in Florida, the sheriff immediately descended on the operation, closed the game rooms, arrested tribal members, and confiscated money and equipment. Like the Seminole, the Cabazon had expected this, and they took the matter to court as well. The Cabazon noted that gaming laws in California were regulatory, not criminal laws, and the courts had already ruled that states didn't necessarily have regulatory power over tribes. The court ruled in the Cabazon's favor. All these rulings brought law and policy in line with sovereign treaty rights and clearly established that tribes could be in the gambling business.

The Cabazon lawsuit wasn't resolved until 1987, but by then, gaming enterprises were already underway across the country, with the biggest concentration of casinos in California and Oklahoma. The court might have been deliberating, but Indians were not. By the mid-1980s, elected tribal leaders had gained forty years of expertise and experience in IRA governments and in dealing with the Bureau of Indian Affairs and state and federal governments. They were prepared to make the most of the opportunity for gaming. Within a year of the Cabazon win, tribal gaming revenue was bringing in one hundred million dollars annually. The door to economic development—at least in the realm of gambling—seemed to have been flung wide open.

But not so fast: the states, a powerful lobby in their own right, were determined to have a stake in Indian gambling. The federal government felt the same way. So in 1988, Congress passed the Indian Gaming Regulatory Act (IGRA), which established the National Indian Gaming Commission. This commission consisted of a chair appointed by the U.S. president and approved by Congress, and two associate or assistant chairs. Only two members could be from the same political party, and two of the chairs had to be held by enrolled tribal members.

IGRA also codified the process by which tribes administered gambling. It established three different classes of gambling. Class I was basically traditional tribal gambling, social games like bagese, moccasin game, or hand game. Tribe members could continue to play these without any federal meddling or oversight. Class II gambling was mostly bingo, but it also included pull-tabs, tip jars, and "non-banked" card games like poker, where players play against one another but not against the house. Tribes had exclusive authority over Class II gaming as long as their state also allowed that kind of gaming and the tribe developed a gaming ordinance approved by the Gaming Commission.

Class III gaming was casino gaming, where the real money lay. The provisions for Class III gaming were the result of a vigorous compromise between the federal government and Indian tribes. The first provision was that whatever forms of gaming a tribe wanted to conduct in a state had to be legal in that state. This meant that in places like Minnesota, where casino gambling was not legal, the state had the power to wrest concessions in the form of taxes in exchange for a state gaming compact with the tribe. The second provision was that tribes must enter into gaming agreements with the state that detailed where and when each casino could be built, how large it could be, how much of the earnings the state took, and the like. The third provision required the tribe to develop gaming ordinances to be approved by the chairman of the National Indian Gaming Commission. IGRA also provided that the FBI, rather than city, county, or state law enforcement, would have jurisdiction over tribal gaming.

Indian gaming boomed after the passage of IGRA. Revenues grew from one hundred million dollars in 1988 to more than thirty-three billion dollars in 2018—more than Las Vegas and Atlantic City casinos combined took in. Despite the influx of money in general, however, gaming changed little for most Indians. Like all American avenues to wealth, casinos privilege the few and leave out the majority. Casinos have had another major effect: they've thrown into stark relief the vexing question of who gets to be Indian at all.

BLOOD QUANTUM AND DISENROLLMENT

America's first blood-quantum law was passed in Virginia in 1705 in order to determine who had enough Indian blood to be classified an Indian—and whose rights could be restricted as a result. You'd think, after all these years, we'd finally manage to kick the concept of "Indian blood." But recently, casino-rich Indian tribes in California, Michigan, Oregon, and other states have been using it themselves to disenroll those whose tribal bloodlines, they say, are not pure enough to share in the casino profits. As of 2017, more than fifty tribes across the country have banished or disenrolled at least eight thousand tribal members in the past two decades. Many different rationales have been used to justify this, but it's telling that 73 percent of the tribes actively kicking out tribal members have gaming operations. What is surprising is the extent to which Indian communities have continued using a system of blood membership that was imposed upon us in a violation of our sovereignty.

In the late nineteenth and early twentieth centuries, the U.S. government entered into treaties with Indian nations that reserved tracts of land for tribal ownership and use and guaranteed annuities in the form of money, goods, or medical care. Understandably, tribes and the government needed a way to make sure the annuities ended up in the right hands. Blood quantum, and sometimes lineal descent, was a handy way of solving that problem. For instance, if one of your grandparents was included on the tribal rolls and you possessed a certain blood quantum—say, you were one-fourth Navajo—the government counted you as Navajo as well.

But blood quantum had another benefit, for the government at least. Officials believed that within a few generations intermarriage and intermixing would eliminate Indian communities, and the government would be off the hook for the annuities.

Indians themselves knew how artificial this category of tribal membership was and used it to their own advantage. Before my tribe, the Ojibwe, established the White Earth Reservation in Minnesota in 1867, Chief Bagone-giizhig lobbied to exclude mixed-bloods from the tribal rolls—not because they weren't Indians but because, most likely, they formed a competing trader class. Bagone-giizhig swore they would rob White Earth. That he was right is a bit beside the point—he probably wanted to rob it himself.

Something similar happened at White Earth after the passage and subsequent amendment of the Dawes Act of 1887, which established the process of allotment. Although excess land could be sold off, full-blood Indians were forbidden to sell. But whites wanted the land and sent in a genetic investigator. In short order, the number of registered full-bloods at White Earth Reservation went from more than 5,000 to 408.

After Congress passed the Indian Reorganization Act in 1934, effectively ending the allotment of land, the provisions of blood quantum became ingrained in Indian communities. They determined if you could vote or run for tribal office, where you could live, if you'd receive annuities or assistance, and, today, if you get a cut of the casino profits. Blood quantum has always been about exclusion. I know full-blooded Indians who have lived their entire lives on reservations but can't be enrolled because they have blood from many different tribes, and I know of non-Indians who have been enrolled by accident or stealth just because they'll get something out of it.

Things were different once. All tribes had their own ways of figuring out who was a member, usually based on language, residence, and culture. In the case of the Ojibwe, it was a matter of choosing a side. In the early nineteenth century, who you were was largely a matter of whom you killed, especially when we were at war with the Dakota, many of whom were our blood relatives.

Who is and who isn't an Indian is a complicated question, but there are many ways to answer it beyond genetics alone. Tribal enrollees could be required to possess some level of fluency in their native language or to pass a basic civics test. (On my reservation, schoolchildren don't read the treaties that shaped our community and aren't required to know about the branches of tribal government or the role of our courts and councils.) Or tribal membership could be based, in part, on residency, on some period of naturalization inside the original treaty area (some tribes do consider this). Tribes don't have armies, but they could require a year of community service. Other nations take these things into account, and in doing so they reinforce something we Indians, with our fixation on blood, have forgotten: bending to a common purpose is more important than arising from a common place.

Of course, just remaining alive and Indian over the past 150 years has been one of the hardest things imaginable. A respect for lineage is a respect for the integrity of that survival, and it should remain a metric for tribal enrollment—but not the only one. Culture isn't carried in the blood. Culture is carried on in many ways—kinship, geography, language, religion, lifeway, habits, and even gestures—but not in blood. Blood matters. And blood is and will continue to be used as a way to determine who is in a tribe and who isn't. But it is useless to determine who is and isn't part of a culture.

What's fascinating to me is that the whole question of culture didn't become part of the conversation about who is and who isn't Indian at all until the period AC—After Casinos. True, *being* Indian (as something one did in addition to something one simply was) began back with the

Red Power movement and was amplified by AIM. But in those early discussions and actions, being Indian was more a matter of politics and emotional affinity than a matter of culture. Even the religions claimed by AIM were antagonistic and political: AIMsters danced the Sun Dance as a way of saying "We're not you" more than as a positive assertion of religious identity. But after casinos began injecting millions and then hundreds of millions and then billions of dollars into Indian economies, culture really came to the forefront in discussions of Indianness.

In part this phenomenon appears to be generational in origin. Many of the Indians who moved to cities in the 1950s, 1960s, and 1970s stayed in the cities. They put down roots, got jobs, went to school, and had families. Their urban and suburban children were raised on story after story of the rez—stories about junky cars and violent sheriffs and selling blueberries or baskets or tamales or necklaces by the roadside; about five or ten or fifteen people living in a shack; about one drunk-scapade after another; about the foibles or idiosyncrasies of this or that elder. These rez stories became foundational myths, benchmarks of authenticity, even though they were all, in one way or another, stories of loss. Nonetheless, for many Indian kids not raised there, the reservation and the mythology around it carried the idea that there was more to being Indian than simply having a tribal ID card.

My mother's tribal ID card uses the misnomer Chippewa. In the last twenty years, Ojibwe tribes have largely rejected this name, which many consider a colonial European mispronunciation. We've replaced Chippewa with Ojibwe, which is what we call ourselves.

The new emphasis on culture may be a matter of class, too. By the 1980s, a recognizable Indian middle class had begun to emerge. The origins of this class can be traced back to the earliest days of the reservations, to mixed-blood Indians who set up shop as traders, foremen, loggers, miners, and the like, relying on both their Indian and their white families. Also, as destructive as the boarding school era was, it had taught many students to not only read and write but to farm, sew, and operate and fix machinery as well. And allotment had made property owners of many Indians. With that added level of security, work and capital were suddenly available to them. World War II and the social programs of the 1960s and 1970s also helped bring a few Indians into the American middle class without necessarily compromising their culture. The advent of casinos could be seen as yet another step in this progression.

The energy around the casinos, and the money derived from them, fed efforts to promote Indian culture, too. Casino-rich tribes—and even tribes like mine that haven't made much from gambling—began sponsoring powwows with large prize purses for dancers and drum groups, resulting in an explosion of contemporary arts and crafts and music. They built and operated museums. They expanded tribal schools where students learned reading, writing, and math but also took classes in Indian singing and drumming, crafts, and tribal languages.

Powwow, Red Lake, Minnesota, summer 2020.

The Seminole now own the Hard Rock Cafe franchise. The Mille Lacs Band of Ojibwe in Minnesota own hotels in Minneapolis. With a little more economic security, Native people can rededicate themselves to our ceremonies and religions—both of which are broadly time and labor intensive.

INDIAN AND IN CHARGE

All in all, by the end of the 1990s there was enough cushion for enough Indians and enough money to begin pondering, in earnest, what being Indian *meant*. Identity politics is a game usually played by people who can afford it. And by 1990 many Indians could afford it. They had enough space in their lives to want to connect to their tribes in ways that were value positive, that didn't see being Indian as a matter of being a full-blood or being enrolled or being simply "dark," as had been the case when I was growing up. Rather, being Indian became a matter of knowing your language, attending ceremony, harvesting game and wild rice or piñon nuts or salmon. Being Indian was still to some degree a matter of blood, but it was also in the process of becoming about much more.

By the 1970s tribes across the country had, for the first time, an "emerging litigation" capability. The legal-services organizations that had helped Helen Bryan with her tax problem were taking root across the country. In the nonprofit sector, legal organizations like the Native American Rights Fund and the Indian Law Resource Center also represented Indian individuals, tribes, and tribal interests in areas such as taxation, undoing the ravages of the Termination Act, and advancing Indian interests and rights internationally. As the Indian legal and professional class grew, the Supreme Court kept pace, recognizing Indian rights in more than 120 decisions handed down since the 1950s that touched on tribal affairs, Indian rights, and tribal sovereignty.

The frenzy of Indian legal activity in the 1960s and 1970s helped secure the idea and fact of Indian tribal sovereignty. Until the 1980s, sovereignty usually had been explored and litigated in terms of treaty rights such as the right to hunt, fish, and gather. Now it expanded to include gaming as the right to administer to the civil concerns of the tribe.

The civil reach of sovereignty was furthered in the Southwest in the 1980s when the Jicarilla Apache were brought to court by oil and gas companies that had long-standing leases on their land. The Jicarilla Apache Reservation in northern New Mexico sat on top of coal, oil, and gas reserves. Those reserves had been tapped by energy companies through lucrative leases with the tribe, written and executed with the heavy hand of the BIA. By the late 1970s, the Apache were no longer content with the deals that had been struck. The tribes, unable to simply change the leases, wanted to tax the oil companies. The Jicarilla Apache constitution, revised in 1968 and approved by the U.S. Secretary of the Interior, gave the tribe the "authority to pass ordinances to govern the development of tribal resources." In 1976 the tribal council adopted the Jicarilla Oil and Natural Gas Severance Tax, applicable to "any oil and natural gas severed, saved and removed from tribal lands." The oil and gas companies sued, and the case wound up in the Supreme Court in 1982. The court found for the tribe. Justice Thurgood Marshall's opinion wrote that the oil companies "avail themselves of the 'substantial privilege of carrying on business' on the reservation . . . They benefit from the provision of police protection and other governmental services, as well as from 'the advantages of a civilized society' that are assured by the existence of tribal government . . . Under these circumstances, there is nothing exceptional in requiring [them] to contribute through taxes to the general cost of tribal government." So much for the myth of Indians as savage people without "real" civilization. And there were other, less tangible shifts that emerged from the sovereignty surge in the 1980s.

My mother, Margaret Seelye Treuer, was born in 1943 in the Cass Lake hospital on the Ojibwe Leech Lake Reservation. She grew up with her three brothers and sister and parents in a two-room cabin in Bena. My grandfather, the World War II vet, and my grandmother didn't make much money. The shack had electricity but no running water, and no heat except a barrel stove. Neither parent pushed education very much, and my mother was pulled from school regularly in the fall to harvest wild rice.

An unidentified Ojibwe woman harvests rice on the Nett Lake Reservation in Minnesota in 1946.

Harvesting rice was awful in her memory. The family sold most of it to buy school clothes, flour, lard, and kerosene. They got thirty-five cents a pound for wild rice in the 1950s. My mother never wanted to do any of that stuff again. So when she was a senior in high school, she decided to continue on to nursing school. When she told her father, he scoffed and sneered. Who the hell did she think she was? Nevertheless, my mother went to nursing school in Duluth, Minnesota, and worked in Saint Cloud for a year before returning to Leech Lake. Shortly after that, she got the Community Action Program job working on health care where she met my father, Robert Treuer. They moved to Washington, D.C., for work in 1968.

After my older brother, Anton, and I were born, my mother wanted something more. My father asked her, *If you could do anything, what would it be?* She demurred. But he was nothing if not persistent. *Just say it, we're just talking. What would you do? No limits.* Reluctantly she said she'd like to be a lawyer because no one had stuck up for her and her family when she was a kid. No one stood up against the cops and the courts and the government.

My father cajoled her into applying to Catholic University in Washington. My mother was admitted provisionally, since she didn't have a four-year degree. Three years later, juggling four kids by that time, she received her law degree. She had interned with the Native American Rights Fund in D.C. and had sat in on Supreme Court hearings for *Bryan v. Itasca County.* In 1979 we moved back to the reservation. My mother and Paul Day, another young Leech Lake Indian who'd gone into law, opened their law offices in the town of Cass Lake.

With my brother, Anton (right), at the 1976 Ball Club Powwow on the Leech Lake Reservation. Anton is seven years old; I'm six.

In the fall my mother made us go ricing, as she had as a girl (though without the pressure to earn). In the summer we picked berries. In the fall she took us hunting. In the early winter she taught us how to hang snares for rabbits. In the spring the family tapped maple trees and boiled the sap into syrup and finished it into sugar. I hated ricing;

it was itchy, uncomfortable work. I shied away from sugaring, too: the fumes from the boiling sap gave me headaches. Much later I asked my mother why she'd had us do all that stuff anyway. Why bother? *I was going to make sure you did well and got into college and went on to find a good job,* she explained. *But I was also going to make sure you knew how we lived, how we lived off the land. That way, no matter what happened out there in the bigger world, you'd know how to take care of yourself back here, on the rez. You'd be able to feed yourself.* Still later, looking back, I see in my mother's actions and attitudes something I surely didn't see then—one of the less visible effects of Indian empowerment and sovereignty. Sovereignty isn't only a legal attitude or a political reality; it has a social dimension as well. Sovereignty carries with it a kind of dignity, a way of relating to the self, to others, to the past, and to the future. As such, for my mother, being Indian wasn't a condition to be cured or a past to be escaped and even improved upon. To believe in sovereignty, to let it inform and define your political and legal existence, your community, and how you move through the world, is to resolve one of the major contradictions of modern Indian life. It is to find a way to be Indian and modern simultaneously. At the Tulalip reservation in Washington State, signs of a possible new way to do all this have emerged.

THE QUESTION OF CANNABIS

In February 2015, amid the cedar masks, canoe paddles, and totem poles at the Tulalip Resort Casino north of Seattle, the talk was all about pot. Indian country had been abuzz about cannabis since the previous fall, when the Justice Department had released the Wilkinson Memo, which seemed to open the way for tribal cannabis as a manifestation of tribal sovereignty. The gathering at Tulalip was technically a CLE (continuing legal education) conference, so you might have expected lawyers. A slew of lawyers in thousand-dollar suits were

there, of course, but so were private equity entrepreneurs, tribal officials, and tribal potheads. Some of the latter didn't talk business as
much as they talked relationships: *We have a relationship with pot.
It's a medicine from Mother Earth. Like, cannabis is tribal.* Wandering among all these people were tribal small business owners, people
who ran gravel companies or sold smoked fish or espresso along the
freeway. They had forked over the five hundred dollars for lunch and a
name tag to explore what marijuana legalization might mean for their
communities.

The lawyers and policy people presented on state laws, the history
of legalization in California, Colorado, and Washington, and its social,
cultural, and political ramifications. Tribal leaders spoke about the ways
in which tribal pot growing could be a whole new revenue stream, if not
a new tribal industry. Behind these discussions were coded questions,
old and new: How to provide for a people in the absence of industry
and opportunity? How to use tribal sovereignty to the best possible
effect? Did tribes really want to invest in another "lifestyle economy"
like tobacco shops, casinos, and tourism? No one knew what to make
of the potheads.

Two months after the "pot summit," I sat across from Eddy Pablo—
something of a jack-of-all-trades: he owns a fireworks stand, dives
for geoduck, and is trying to make commercial cannabis a thing at
Tulalip—in the same casino. He had come armed with notes and
handouts about marijuana legalization, medical uses of marijuana,
and tribal dispositions about legalization and capitalization at Tulalip
reservation. Eddy is about five foot ten, with an absurdly strong build,
dark skin, small eyes, and spiky black hair in a neat crew cut. He's thirty-
one with three children. "I've lived here my whole life. Both my parents
are from here. I'm thankful for it." He is soft spoken but gives off that
uniquely Indian sense that nothing bothers him. Yet there is plainly a
kind of seething, sliding, waiting energy underneath his social self. He

speaks of the business aspects of marijuana in the same tone of voice as he tells the story of how he almost died while diving. "I was diving for geoducks [a giant, burrowing mollusk] and the compressor ran out of gas. It feeds oxygen down to me where I was, about forty feet down. The guys on the boat thought I was dead when I was hauled up. They asked me if I was all right. And I was like, 'No, I'm not all right.' Man, I'm happy to be alive."

But to be Indian and alive is no easy thing. "My high school was a subtle racist high school. Not so much the kids. But the teachers had no expectations for us. If you have low expectations, then that's all the kid will strive for." Eddy made it to community college but it didn't stick. He ran afoul of the law and landed in jail. After he got out, he got hooked on geoduck diving. "You don't get to dive very much. Maybe eight days a year. But a boat can make thirteen K [thousand dollars] in three hours." Eddy becomes more animated when he talks about being on the water.

The next day he picks me up to go digging for clams on Cama Beach Point. His car is packed with five-gallon buckets, shovels, rakes, and his son, Cruz, tucked in the back seat. As we drive, Eddy points out the landmarks. The Tulalip Reservation—twenty-two thousand acres of Indian land—sits between Interstate 5 and Puget Sound just north of Seattle. It is indescribably beautiful. "That's where I grew up," he says, pointing at a nondescript house among a handful of other HUD homes facing a silty bay that was, until relatively recently, thick with salmon. Cedar grew down to the shore not too long ago. The winters are mild and the summers temperate. The entire sound was filled with Indians who pulled their lives from the waters. It's a testament to the perseverance of those Indians that there are still many of them left on Puget Sound even though the cedar have been cut down and the salmon run is a trickle of what it once was. The Tulalip Reservation itself, established in the Treaty of Point Elliott in 1855, is made up of seven intermingled peoples—Duwamish, Snohomish, Snoqualmie, Skagit, Suiattle, Samish, and Stillaguamish—all considered Coast Salish. There are about forty-eight hundred enrolled tribal members, but only about twenty-five hundred live within the borders of the reservation. There are also about three thousand non–tribal members who live within its boundaries, making Tulalip like a lot of other reservations whose lands were subject to allotment legislation in the late nineteenth century. And just as on those other reservations, the nicest parcels in Tulalip, those right on the sound, are largely owned or leased by non–tribal members.

But unlike most tribes, people here are doing all right, economically speaking. The median household income at Tulalip in 2020 was $90,068 per year, more than fifty-four thousand dollars above the national average. (Tribal members do get a per capita payment from the casino profits; in 2020 that was $42,037.) The Tulalip, as a collective, as a *business*, is doing well. Where once the tribe's wealth could be measured in fish, it can now be measured in income and infrastructure.

As for Eddy, without a college degree and with three kids to support, he hustles. He dives for geoduck. Crabs. Fishes. Harvests sea cucumber. And he owns a fireworks stand. All of this together somehow makes a living. He sees marijuana as something that can be added to the mix. "We should get in the business," he says. "Our sovereignty can give us a leg up. We should grow, process, and dispense. We could control the whole chain."

The cannabis industry has started modestly at Tulalip. The tribe opened a marijuana dispensary in August 2018. Some of the profits go toward helping addiction and mental health issues on the reservation. Tulalip is also funding research at Stanford University on medicinal attributes of pot, including how cannabis oil may help with treatment of opioid addiction.

Les Parks, the former tribal vice chairman of the Tulalip, was an early champion of the tribe getting into the cannabis business. He's the one who put together the 2015 "pot summit." Les, in a bolo tie and boots, picked me up in a very large, very new pickup truck. We drove around the rez in what I can only call an effort to roll out the salmon-colored carpet. We began at the casino, with its Four Diamond award-winning hotel, twelve stories, 370 rooms, nearly 192,000 square feet of gaming space, and seven restaurants. Then we drove the winding, oddly suburban roads of Quil Ceda Village. Quil Ceda is a consolidated borough on the reservation that's a shopping-food-entertainment hub, the only federal municipality in the United States other than Washington, D.C., and the only city with a permanent population of zero. Instead it contains 110 outlet stores, a Cabela's, a Walmart, a Home Depot. (Since my visit, a cedar-clad youth center, a four-hundred-thousand-dollar skate park, and the pot dispensary opened.) I hear about the modest origins of the reservation itself, then we drive past the Tulalip tribal offices, a thirty-two-million-dollar glass-and-cedar beauty, the Early Learning Academy, and the museum. Tulalip is very much like many of the other 326 (the BIA says there are "approximately" 326) reservations in America. Instead of the wasteland that is the popular notion of rez life, it is a patchwork of businesses, Indian homes, non-Indian homes, trees, and land.

Les is proud of his community. Our tour turns personal, and so does

The Tulalip Tribes of Washington opened the Hibulb Cultural Center and Natural Preserve in 2011. The center houses important art, artifacts, and exhibits that help sustain tribal community and culture and preserve and present Tulalip history.

the talk, when Les veers down a long, narrow road that ends near a creek feeding into the sound. This is where his family's original allotment was. "My great-great-grandfather must have been important because this was a good place to live, right next to the creek. It would have been full of salmon." But Les has suffered like so many Indians have suffered: he lost his mother to a drunk driver, his father wasn't around very much. The rough-cut lumber and tar paper house he grew up in is long gone. He had a lot of brothers and sisters. There wasn't much to go around. Here as elsewhere, survival was the principal challenge for Indians for well over a century. And from Les's story, like others, it's clear that a certain tolerance for conflict, pain, and uncertainty has been necessary to that survival. What, then, allows growth? What are the ingredients necessary for a community not only to make money but to grow real wealth? Les seems torn as he responds.

"My sister-in-law got Parkinson's disease. It was horrible to watch. Pot helped her. It helped her pain a lot." But Les doesn't want the tribe to sell pot. Or to *only* sell it. "I want us to use our sovereignty to fast-track clinical trials for the uses of marijuana extracts. There are a lot of uses for extracts. There's even some research that suggests cannabis extracts can be used to cure type-two diabetes. Think about that. Think about an Indian company, a tribal pharmaceutical company, that could cure the greatest threat to our health."

Fifteen percent of American Indians have diabetes, and in some communities in the Southwest, the rate is as high as 22 percent. And diabetes is only part of the problem. Along with high dropout and unemployment and poverty rates, Indians have a mortality rate from accidental death that is twice the national average. (The only thing it seems we have going for us is that we beat everyone out on the cancer scale. For some reason we don't get it as often.) Life, for many of us, is not merely bleak: it's short, poor, painful, unhealthy, and tumultuous. All of which makes Les's dream and the reality of Tulalip the more remarkable.

His own journey has been remarkable, too. Out of high school Les took part in a federally funded vocational training program and studied to become an electrician. He parlayed that into a job with the tribe. From there he started his own construction company. Along the way he did what a lot of the people at Tulalip seem to do, which is to say a bit of everything: fishing, fish wholesaling, selling fireworks, buying land, and eventually running for office. There is a steady arc to Les's life that resembles the one that was supposed to move Americans from being poor into the middle class from the post–World War II years through the 1970s. For many Americans that arc collapsed in the 1980s, but it still seems available to at least some of the people at Tulalip. Just as Les moved from poverty to relative comfort in about thirty years, so, too, has the tribe: the original tribal offices, a small clapboard house near the marina built in 1935, could fit inside the multimillion-dollar tribal offices up on the hill many times over. That's a long way to go in a relatively short amount of time. According to the Tribal Employment Rights Organization (TERO), there are 57 registered small businesses owned and operated by Indians on the Tulalip Reservation right now; that swells to more than 160 when there's a big project on the books. And that figure doesn't seem to include fishing boats, the 139 tribally owned and operated fireworks stands at Boom City, a famous annual marketplace, or tribal businesses in nearby areas that are technically off the reservation. Despite historical oppression and in contrast to stereotypes about Indians, there is an active and thriving entrepreneurial class at Tulalip.

Tribal power is an interesting thing. Most tribes are caught between maintaining political and economic stability, on which sovereignty depends, and the urgent need to change the economic and social climate. Often, doing something about all this means empowering people who work for the tribe but come from outside it. People like a white corporate lawyer named Mike Taylor.

Taylor represents the kind of force—the man behind the man behind the man—who has helped shape Indian country for the better part of more than forty years. He sought me out and pinned me down on my last day at Tulalip. "You have to understand. In the bad old days, there was no police here, no court. Embezzlement is what you got . . . Politics was only a way to mitigate your own poverty, not a way to help other people. Tulalip was a dangerous place. There was really no one to call. Women, children, elders: they were all in danger." A few things, however, came together. The Boldt decision in 1974, wherein a federal judge awarded 50 percent of Washington State's annual catch to tribes with treaty fishing rights, was a great boost not only to individual Indians but to a sense of tribal purpose as well. And then *California v. Cabazon* helped open up gaming in the 1980s. These court decisions have had a huge impact on tribal enterprise, at Tulalip and elsewhere. Both cases resulted from Indian civil rights cases.

Those decisions affected all tribes, but not all tribes have grown in the way Tulalip has. "At Tulalip," says Mike, "you can point to the role of Stan Jones . . . He was on tribal council for over forty years and had a unique view of what tribes should aspire to. He had this kind of history: fishing, running his own business. He had plenty of reason to be dyspeptic with white people, because of things that had happened to him. It occasionally surfaced. Here's an example: We put out bids for the hotel. We got bids from PCL, a big company, and we were negotiating the construction contract with them. We were almost done. All that was left was the clause about dispute resolution. They wanted state court. Stan said tribal court. The president of the company came down and in the meeting he says to us, 'You have your culture and we have ours. We aren't going to use tribal court.' Stan stood up and made a speech, the essence of which was: 'We're not doing this.' And we went to the second bidder, who agreed to arbitrate in tribal court if necessary. They built the casino. Stan was tough but also a smooth operator. He got the Marysville Chamber of Commerce to move onto tribal land. He would do anything that would benefit Tulalip. He felt the people here deserved more than they were accustomed to. Most of the leadership we have now were schooled in the world of Stan Jones." (Stan Jones, the "Chief of Chiefs," died on November 5, 2019. Hundreds turned out for his funeral.)

I think Mike Taylor, a lawyer, had much to do with it, too. After he arrived at Tulalip, he pushed to establish a court system and tribal police force. "Tulalip is now a safer, more productive place. The key to growth is stability, accountability, and separation of powers. We've got all that here now."

Mike Taylor, and people like him, have shaped tribes the country over. And it's a testament to the Tulalip tribes that Mike has been allowed to do the work he has. But agitation from within the tribe but outside its political structure is also important. At Tulalip that agitator was Ray Sheldon.

When I visited Tulalip in 2015, Ray was alive, well, and not hard to find. (He since passed away on January 30, 2019.) Ray's home and business were located on Tulalip's main drag. All you had to look for is a large fiberglass chicken on a pole and the sign for smoked fish, with its ever-changing digs at tribal officials. (That day it said: DID THE BOARD GET A BIG PAY RAISE? And below that: BOARD SAID NO TO PAY INCREASE FOR ELDERS, WHY?) Oh, and there's also the cell tower Ray leased, which rises above the trees and can be seen for miles around. However, it was hard to know where exactly on the property to find him. There was a jumble of buildings—a shop for selling the fish, a machine shop, a house, a few more outbuildings I couldn't quite iden- tify, and heavy equipment and building materials stacked here and there. To some it might look like a mess, but to me it looks like money. I finally located the office, and Ray met me at the door.

"Try this," Ray says, handing me a package of smoked salmon. "You got to eat that right now. Not later." So I do. There is no preamble, no getting to know each other, no feeling out.

"Okay," he begins, "one thing the government did to poorer Indians, not us, but like the Navajos, poor Indians out in the sticks, they didn't put enough into Indian enterprises but they gave them Indian agents money to set up shop." The Bureau of Indian Affairs has earned its reputation as one of the most mismanaged and corrupt federal agencies. Between 1973 and 1992 alone, audits show that the BIA stole or lost more than $2.4 billion of Indian money from oil, gas, timber, and grazing leases. And that's for just nineteen of the roughly 150 years that the BIA has been managing Indian money.

In that kind of climate, starting any kind of tribal or private business is dicey. But it didn't deter Ray. And by the end of the day, I'm not sure if anything could deter him.

"I got where I am because I worked," he says in his age-thickened voice. "I started in logging, and then fishing. Then I joined the Marines in Korea. I worked in logistics and supply because I had a year and a half of college going in. After the war I studied on the GI Bill. I got my BA in business! I went on to operating heavy machinery, grading, gravel, excavating. I opened my store in 1985 with a loan from the bank. I didn't get one from the tribe."

Ray has had firsthand experience of how the cronyism of the Indian service seems to live on through tribal government.

"I'm always on their case," says Ray Sheldon. "What annoys me is when people in high echelon forget who they are." According to Ray, the contracts for building Cabela's on the reservation went to a non-Indian contractor when Ray and his family had hoped to get it. Construction bills ran to twenty-one million dollars. Ray wonders about insider deals. "One thing that really bothers me," he says after naming many other things that bother him, "I've been fighting for children for quite a while. One of the biggest things the tribe is being confronted with is sex abuse. Women getting sex abused. Kids getting sex abused. They aren't putting enough money or time into that program. Nothing is really being done about it." Ray has a way of being fiercely disgruntled about tribal matters while he clearly loves and cares very deeply for his community.

It seems to me that the tribal government at Tulalip is, overall, pretty good, pretty healthy, even though some tribal members, like Ray, feel it could be better. (And the Tulalip have done something to intervene into cycles of abuse.) There is a tribal council that tends to the needs of the people and there is a business council that runs Quil Ceda Village, which generates income for the tribe. The Tulalip empowered their own citizens in governance, law (80 percent of Tulalip's legal team is Indian), and enforcement. Now Tulalip has secured a federal highway project to rebuild an overpass and on-ramps on the north end of the reservation. The tribe is currently negotiating with the State of Washington and looks likely to be awarded a big chunk of the sixteen billion dollars earmarked for roadwork in the region. Teri Gobin, the 2020 Chairwoman of the Board of Directors of both Tulalip's Tribal Council and TERO program (and the daughter of Stan Jones), makes a good point. "They're having booms in other places—like the oil fields in North Dakota—and a lot of Indians are getting in on it and doing good business. But we are trying to create stability, develop skills. The tribal vocational skills program is the only tribal accredited vocational training program in the country. It's free," says Teri. "It's free for any Natives from any community, and it's free for their spouses, too. We've even built houses for the homeless in Seattle."

So what does it take to follow Tulalip's success story? Because, caveats aside, it *is* a success. Location. Leadership. Separation. Structure. Opportunity. And hustle. It takes people like Stan Jones and Teri Gobin. It takes young people who've paid their dues and want to do good, like Eddy Pablo. It takes a kind of vision like Les Parks'. And if you want to see where modern Tulalip entrepreneurship began, you've got to go to Boom City.

BOOM CITY

Boom City is exactly how it sounds. For two weeks leading up to the Fourth of July, the largest fireworks bazaar west of the Mississippi rises from the gravel on a vacant lot near the Tulalip casino. Plywood shanties are trucked to the site and arranged in neat rows. The awnings are opened and the sales begin. Each of the 139 stands is stuffed with fireworks. All of the stands are Native owned, and the action is administered by a board of directors, which in turn is administered by the tribe. All of the stands are painted brightly, and many bear equally colorful names: Up in Smoke and One Night Stand. Others bespeak proud ownership: Mikey's, Junior's, Eddy's.

It's slow when I arrive at Eddy Pablo's stand, but even so there is a lot of money changing hands. Fireworks—like gaming and, to a lesser extent, tobacco—are regulated by the state. As sovereign nations, Indian tribes in states like Washington where fireworks are illegal enjoy a sales monopoly. I find Eddy deep in his stand, trying to avoid the sun. He nods at the carpet in front of his stand. "That stops 'em," he says. "Walking around on that gravel all day hurts your feet. And then they walk on this. It's a little thing, but the little things add up to business. You can make fifteen to twenty-five thousand for the season. More if you're smart." I can't help noticing the carpet is salmon-colored.

The day burns on and on. In the afternoon the sound of fireworks can be heard nearby. Just as fireworks can be sold on the rez, so, too, can they be exploded on the rez. And Boom City is happy to provide a field where you can set them off. It's a free-for-all. Rockets, mortars, roman candles, spinners. They're all going off simultaneously and nonstop. Tribal members will light off upward of a thousand dollars' worth of fireworks as a "memorial" for someone in their family who has passed on.

I wander back to Eddy's stand dazed by the fireworks and by everything else I've seen at Tulalip. This reservation that dates from 1855 really seems to have been born in the past forty years. It has come alive and done exactly what federalists have always wanted Indians to do: become a self-sufficient, self-supporting, entrepreneurial, relatively rich version of the American Dream—a people, a community that works hard and makes things work and gets ahead. Pretty much every reason for underperformance offered by other tribes—lack of access to education, lack of infrastructure, intergenerational sexual abuse, boarding schools, forced religious conversion, historical trauma, exploitation and loss of natural resources—has been experienced at Tulalip. Tulalip is a conglomeration of separate tribes that came together by choice, circumstance, and under pressure to form a nation. It has suffered its own internal divisions and traumas. It has endured natural and civic disasters, gone through recession and poverty and joblessness. But it has found a way to provide free health care for all its citizens, free education for those who want it, free excellent childcare for working parents, a safe and comfortable retirement option for its elders, and a robust safety net woven from per capita payments that are enough to encourage its citizens to venture into enterprises small and large. The Tulalip Nation provides for its most vulnerable citizens—the young and the old. And it provides enough security for the people in between life's beginnings and ends so that they can really see what they might become.

This is Tulalip. This could also be America if only the country would pay attention. It seems antithetical, even nonsensical, to consider that in order to find America you need to look at Indian communities and reservations. But it's true. The questions posed by America's founding documents and early history—What is the reach of the federal government? What should it be? How do the rights of the individual balance against those of the collective? What is, at the end of the day, the proper role of the federal government in our social structures and lives? How to weigh the demands of community and modernity? How to preserve, protect, and foster the middle class?—are answered by looking at Indians, at our communities, and at our history.

Americans were forever trying to create Indians in their own image. And in some ways they've done it. At least they might have gotten Indians to buy into the American Dream. But it is quite possible that Indians dream differently. The American Indian Dream is as much about looking back and bringing the culture along with it as it is about looking ahead. The Tulalip are far from achieving that dream: fewer than a dozen first-language speakers of Lushootseed remain (but activists and educators are aggressively offering Coast Salish language classes in the area), and the old lifeways tied to the sea are as endangered as the sea itself. But they are dreaming, they are trying nonetheless.

The lights are bright between the Boom City stalls. Brown and white and Black people walk and talk excitedly, their eyes gleaming and taking in everything their money can buy. Eddy watches and pauses. "Just because we are successful doesn't mean we don't have all sorts of problems. We've got a lot of money. More than most. But we still die young. We've got a bad heroin problem. We still have a lot of domestic abuse and sex abuse. Money hasn't changed that, not yet. But if we don't get a handle on those things"—he raises and opens his hands—"all our wealth could disappear." It could. But it hasn't yet. It's rising up in the sky and—boom—it goes and then the ash drifts down to settle on our upturned faces.

DIGITAL INDIANS
2015 ONWARD

◆◇◆◇◆◇◆◇◆◇◆

ON JUNE 26, 1992, REPLICAS of the *Niña, Pinta,* and *Santa María* docked in New York City after a three-hundred-day voyage retracing Columbus's route from Spain to the Caribbean. Built by the Spanish government to celebrate Columbus and "the friendship of the Spanish people," the boats were met by well-wishers. For five dollars you could tour the ships, and for nine dollars you could buy a reproduction of Columbus's log—presumably a highly expurgated version that made no mention of rape, torture, or slavery. The boats were also met by a handful of people protesting Columbus, colonization, genocide, and the very idea of the discovery of the New World.

The U.S. federal government had also long planned a Quincentenary Jubilee to kick off 1992, to end with its own replicas of the *Niña, Pinta,* and *Santa María* sailing beneath San Francisco's Golden Gate Bridge. But corporate sponsors retreated and the jubilee never happened. A parade and celebration in Washington, D.C., were hastily canceled when Indian activists threatened to show up in force. Parades and celebrations in Los Angeles and Denver suffered the same fate. Protesters dumped red dye in the Fox River in Chicago to protest the genocide of Native Americans, and the city of Berkeley rebranded Columbus Day as Indigenous Peoples Day. In 1994 the United Nations declared August 9 as the International Day of the World's Indigenous Peoples. Times were changing. And it wasn't just the public conscious that was changing as we neared the end of the twentieth century; the real lives of Indians across the country were changing, too. Natives and Native communities were strong enough in 1992 to do what they had been unable to do in 1492: turn the ships away.

Now in the twenty-first century, local tribal knowledge and global modern life have started coming together in unlikely places. One of those places is on the plates served by Sean Sherman. Sherman is founder of the Sioux Chef, a multi-tribe team of "chefs, ethnobotanists, food preservationists, adventurers, foragers, caterers, event planners, artists, musicians, food truckers, and food lovers" in Minneapolis. He's also an award-winning chef, cookbook author, culinary community activist, and cofounder of North American Traditional Indigenous Food Systems (NāTIFS), a nonprofit dedicated to using food as a tool to address economic and health inequalities in tribal communities. NāTIFS opened the Indigenous Food Lab in Minneapolis in August 2020. The Lab is a restaurant and a training, research, and educational center to promote understanding and use of Indigenous food and native foodway. Another of its projects is cooking up four hundred hot meals a day for Minnesotans in need.

The first concoction of Sean's I ever tasted was cedar tea sweetened with maple syrup, served at a special gathering of foodies and chefs convened in Sean's honor. One sip, and the barstools and track lighting and tile disappeared; the space rearranged itself into a snow-covered path crowded with spruce and red pine on one side and tag alder and birch on the other. This is the trail my older brother and I walked in the winter when we were kids. It ran straight out of our backyard through plantation pine and on between a hill and a swamp before reaching another small hill covered in old-growth pine and a sprinkling of birch. We'd walk up the hill and look down on the Mississippi. Then we'd make a campfire and pick cedar and boil up swamp tea in an aluminum pot, while the wind scudded snow off the branches and the snow hissed at the fire's edge and a jay called in the distance to the stuttering annoyance of red squirrels around us.

The rest of the meal Sean made was equally memorable. It included smoked walleye spread with fresh blackberries and sorrel, duck pâté and maple-brûléed duck in an apple broth, a salad of foraged greens topped with tamarack blossoms, and cedar-braised bison with a flint corn cake. Dessert was a sunflower-and-hazelnut crisp with popped amaranth. Sean's recipes call for combining Indigenous ingredients in both old and surprising new ways. "Our philosophy and politics is: Indigenous, Indigenous-produced, local, organic. In that order." He isn't interested in "Indian" food per se (salmon on a cedar plank) or even in dressing up Indian comfort food (fry bread or macaroni) in some new way. "I try to cook only with the foods historically available to the Indigenous people of the area I'm working in. So for me that means Lakota/Dakota and Ojibwe ingredients." Like? "There's so much. So much all around us," Sean answered as he, his life and business partner Dana Thompson, and I took a trip to Wozupi Tribal Gardens, just south of Minneapolis. "See that?" He pointed at a brown weed in the ditch along Highway 13. "Remember what we ate on Monday? Amaranth? That's amaranth. It grows all over around here. And goosefoot. And sorrel. Not to mention berries, wild rice, squash, and corn."

The Sioux Chef team works with the farm team at Wozupi Gardens, a project of the Mdewakanton tribe, established in 2010. Wozupi produces an incredible array of heirloom, organic, and what can only be called historical Indigenous varietals. Cherokee beans. Potawatomi lima. Oneida corn. Arikara yellow squash. Hidatsa shield beans. Lakota squash. Gete-okosimaan (Ojibwe "old time" squash). The goal is to get these goods into all the Mdewakanton restaurants and casinos, as well as other restaurants and private homes.

Sean Sherman is Oglala Lakota and grew up on the Pine Ridge Reservation in South Dakota. As a teenager he worked in restaurants. Right out of high school, he worked as a field surveyor for the U.S. Forest Service in the Black Hills. His job was to take a sample of all the plants growing within certain coordinates. He came to know pretty much everything that grew in that environment and, being curious and having worked in restaurants, he learned which plants a person could eat.

In 1997 Sean moved to Minneapolis and worked in a variety of restaurants there. Each cuisine he mastered he followed down to its root. And now what he makes is not "artisanal" or "Indigenous-inspired" but rather, archival food, in combinations that are delicious and inspiring.

The Sioux Chef debuted in 2014 as a caterer and food educator. Since then, Sean has experienced a level of attention and success that most chefs only dream of. He's featured on radio and in magazines and at symposia. He's all over the place in Minneapolis, cooking for summits and special events, hosting pop-up dinners. He's helped the Little Earth housing project establish the Tatanka food truck, developing the concept and menu and training the staff. The truck, like Sean's own brand, is adamantly, proudly, and creatively Indigenous. Among a chronically malnourished and diabetes-stricken community, to serve bison and turkey and walleye pike, cedar tea, and corn is something of a revolution. And Sean's cooking has found a loyal and enthusiastic base not only among foodies and wild-food devotees who flock to Owamni, the popular restaurant he opened in downtown Minneapolis in 2021, but also among reservation and urban Indians, both rich and poor. To my mind, that's because the politics of Sean's food confront the private demons of pretty much every modern Indian. Whether we are urban or reservation, our story—the story of "the Indian"—has been a story of loss: loss of land, loss of culture, loss of a way of life. Yes, Indians remain; we remain across the country, as modern Americans and modern Indians. But inwardly we wonder: How much of our culture actually remains? How authentic, really, are we? At what point do we cease being Indians and become simply people descended from Indians? Sean's food, the whole conception of it, affirms us: All is not lost, it tells us. Much remains of our cultures, our knowledge, our values. It literally rests at our feet and over our heads; all we need do is reach out and pluck it. This is a profound politics.

As singular and exciting as Sean's approach to cooking is, he is part of something much larger afoot in Indian country.

INDIGENOUS KNOWLEDGE

For so long the Indian struggle for survival was a strategy aimed outward: to cajole, scold, remind, protest, and pester the powers that be to rule the right way in court cases, to pass the right legislation to protect tribes and tribal sovereignty, to honor treaties, and to simply remember both our past and our continued existence. But the 1990s marked an inward turn. People like Sean Sherman are engaging in a new brand of activism. Instead of, say, occupying the BIA office in Washington, D.C., they occupy a cultural, social, and political space where they actively remember and promote Indigenous knowledge—and not just because it serves Indians but because it serves modernity.

Federal Indian policy seems to have settled into the track laid down during the Nixon administration: that of self-governance, self-determination, and a government-to-government relationship between the federal government and the tribes. Tribes still do battle with the government—and federal Indian law can twist and turn in the most surprising ways.

On July 9, 2020, the U.S. Supreme Court ruled in favor of Jimcy McGirt, a Seminole of Oklahoma, in *McGirt v. Oklahoma*. The justices' ruling ended nearly twenty-four years of wrangling over the boundaries of Indian jurisdiction and opened up a whole new set of opportunities and problems in Oklahoma.

McGirt was convicted of sex crimes against a child by an Oklahoma jury in 1997. He was sentenced to life without parole. That same year,

McGirt appealed on the grounds that he was Native, and that the crimes had taken place on land that was part of the Muscogee (Creek) Nation reservation. McGirt's legal team argued that the Oklahoma Enabling Act of 1906 never disestablished Native sovereignty over a vast area of Oklahoma. Therefore, these three million acres rightfully fell under the jurisdiction of the Muscogee Nation, not the state of Oklahoma, which therefore couldn't have legally prosecuted and convicted McGirt in this case. The U.S. Supreme Court's ruling did not absolve McGirt of his terrible crime (he's now serving his time in federal instead of state prison), but it is a huge victory for tribes in Oklahoma: in effect, the justices ruled that the eastern third of the state was, has always been, and still is Indian land.

Activism is a permanent necessity, as Standing Rock and dealing with COVID-19 bear witness. But we've also turned inward. Across Indian country, a new generation of activists are focusing their attention and energy and working hard to strengthen their communities from the inside. Several factors precipitated this sea change. Many younger Indians now have educational opportunities long denied previous generations. They have the economic means to travel and to return to their culture. And thanks to the sovereignty wars, they once again have the dignity and legal rights of a sovereign people, born up by their cultures, community, and government.

In the 1960s and 1970s, to be a "woke" Indian might have meant joining the Trail of Broken Treaties and caravanning to Washington to occupy the BIA. Now it just as likely means sitting in a classroom at a state university and learning a tribal language. In 1994 I moved back to Leech Lake Reservation, the place I had hoped to escape when I graduated from high school in 1988. It was an important return for me. I had found graduate school both stressful and sterile. And my connection to my tribe felt tenuous. If any of the rest of life's efforts was going to make sense, it had to, for me, make sense in relation to my tribe and my culture. I moved home and began working for a nonprofit dedicated to strengthening Ojibwe language and culture and establishing an Ojibwe language immersion school at White Earth Reservation to the west of Leech Lake.

It was hard work. When a community is whole, language grows out of the web of relationships that make that community. However, at White Earth (and other Indian communities) it was hard to find that wholeness. There was intergenerational abuse—physical, domestic, sexual, substance. There was a pronounced lack of continuity between people and institutions. It felt like everything was a mess. My coworkers and I puzzled over a very basic hurdle: the Ojibwe language wasn't important to that many people. Young people were especially uninterested. We had to, in some way, make language and culture cool. And if we could do that, the rest would likely fall into place. Language work felt crucial to us. Culture contains kinship, politics, lifeway, traditional activities, or is contained in them, but language has a special role as a carrier of culture. More than that: our Ojibwe religion is vested in our language. It cannot be practiced in English. The death of our language would likely be the death of us, certainly the death of our ceremonial life.

We did not feel alone in our work. Even scattered on reservations and cities in six states and three Canadian provinces, and in tribes across the country, the Ojibwe displayed a marked change in not only attitude but direction. In the 1960s and 1970s, AIM and the Red Power movements looked outward. For them, Indian country remained a problem to be solved, a problem with which to confront America. This shifted inward in the 1980s and 1990s, as tribes and individuals dedicated themselves to cultural and linguistic revivals. My brother Anton, who worked with me on the language project, put it this way: "The U.S. government spent two hundred years trying to kill us, trying to take our land, language, and culture away from us. Why would we look to them to fix it? We must look to ourselves to do that."

Although Native American languages have been on the decline since 1492, and only twenty of them out of many hundreds are expected to remain viable into the twenty-second century, programs teaching these vanishing languages are on the rise. These programs are intent on bringing the Indian past into the present, and bringing the present into Indian lives. Manuelito Wheeler, a Diné language activist, recruited Diné voice actors from across the Southwest (there remain more than one hundred thousand Diné speakers in the United States) and dubbed *Star Wars*, and later *Finding Nemo*, into that tongue. Speakers of Ojibwe and Choctaw and a host of other Native languages are using Facebook, YouTube, and Twitter to speak, promote, and communicate in the languages of the First People. Indians are founding and attending tribal and community colleges on reservations—more than thirty-five of them across thirteen states at last count—to study Native languages alongside computer science, math, English, history, and business administration. Transforming education into something that we do for ourselves, rather than something that is done to us, goes a long way toward healing the long rift between Indians and the educational system.

A RADICAL CHOICE: HEALTH

Similar forces are driving one of the areas that Indians are just now beginning to address: personal and community health. The U.S. government did its best to exterminate the bison, then gave us flour and lard as replacements. Poor diet did damage to our culture and our health. Obesity, diabetes, heart disease: these are the products of oppression. Sarah Agaton Howes is one of those fighting not just against a system but for her community.

We are in a coffee shop in Cloquet, a former logging town just off the Fond du Lac Reservation in northern Minnesota. Sarah, a mother of three, is cheerful and funny and pretty. She originally opened House of Howes, a contemporary Ojibwe design, art, and lifestyle store, then moved it online in 2014 as Heart Berry and expanded its mission. Heart Berry showcases the work of Indian artists through its Inspired Natives Project and offers classes on cultural art making. Howes is also a passionate runner who is known as "the Run Stalker" of the reservation. She pretty much lives in activewear.

I had first met Sarah, who is also Creek, at Ojibwe ceremonies in Wisconsin. She grew up in Cloquet; her dad was a cop. "The only Native cop in the whole county. He had a full-time job. That was rare for men around here back then." Her father's job influenced the family. "He knew all the bad things that were happening in the community and I think that kinda pulled us away from what was going on there." So the family kept to themselves. Sarah did spend a lot of time with her cousins, but her Ojibwe life withered. Surprisingly, it was their diet—or the consequences of it—that changed things. When Sarah was eleven, her father had a heart attack. The event shook him. "He completely changed his life. He went back to ceremonies, he went back to our roots. Everything shifted at that point." Her parents divorced, and Sarah stayed with her mother. Her father was secretive about his newfound ceremonial life, so she didn't know much about it, and she never got the chance to find out. Her father had developed diabetes, and like his own father, he died at forty-nine, when Sarah was twenty. "Average for an Indian in those days," she says. "Unhealthy eating, too sedentary, genetics, and stress." Now she has brothers who are into their forties, and she worries about them, too.

Her father's late-life connection with traditional ways "created the possibility of other directions for me," Sarah says. "So in my twenties it was me trying to find that life, basically. Trying to find my way back to it." After high school and college, she married and got pregnant. During a postnatal checkup, a doctor tried to talk to her about her weight. "I was really heavy then. I weighed about two hundred eleven." The doctor told her she was likely to develop diabetes within ten years if she didn't change something. "I'm feeding him [her son] organic squash and stuff like that. And me? I'm eating potato chips and grilled cheese!" Sarah came from a place where everyone was significantly overweight. But she didn't want to end up with her son eating chips and cheese and "I didn't want him to watch me take shots, or watch me in the hospital."

That was when she started going back to ceremony. Many tribes, ours included, feel that our ceremonies are to be protected. We joke that our ceremonial traditions are a bit like Fight Club, and the first rule of Fight Club is: you never talk about Fight Club. So Sarah "had no idea of even what was going to happen. But it was like . . . I had to get to a better place. A good place physically, spiritually, mentally."

Choosing to deal with her worries through ceremony was one of the first big healthy choices Sarah had made in her life. She began to see how her physical health was connected to her spiritual and mental health. But she didn't know many physically healthy Indians. One woman from her reservation, who also attended ceremony, had run a half marathon. "I was like, 'no way.' But internally, she must have planted a seed in me." Sarah did a 5K race. "It took me so long the police car had to drive behind me at the end, like I was the president!" She laughs, and it's a great laugh. "I remember getting to the finish line and people were cheering for me. It was a major moment. I want my son to see me be a fully vibrant person. I wanted to know what it would feel like not to be a prisoner in my own body."

After she ran that first 5K, Sarah joined a Weight Watchers group on the reservation. She didn't know anything about cooking or nutrition, but she followed the program. Her husband did it with her. She lost eighty pounds in six months, got pregnant, and had a healthy daughter. Then she set about losing the weight she'd gained in pregnancy. "People asked, 'Are you on meth? Are you eating?' I had to *show* people I was eating and was being healthy. Those models weren't out there."

Sarah began running with other Indian women. "The first time I ran on a trail with a group of Indian women I was like, 'What is happening right now? All these Indian women running through the woods? It hasn't happened in a hundred years around here!' And it was one of those clear moments in life. One of those moments you *know*: This is *exactly* what I'm supposed to be doing right now. This is perfect."

From there, Sarah started organizing the group; at least three and as many as seven of them have run together, long runs of ten miles or so, at least once a week, kids and jobs notwithstanding. She started a Facebook group for women called Kwe Pack. "We need our own spaces; it's important we learn how to support each other as Anishinaabekweg [Ojibwe women]." It might seem like a small thing Sarah is doing, gathering a dozen or so women to run in the woods, but in Indian country, perhaps the most radical mode of resistance is to choose to be healthy. "We're trying to make it *normal* to be healthy." When she first moved back to the reservation, passing cars would slow down to get a look at her, wondering if she'd escaped from the nearby treatment center. "Or they'd ask me if I got a DWI, because I wasn't driving. It was so abnormal to see Indians out running." Now everyone knows who Kwe Pack are.

Chelsey Luger is also part of the force that's creating the shift toward Indian health. We met at Urban Stampede Coffee in Grand Forks, North Dakota. Chelsey is short, lean, and muscular. Her mother is Ojibwe from the Turtle Mountain Reservation in North Dakota, and her father is Lakota from Standing Rock Reservation, also in North Dakota. Being Indian in Grand Forks meant having white friends. Chelsey was a hockey and basketball cheerleader, but also "always the girl in class that they couldn't joke around with. They couldn't joke about Native people or Black people or gay people. I'd speak up." Her friends would say, "Yeah, but you're different, your parents have good jobs." It was true that Chelsey's upbringing defied the stereotypes about Indians and Indian life. Her parents not only had college degrees and solid achievements but also were deeply invested in their children's education. As Chelsey did not hesitate to point out to her classmates, many Indians' lives defy the stereotypes.

Despite being viewed as an exception, Chelsey didn't have it easy. Racism and exclusion run deep in places like Grand Forks. "By the time I was in high school, I was really a spitfire. I was just pissed off all the time. I was so angry." She got in physical fights, verbal fights, both in Grand Forks and on the rez. "On the rez I was White Girl, and here in Grand Forks I was that Indian girl. I felt like I couldn't win. I'm grateful for it now. It turned me into a chameleon. I can go anywhere. I can do anything." Where Chelsey wanted to go was out. She applied and was accepted at Dartmouth College in New Hampshire. "When I first got in, people always asked, 'How did you get into that school?' They thought I got in because I was Native. I mean, I had great ACTs and straight As. How the hell do you *think* I got in? And I wrote a really good essay, I have experiences, and I have something to contribute."

Dartmouth is home to the oldest program serving Indian students in the country and had made recruiting them something of a mission, resulting in the largest and most robust Native student organization of any elite college in the country. But even there, prejudice followed her. The privileged student body was tradition-bound and conservative. There was also a heavy binge-drinking culture. As in high school, Chelsey was accepted, but she'd never partied as she did at Dartmouth. And she was still angry. Yes, she was with people from all around the world, but she couldn't find her niche. Eventually she recognized that she wanted "to carry myself with a certain sense of dignity. And I didn't want to allow people to make me angry."

Chelsey got involved with the Native community at Dartmouth. She had no intention of majoring in Native American studies. "I go to ceremonies. I know my culture. Why would I study it?" she thought. But then an older student told her to take a course with a particular professor and, she says, "My eyes were opened." She took another course, and another. "Eventually I learned there was all this stuff I never knew I needed to learn." She became immersed in Native American studies, stopped partying, and did well in her classes.

After Chelsey graduated from Dartmouth, she moved to New York and began working in the sex crimes unit of the DA's office. "I didn't realize it, but I was becoming very unwell. I was so wrapped up in my life in New York." She was becoming increasingly materialistic and fixated on finding a way to make money and become powerful and make a name for herself. "I was lost. So, so lost. I gained weight."

Chelsey started working out again, harder than ever before, and started serious weight training for the first time. Then other changes occurred, too. She stopped drinking entirely. "I woke up one morning and I was feeling like, 'Damn, it's time to realize, it's time to *know* this substance has a spirit. It's dangerous. It's out to get me. It's out to get my people. And it's doing its job. I'm going to reject this.'"

Bit by bit, Chelsey got control over her life. Like Sarah Agaton Howes, she realized that her poor health and poor choices were related to her distance from her culture, religion, and ancestral self. Over social media, she met Thosh Collins, a photographer who worked for the Native Wellness Institute. On the way to a photo shoot with him, Chelsey got a call. "Something with my dad was going down in North Dakota and it broke my heart. I started crying." When she apologized for her outburst, Thosh told her a similar story from his own family. It helped. "And since then, we've been close. He was born and raised on the rez, Pima from Salt River, Arizona. We really connected . . . We started talking about Indigenous fitness. About warrior strength."

Becoming healthy physically and mentally, Chelsey found, enabled her to relate differently to other Native people, too. Returning to culture, to her Indian self, to an Indian self separate from all the hurt her people have felt, changed her. "All of it instilled in me an incredible sense of pride. I was better able to articulate my thoughts and feelings and better able to understand why my people were in the condition they were in. When you're able to defend yourself with thought, when you have those tools, you become less angry. Anger is easy. Jealousy is easy. It's more difficult to feel compassion."

As with Sarah, it was social media—being a digital Indian—that enabled Chelsey to extend her reach out to other Native people and back to the very best parts of being Native. Thosh and Chelsey put their heads together and formed Well for Culture (WFC), an organization that put into practice what they and others had been feeling. WFC is a hybrid beast: part Indigenous knowledge clearinghouse, part lifestyle and fitness resource, part political exhortation for Indians to think about their health, and part a platform for Thosh and Chelsey to work with tribes and schools on issues affecting Indian youth. "Our people have been healthy for centuries, and it's only a short while we've been unhealthy." They talk to Natives of all ages about how being well for themselves and their families is also a way of being well for the culture. "Because without wellness we can't have our culture. You can't go to a ceremony if you're drunk. You can't do that stuff if your body doesn't function properly. You can't hear stories and get teachings from elders if you're not well. You can't sustain your family or teach your children. So if you're not well, there goes your culture. And it goes the other way, too. It was my culture that brought me to real fitness." Ancestral knowledge, she believes, is a way to move forward, not back.

Chelsey is quick to remind me that she and WFC are part of a movement. "We're not the leaders. We're not gurus. We're just facilitating this digital space, we are bringing people together." She and Thosh see themselves as ambassadors. They don't pressure or guilt-trip, but they do encourage people to change. When kids bring up fry bread, they explain that the flat, fried dough is not actually traditional and Indigenous; fry bread was survival food when Natives were forced onto vegetation-poor reservations in the nineteenth century and given rations of flour and lard. "We say we grew up with it and like it and we say fry bread is not power. We say fry bread kills our people. It's that serious. It causes diabetes and heart disease. We have to look at those colonial foods as a kind of enemy." Chelsey and Thosh see signs of a new sense of direction in the next generation. "These Native kids pay attention. Something is changing, you can feel it."

Changes could be felt legislatively as well. In the 1990s and 2000s, a slew of laws affirmed the kind of shift in Indian life that had occurred in the lives of Sean, Sarah, Chelsey, Thosh, and many thousands like them. In 1990 Congress passed the Native American Languages Act (NALA), the Indian Arts and Crafts Act (IACA), and the Native American Graves Protection and Repatriation Act. (NAGPRA). NALA put money behind efforts to undo the damages done by residential boarding schools in trying to eradicate our languages. The IACA protects Indian artists by making the sale and distribution of "Indian" art made by non-Indians and advertised as "authentic" a crime. And as we've seen, NAGPRA facilitates the respectful return of or control over the remains of Indians as well as of sacred or cultural objects.

In 2013 the Violence Against Women Act (VAWA) that had been passed in 1994 was reauthorized and significantly revised. Among the new provisions was the empowerment of tribal courts to charge and prosecute non-Natives who raped or assaulted Native women on Native land. This was important legislation for Indian communities. According to the National Institute of Justice, four out of five Indian women are assaulted in their lifetime, and more than half of Indian women have been raped or otherwise sexually violated. The majority of Native women are married or partnered to non-Natives, and the majority of rapes and assaults take place in or near their homes. Yet for decades, those who attacked Indian women were able to escape prosecution through jurisdictional loopholes or simply because local authorities were reluctant to prosecute. The revised VAWA is a potent weapon for the defense of Indian women. Still, the congressional bill expired in February 2019 under the Trump administration. It was reintroduced and passed in the House of Representatives in March 2019, and finally passed in the Senate in March 2022.

◈

Meanwhile, people like my cousin Nicole Matthews keep the struggle going.

Nicole has been the Executive Director of the Minnesota Indian Women's Sexual Assault Coalition (MIWSAC) for years. She is at the forefront of efforts to address the violence in and around our communities as it affects Indian women. I caught up with her on the phone between trips to Guam, where she leads training sessions about Indigenous sexual assault and violence prevention.

"I grew up in Minneapolis and went to Roosevelt High. My mom was a single mother for most of my childhood, but my grandma and grandpa came down to the [Twin] Cities and brought me back to Bena to spend time on the rez a lot when I was a kid." Nicole's mom, Lynett,

Nicole Matthews, executive director of the Minnesota Indian Women's Sexual Assault Coalition and a tireless advocate for Native women, gave a TEDx talk in 2021 on how Indigenous values can help sexual violence victims heal.

was one of nine kids, one of whom—Lissa Babe—died when she was two or three. "She'd broken her arm, so was using her left hand, and poked the scissors in her eye; she died on the operating table. I remember my mom telling me that's when my grandpa started to have doubts about everything. He'd been to [Indian] boarding school and sent all his kids to the Catholic church. But when he and my mom went to the priest and asked him to do last rites on Lissa Babe, the priest wouldn't do it. He said 'he had to get up early to go ice fishing and he didn't have time.' It was the first time my mom saw my grandpa cry."

Nicole didn't graduate from high school. "I was in an icky relationship with my oldest daughter's dad and I was going nowhere fast. I was always super smart, but I didn't want to go to school. I dropped out. But when I got pregnant I was like, Oh, I've got to be responsible for someone else.' My daughter's dad ended up in prison for eighteen years. My mom wanted so badly for me to succeed and I felt like such a disappointment to her. And so, after my daughter was born, I redeemed myself and did it all as a single mom. I got my GED. I took my placement exams for college, went to school, and graduated with honors with my degree in applied psychology and a minor in human relations and multicultural education.

"That's when I got into advocacy. While in college, I took a forty-hour sexual assault advocacy training class. I was already volunteering at the women's center on campus and did my internship at a sexual assault organization in Milaca [a city in Minnesota] and we worked with a lot of [Ojibwe] people from Mille Lacs. That's where I got introduced to the work that I do now."

Violence against Indian women and girls is not a new issue, but it is finally creeping into the national discussion because of people like Nicole and others in the Missing and Murdered Indigenous Women (MMIW) movement. Since 2016 more than 5,712 Native women have gone missing or been murdered and Native women experience violence at ten times the rate of other women in the United States. The MMIW movement, which has a highly visual social media presence, also includes nonprofits like MIWSC and grassroots organizers in support of the federal Violence Against Women Act (VAWA).

Minnesota leads the nation in terms of MMIW activism and Nicole was part of a task force there that spent nearly two years gathering information and statistics about violence against Native women. "The official DOJ [Department of Justice] stats are that the rates of sexual violence among Native women are two times higher than for all other races. Over seventy percent of the violence against Native women is perpetrated by non-Native men. Native women have higher rates of victimization than any other group in the country." This isn't exactly news to me though I am shocked every time I hear those numbers. And though I know better I can't help but blurt out: *Why?*

"It's complex," Nicole responded. "You have jurisdictional issues. The current VAWA expands that jurisdiction over non-Native perpetrators of sexual violence. The Tribal Law and Order Act, which was put into previous versions of VAWA, gave tribes jurisdiction over non-Native perpetrators of domestic violence. But the tough part is that in order to make use of those provisions you have to, essentially, be set up like a mainstream [white] court. We also have to look at the effects of colonization. We have generations of kids who were abused in residential boarding schools where they were stripped of their language and cultural teachings and practices and identities. They go home and have kids and families and they're trying to raise their families with that trauma. We have all of the ways in which we've been othered and ignored. A lot of people think we don't even exist anymore. When we interviewed people for a research project on trafficking we were working on, one sex buyer said to a [Native] woman, 'I thought we killed all of you.' Another sex buyer wanted a woman to roleplay that he was John Smith and she was Pocahantas.

How disgusting is that?" Nicole brings her point home by mentioning a sex trafficking ring in Minnesota that referred to itself as "The Minnnesota Nice Guys" led by a former Hennepin County attorney named John St. Marie. The men were arrested.

"We interviewed one hundred and five Native women who were used in sex trafficking in Minnesota. Some of the stuff we learned is that homelessness and poverty play a huge issue in terms of risk factors. Among the women we interviewed, ninety-eight percent were or had been homeless. So when you think of risk factors for being assaulted or trafficked, certainly being on the street and not having money to feed your kids is a pretty big risk factor. Seventy-nine percent were abused as children by an average of four perpetrators. So we have to look at childhood trauma, and we have to focus on healing."

It makes sense to me that Nicole and other women's work on the abuse issue is holistic: they emphasize over and over the positive power of culture and cultural connection, of strong families, of access to cultural and spiritual resources, not to mention policy changes at the local, state, and federal levels. Minnesota, for example, has the first MMIR (Missing and Murdered Indigenous Relatives) office in the country, with permanent funding and a staff. As Nicole explained, "They won't be the ones directly responding to problems necessarily, but they will be working with all the agencies and organizations tasked with responding. They'll work to be sure our systems are changing, and be responsive to families and communities." For example? "For example, we heard several stories from families about Native women who were murdered, but the medical examiner called it a suicide. The women's families know it was murder, the community knows it's murder. There was this one woman who was found hanging from a tree in the woods and they tried to call it a suicide. But because of the work of the MMIW Task Force, the Minnesota Department of Heath is starting to do psychological autopsies where they will look at the whole picture and take a bigger look at what happened, rather than just examining the body. That will be impactful." And, Nicole added, the Minnesota MMIR office will be doing other work, too. "If you're homeless and go missing, who's looking for you? If you're homeless you're not missing from anyplace. Most of the people we talked to for our research on [sex] trafficking had known someone who had gone missing and was never found. Remember when Gabby Petito went missing? The [white] woman who was killed by her fiancé when they were traveling across the country in their van? When the Gabby Petitos go missing we see all their cute pictures; it makes us feel sad and it *should*. But when you see a picture of a Native woman who's gone missing, you know what they show us? Mug shots. Which then makes people feel another kind of way. It makes people wonder what we did to make this happen to us. The MMIR can help combat even the optics of missing Native women."

I wonder out loud how my cousin stays sane and stable. Not surprisingly, Nicole talks about the things she hopes will also help with generational change in Indian country. "Prayer is important and ceremony and trying to be as grounded as I can in things that bring me joy. The reality is that I didn't choose this work and it chose me. It's my purpose. My work is about me and my community and my family—we want something better for our future generations. I can't let all the trauma

A red handprint, like the one worn by this unidentified MMIW protestor at Beth Schmidt Park in Elon, North Carolina, symbolizes the ways in which Native women have been silenced, most alarmingly, by their murders and disappearances.

swallow me up 24/7. I have to remember the good things. Like VAWA. It's a huge win."

It's been all too easy for Native people to see ourselves as isolated and disempowered and disconnected. But just as Native people once used all the parts of the bison we killed, we now use all the parts of digital technology: from internet sites and search engines to apps like TikTok, Instagram, Snapchat, YouTube, Facebook, and Twitter. We use these parts of the web to connect and to fight, to raise awareness and to encourage one another. It's not all positive, of course, but it is certainly profound. Clearly, things are changing in Indian country and Indians are making those changes. In 2007 Senator Sam Brownback of Kansas introduced "a joint resolution to acknowledge a long history of official depredations and ill-conceived policies by the federal government regarding Indian tribes and offer an apology to all Native Peoples on behalf of the United States." The resolution was eventually passed and signed by President Barack Obama as a rider on a defense appropriations spending bill. It had no teeth whatsoever: the resolution included a disclaimer making it clear that the "apology" did not authorize or support "any legal claims against the United States, and the resolution does not settle any claims."

Still, a half-felt apology to Indians is better than fully formed policies detrimental to our existence. All in all, during the period 1990–2015, a picture of Indian survival, resilience, adaptability, pride, and place in modern life came into focus. Many of these points came together on and near the Standing Rock Reservation in North Dakota during the Dakota Access Pipeline (DAPL) protest that erupted in 2016.

STANDING TOGETHER AT STANDING ROCK

The DAPL's original plan took it past Bismarck, North Dakota, but that route was rejected because it was too close to the municipal water supply. The alternative put the pipeline across the Missouri River just upstream of the Standing Rock Sioux Reservation. And this is where the pipeline became an Indian problem.

The project was fast-tracked. The permitting process was stream-lined: DAPL, along with its parent company, Energy Transfer Partners, was not subject to the usual permitting process for large interstate projects except where the pipeline was to cross major bodies of water and where it might affect ceded, historically important, religiously significant tribal lands. This meant DAPL had to conduct cultural and environmental impact surveys in liaison with the state of North Dakota and with tribes whose homelands the pipeline crosses. DAPL was legally obligated to consult the Standing Rock Sioux, among other tribes. Which it did. Kind of. While the pipeline route was being planned, Energy Transfer Partners engaged in extensive surveying. According to documents filed in federal court: "By the time the com-pany finally settled on a construction path, then, the pipeline route had been modified 140 times in North Dakota alone to avoid potential cultural resources . . . All told, the company surveyed nearly twice as many miles in North Dakota as the 357 miles that would eventually be used for the pipeline."

Three other tribes in North Dakota met and conferred with DAPL planners, and the pipeline was moved accordingly. And then the com-pany tried to meet with Waste'Win Young, the tribal historic preserva-tion officer for the Standing Rock Sioux. The DAPL liaison spoke to Young on the phone a few times after the pipeline plan went public, but then, according to court documents, it seems the company had trouble reaching her. The Army Corps of Engineers was also duty-bound to make sure the pipeline worked with the state and with tribes. They tried to reach out to Young, but to no avail. The Corps also arranged a meeting with the tribal council and Dakota Access on the Standing Rock Reservation. When the Corps arrived, Tribal Chairman David Archambault II told them that the meeting had started earlier than planned and was already over.

I don't know why Young and Tribal Chairman Archambault didn't meet or consult with DAPL when the window to consult was open. On the day the Army Corps of Engineers green-lit the project publicly Young registered a complaint. This was in December 2014. Deadlines were once again extended. Meetings were once again scheduled and canceled. Again more deadlines came and went. A year passed like this. But finally, in the spring of 2016, the tribe and the Corps and DAPL representatives met no fewer than seven times. The Standing Rock Sioux had a chance to bring its own experts to bear on the question of cultural impacts. Meetings were held on and off the reservation; the Corps, DAPL people, and tribal officials visited the actual sites in question. As a direct result, DAPL reopened consultations with tribes. Three tribes identified previously overlooked sites and the pipeline was adjusted accordingly. Standing Rock, however, declined to participate in these surveys because of "their limited scope" and instead "urged the Corps to refine the area of potential effect to include the entire pipeline." This wasn't going to happen. The tribe refused to give input, the pipeline construction began.

The Standing Rock Sioux set up a protest camp in April 2016 even as the tribe filed an injunction against the proposed pipeline crossing. The camp quickly grew to include Indians from more than three hun-

The #NoDAPL protest camp at Standing Rock was the largest gathering of Indians in the United States since the Lakota, Cheyenne, and Arapaho formed the tribal armies that defeated the U.S. Cavalry at the Little Bighorn nearby. Demonstrators at the site called it the Mni Wiconi protest; mni wiconi means "water is sacred" in Lakota.

dred different tribes, professional activists, and foreign rights organizations. The tribe and the protesters were working together, and this in itself was novel. Tribal authorities from all over the country sent food, firewood, and supplies. By October more than a million people had checked in on the Standing Rock protest via Facebook.

Things got violent fast. The protesters were determinedly pro–peaceful direct action; the private security teams brought in by Energy Transfer Partners, not so much. They loosed attack dogs on protesters. The activists were pepper-sprayed, arrested, hosed down with water cannons, and shot with rubber bullets. All along government officials, security forces, and company representatives decried how the Indians were trespassing on private property, as though this was the greatest crime in which you can engage on a land.

Meanwhile, in court the Standing Rock Sioux officially objected to the pipeline on the grounds that it violated the National Historic Preservation Act. This is important. As much as the tribe, as a sovereign Indian nation, talked about water and tribal lands, their objections were rather narrow. They did not file legal motions under the Clean Water Act or the Rivers and Harbors Act. The protest, however, was more wide-ranging. While the Standing Rock Sioux argued in court that the pipeline would destroy sacred sites, the protest on site was primarily about fighting the danger to drinking water posed by the pipeline. The latter argument is bigger, because it hinges on tribal sovereignty and the protection of natural resources. The protesters referred to themselves as water protectors. They made a broad call about the need to protect sacred sites *and* clean water and to push the country to think harder about clean energy. The "story" of the protest, however, is largely a story we've heard before: that the government has always undervalued the rights of Indigenous people and continues to do so, that Indigenous people are the stewards of the land, that Indians continue to get shafted by the government. But to rest on that story alone would be to miss the bigger and more fundamental one.

The story of the Dakota Access Pipeline is not another iteration of the "Indian problem": that Indians, sadly, lost, and with them having lost, it's hard to know what to do with them, especially when they are in the way. Rather, the Indian problem has always been a government problem. And how the government does business affects us all. It's not just what the government is willing to do to Indians, or what the government is willing to allow to happen to the land and the water. It is that *we created a government that is doing this to us*. It is the government *we* empowered that privileges private ownership over the common good; that fast-tracks enormous projects at great environmental cost in order to assure us of cheap energy to fuel our out-of-control consumption. We have, with our votes and our energy, opted for smaller government that is unable and unwilling to do the job of detailed overseeing, thus creating the opportunity for enormous environmental and social crimes by corporations. Government agencies like the EPA and the Army Corps of Engineers often seem to exist to safeguard business interests rather than the public interest. The protesters at Standing Rock were making a stand on behalf of all Americans for better processes, better decisions, and better laws for our energy future, to protect all of us.

Standing Rock, just like the record-breaking Women's March of 2017, the 2018 student-led gun control March for Our Lives, the 2019 Global Climate Strike, the Black Lives Matter movement, the epic national protests after the police murder of George Floyd and other Black citizens in 2020, and the massive voter turnout in the 2020 presidential election, proves we have to show up to get up. We have to participate, at cost and peril, in shaping our government and thereby shaping its processes—including how, where, and why pipelines are approved, permitted, planned, and built. The success of any social justice movement is vested in the degree to which activists voluntarily endure injustice and injury to march in the streets and line up at the voting booth. Even in the face of setbacks.

The ten-month protest at Standing Rock Reservation was shut down in February 2017, soon after President Donald Trump took office. The protest camp was forcefully dismantled by the government. The Dakota Access Pipeline became operational on May 14, 2017, and started carrying more than 400,000 barrels of oil a day from the Bakken oil fields in northern North Dakota to Patoka, Illinois, over 1,172 miles, across four states, and under the Missouri and Mississippi Rivers. Even though the protest itself wound down, the legal fight continues. In 2017 a federal judge ruled in favor of the Standing Rock Sioux and against the pipeline; the court found that the Army Corps of Engineers broke the law when it approved the pipeline without fully consulting Standing Rock's experts. The court ordered the Army Corps to study the issue of environmental, historical, and cultural degradation more fully. It did not. In fact, it seems that the pipeline people actually wrote the Corps' subsequent findings for them. The tribe filed a motion for summary judgment in March of 2019 and by the end of the month, the U.S. District Court in Washington struck down the federal permits for the pipeline. But surely this is not the end of the matter: there's too much money involved. As on my own reservation, other tribal governments contemplating granting easements to pipelines across their ancestral lands now have to contend with a newly awakened tribal population that has been educated about pipelines and their consequences. Other rural communities—farmers, municipalities, and the like—have also become involved. What might have been seen as only an Indian problem is now seen as an American problem. The Standing Rock protest made the difference. And the next time it won't be so easy.

THE TWENTY-FIRST-CENTURY FRONTIER

For modern Indians, the past is coming into contact with the future through the persistent, creative efforts of Indians working in environmental fields, education, language revitalization, cuisine, and health. Those efforts became particularly urgent when the COVID-19 pandemic first spread in 2020. The coronavirus disproportionately impacted Native communities. (The Navajo Nation on the largest and most populous reservation in the United States was particularly hard hit.) According to a report released by the Centers for Disease Control and Prevention in August 2020, in twenty-three states, COVID was confirmed in American Indians and Alaska Natives at three and a half times the rate of non-Hispanic white populations. Because many Indians suffer from diabetes, heart disease, and other chronic conditions, the susceptibility to and complications of COVID-19 were even greater. Efforts to contain the pandemic meant casinos, tourist sites, and other revenue-generating tribal business closed. Income, which would have gone to governing, social services, education, and health care for a tribe, was therefore much reduced. The COVID economic impact was harsh for many Indians, as it was for other Americans crushed by health care, housing, and income disparities. The Navajo Nation, for example, had COVID-19 infection rates higher than any other place in the country. This was in large part because, during President Trump's time in office, the BIA and the Indian Health Service ignored their treaty and trust obligations with tribes. They didn't deliver the food, water, medical staff, and personal protective gear the tribes needed and that they were owed.

The political landscape of who will be there to represent Indians when measures like coronavirus relief are needed is changing, too. In 2018 more than eighty Indians ran for public office across the country, at every level. Voters elected Deb Haaland (Laguna Pueblo) and Sharice Davids (Ho-Chunk) to the House of Representatives for New Mexico and Kansas, respectively. They are the first Native women to serve in Congress. Democrats Haaland and Davids joined Republican representatives Tom Cole (Chickasaw) and Markwayne Mullin (Cherokee), both from Oklahoma. Peggy Flanagan (Ojibwe) won the race for lieutenant governor of Minnesota. Across the country, thirty-one Native women campaigned for seats in state legislatures, three in gubernatorial races, and four for Congress.

Give "staying home" a new meaning.

Connect with your home in nature. Stay home to save a life.

#Coronavirus
#WellnessWarriors
caih.jhu.edu

One of the posters about COVID-19 safe practices created by the Johns Hopkins Center for American Indian Health, which works with more than 140 tribal communities in twenty states.

In the 2020 elections, twelve Native candidates ran for Congress: nine for House seats and three for the Senate. Proving the diversity of Indian country, there were again Republican and Democratic candidates. Deb Haaland and Sharice Davids hung on to their House seats along with Tom Cole and Markwayne Mullin. They were joined by New Mexico Republican Yvette Herrell (Cherokee) and Democrat Kaiali'i Kahele (Native Hawaiian). The Native vote in places like Wisconsin and Arizona swung those states for the Joe Biden–Kamala Harris ticket in very tight races. President Joe Biden nominated Deb Haaland for Secretary of the Interior. When she was confirmed by Congress on March 15th, 2021, she became the first Native cabinet member.

Deb Haaland (hand raised) is sworn in as Secretary of the Interior by Vice President Kamala Harris (right) on March 18, 2021.

The old western frontier might have been closed in 1890, but the modern Indian frontier doesn't face that direction anyway. The biggest shift I can see in my own lifetime is a kind of collective determination to do much more than just survive. Our identity politics reflect this. When I was a kid on the reservation, who was or wasn't authentically Indian was determined largely in those endless clashes over how dark you were, whether you were enrolled in the tribe, whether you came up hard, how much damage you could do to yourself and others and still keep on living. This is no longer true. To be Indian today seems to be more a matter of action. I hear it all around me, at powwows and ceremony and online. *Do you speak your language? Gidojibwem ina? You hunt? Did you go ricing this year? You headed to the drum dance? Did you go to Standing Rock?* Less and less do we define ourselves by what we have lost, what we have suffered, what we've endured.

We have grown diverse in Indian country. The numbers tell part of the story. The total of those who identify on the U.S. Census as Indian has risen from about 237,000 in 1900 to over 9.7 million by 2020. In the last decade alone, the Native population increased by 86 percent. Of this ever-increasing population, in 2020 roughly half of all Indians lived in or near urban areas, continuing the trend begun in the years after World War II. Census updates also showed that overall, Indians are young, too: the median age of Native folk in 2020 was thirty-three years old as compared to thirty-eight years old for Americans generally.

These demographic changes have begun to erase many of the old hurdles and divides. Reservation people go to the city and bring the reservation with them, and city Indians go back to the reservation and bring the city with them.

The net effect of all this diversity is a sense that we Indians are surging. We seem to be everywhere, and doing everything. Social media helps connect us. Sarah and Chelsey and Thosh and Nicole and the water protectors and powwow Indians and health workers and corporate types and artists and writers and college kids and Indian soccer moms and everyone else are in increasingly close contact. I can't help feeling we are using modernity in the best possible way: to work together and to heal what was broken.

EPILOGUE

❖❖❖❖❖❖❖❖❖❖❖

AFTER THE MASSACRE AT WOUNDED Knee in 1890, there were a few skirmishes in South Dakota, Utah, Nevada, Arizona, New Mexico, and Minnesota. But most of the most famous chiefs—Sitting Bull, Crazy Horse, Geronimo, Chief Joseph, Red Cloud, Bagone-giizhig, Tecumseh, Black Hawk, Cochise, Quanah Parker—were either dead, imprisoned, or in retirement. At the time of first contact, around 1500 CE, Indian populations in North America had been, according to sober estimates, around twenty million. There were more than five hundred distinct tribes spread over the entire continent—from the Florida Keys to the Aleutian Islands.

The story of the land parallels that of the population. The United States comprises 2.4 billion acres. By 1900 Indians "controlled" only seventy-eight million acres, or about 3 percent, and there were only 237,000 Indians left. As we've seen, this outcome wasn't the result of a single regime or episode or factor, and it didn't happen overnight. But Wounded Knee came to stand in for all of it: the final blow, a full stop to a long sentence of pain and dispossession. The frontier was closed, and its memory was already being turned into myth in dime novels, westerns, and Wild West shows. Indians were on the way out, moving from a life in the world to a kind of museum existence.

But not so fast.

As I've tried to show in this book, Indians lived on, as more than ghosts, as more than the relics of a once happy people. We lived on increasingly invested in and changed by—and doing our best to change—the American character.

It pains me to think about Wounded Knee. It also pains me, for different reasons, to read about it in books like Dee Brown's. What hurts is not just that 150 people were cruelly and viciously killed. It is that their sense of life—and our sense of their lives—died with them. We know next to nothing about them. Who among them was funny? Who kicked his dog? Were they unfaithful, or vain, or fond of sweets? The tiny, fretful, intricate details are what make us who we are. And they are lost again and again when we paint over them with the tragedy of "the Indian." In this sense, the victims of Wounded Knee died twice—once at the end of a gun, and again at the end of a pen.

We Indians die, too, in our own minds. And this is perhaps the saddest death of all. I cannot shake the belief that the ways in which we tell the story of our reality shapes that reality: the manner of telling makes the world. And I worry that if we tell the story of the past as a tragedy, we consign ourselves to a tragic future. If we insist on raging against our dependency on the United States and modernity itself, we miss something vital: as much as our past was shaped by the whims and violence of an evolving America, America, in turn, has been shaped by us.

This book is an attempt to rescue the dead from the enemy by looking beyond Wounded Knee. It is not about the heart that was buried in the cold ground of South Dakota but rather about the heart that beats on—among the Dakota, to be sure, but also among the Diné, Comanche, Ojibwe, Seminole, Miwok, Blackfeet, and all the other tribes around the country. And while Wounded Knee was the last major armed conflict between Indian tribes and the U.S. government, there have been many battles since 1890: battles fought by Indian parents to keep their children, and by the children far away at boarding schools to remember and keep their families and their tribes close to their hearts; battles of Indian leaders to defeat allotment and other destructive legislation; battles of activists to make good on the promises their leaders couldn't or wouldn't honor; battles of millions of present-day

Indians to be Indian and modern at the same time. We are, in a sense, the children and grandchildren and great-grandchildren of those hundreds who survived Wounded Knee and who did what was necessary to survive and then—bit by bit—to thrive.

The *how* of the telling shapes the *what*. This book is meant to tell the story of Indian lives, and Indian histories, in such a way as to render those histories and those lives as something much more, much greater and grander, than a catalog of pain. I have tried to catch us not in the act of dying but, rather, in the radical act of living. Because at the heart of the political convulsions that now grip the nation we love is a human question. A simple one:

What kind of country do we want to be?

It has always bothered me that the very idea of paying attention to Indian history is tinged with the soft compassion of the do-gooder, as if it's a kind of voluntary public service. But if we treat Indian stories this way, we do more than relegate Indians themselves to America's deep and sometimes dark past. We also miss the full measure of the country itself. If you want to know America—if you want to see it for what it was and what it is—you need to look at Indian history and at the Indian present. If you do, if we all do, we will see that the issues posed at the founding of the country have persisted. To ignore the history of Indians in America is to miss how power itself works.

Founding Father John Adams, writing to Thomas Jefferson in 1816, urged him to remember "Power always thinks it has a great Soul, and vast Views, beyond the Comprehension of the Weak." If anything, the lives of Indians remind us that our souls have great power. We need to recall the mute agony of the Indian woman, her name lost to history, who was abducted by Columbus, sold, traded, raped, and likely consigned to the sea. We need to remember the strength and dignity of the Otoe chief Medicine Horse, who responded to the federal commissioner trying to take his land in 1873 by saying, "We are not children.

We are men. I never thought I would be treated so when I made the Treaty." We need to remember the anguish of the Indian father who received news of his daughter's death at Flandreau Indian School in 1906: "I am very sorry that you could not have seen your daughter alive, for she had grown quite a little and improved much since you let her come here with me." To remember these stories and all the others is to remain humble in power, and to be called to tend to the troubled soul of the country. It is to remember that our very lives exist at the far side of policy. It is to remember the good and the bad, the personal and the social, the large and the small. It is not to capture Indians, per se, but to capture the details of our lives. We are, for better or worse, the body of our republic. And we need to listen to that body, to hear the sound, faint at times, stronger at others, of a heartbeat going on.

ACKNOWLEDGMENTS

◆◇◆◇◆◇◆◇◆◇◆

I BEGAN WRITING THE ORIGINAL, adult version of this book the week my father died in the winter of 2016. Not an easy time. I have felt both the loss of him and his presence every day since. And in the ultimate balance of things his presence is felt more keenly. But it was the living who made all the difference as I wrote and it is them I would like to thank. It is, of course, largely impossible to thank everyone who needs to be thanked here. This book sat in my mind for years before I sat down to write it. And when I did finally begin, that, too, took years. I owe a great debt to everyone at Riverhead Books and to my editor, Becky Saletan, in particular. You were patient, and brilliant, and when you said you wanted my best work, not my fastest, I took you at your word. It was a pleasure to then create this edition with the team at Viking: Ken Wright, president and publisher; editor Sheila Keenan; Lucia Baez, designer; Claire Tattersfield, who helped with photo research, and the copyediting team of Krista Ahlberg, Abigail Powers, Stéphanie Rushia, and Kelley D. Salas. I would also like to thank my agent extraordinaire, Adam Eaglin, for seeing the book inside the idea and for making everything possible. The School for Advanced Research in Santa Fe housed me for five months. The writing began there and wouldn't have been possible otherwise. The peace and quiet coupled with the energy of brilliant colleagues was indispensable. I would also like to thank my students and colleagues at the University of Southern California. You kept me company through the long birth of the book and supported me intellectually and materially. Being a teacher keeps me awake, it keeps me alive and engaged. I owe you all. Most of all, I am indebted to my fellow Indians across the country. Bobby Matthews, Santee Frazier, Sterling HolyWhiteMountain, Red Hall, Pat Schildt, Dave Schildt, Sierra Fredricksen, Eddy Pablo, Gabe Galanda, Ray Sheldon, Sarah "Southside" Agaton Howes, Chelsey Luger, Nicole Matthews, and more (many more) opened their homes and lives and hearts to me. If I didn't have space to mention you here, or if your stories didn't end up in the book: you are not forgotten. Thank you. I like to think each of you in your own way did it not for me but to have a chance to come together to talk out our past with the idea that it will help create a better future for our people. I would also like to thank my family. My father and mother—Robert Treuer and Margaret Seelye Treuer—have always inspired me. I was not an easy child, and I apologize. I am not an easy man, and for that I also ask your forgiveness. My children endured long separations from me when I was on the road. I love you. More than anyone else, this book is for you. You are cheerful and smart and funny and interesting and curious and kind: everything I hope to be someday. Also thanks to my inspiration and my love: Abi Levis. I couldn't have done this without you.

NOTES

THIS BOOK CONTAINS NO COMPOSITE characters or pseudonyms. All dialogue in quotation marks was recorded digitally. Reconstructed dialogue appears in italics. I have tried my best to frame opinion as opinion and fact as fact, if for no other reason than that Indian lives and Indian history have long been given the fancy treatment of poetic and loose interpretation. This book is a combination of history, reportage, and memoir. It is also my take on things, my read of our shared Indian past, present, and future. Errors of fact are mine. For better or worse, this book is mine.

Notes for caption text are italicized.

PROLOGUE

2   By the late 1870s, an estimated: "Time Line of the American Bison," National Bison Range Wildlife Refuge Complex, U.S. Fish & Wildlife Service, www.fws .gov/bisonrange/timeline.htm.

4   "Helpless children and women with babes in their arms": John A. Haymond, *The American Soldier, 1866–1916: The Enlisted Man and the Transformation of the United States Army* (Jefferson, NC: McFarland, 2018), 237.

5   "greatest concentration of recorded experience and observation": Dee Brown, *Bury My Heart at Wounded Knee* (1970; New York: Henry Holt, 1970, 2000), xxiii.

6   "If the readers of this book": Brown, xxv.

FATAL ENCOUNTERS 10,000 BCE–1890

13   Both sites may stretch back nineteen thousand years: Ann Gibbons, "Oldest Stone Tools in the Americas Claimed in Chile," November 18, 2015, *Science*, www.sciencemag.org/news/2015/11/oldest-stone-tools-americas-claimed -chile.

14 Archaeological evidence: John E. Clark and Dennis Gosser, "Reinventing Mesoamerica's First Pottery," in *The Emergence of Pottery: Technology and Innovation in Ancient Societies*, ed. William K. Barnett and John W. Hoopes (Washington, DC: Smithsonian Institution Press, 2015), 209–19, retrieved at users.clas.ufl.edu/dcgrove/mexarchreadings/reinventing.pdf.

16 "to encourage them [Indians] to abandon hunting": "Jefferson's Secret Message to Congress," January 18, 1803, *Rivers, Edens, Empires: Lewis & Clark and the Revealing of America*, Library of Congress, www.loc.gov/exhibits/lewisandclark/transcript56.html.

17 When it was over, the United States secured: Charles Flowers, Peter B. Gallagher, and Patricia Wickman, Seminole Timeline, Seminole Tribe of Florida, History, www.semtribe.com/History/TimelineText.aspx.

17 *"I will make the white man"*: Quoted in "Billy Bowlegs in New Orleans," *Harper's Weekly*, June 12, 1858, 376, archive.org/stream/harpersweek100bonn#page/376.

18 At a cost of nearly sixty million dollars: "The Causes and Effects of the Seminole Wars," Florida Memory, State Library & Archives of Florida, www.floridamemory.com/onlineclassroom/seminoles/lessonplans/4thgrade/4th-causes.php.

19 Life appears to have been particularly good: Alice B. Kehoe, *North American Indians: A Comprehensive Account*, 3rd ed. (New York: Routledge, 2005), 209.

20 In 1592, before the Seneca had direct: Mary Ellen Snodgrass, *World Epidemics: A Cultural Chronology of Disease from Prehistory to the Era of Zika* (Jefferson, NC: McFarland, 2017), 56.

22 In Ohio some mounds were found to contain: Alice Kehoe, *North America Before the European Invasions*, 2nd ed. (New York: Routledge, 2016), 85.

22 One burial mound at the Mound City: "Hopewell (1–400 A.D.)," Heilbrunn Timeline of Art History, The Metropolitan Museum of Art, www.metmuseum.org/toah/hd/hope/hd_hope.htm.

22 Large villages replaced small seasonal camps: "Mississippian Period AD 1100–1541," Fort Smith National Historic Site (Arkansas), National Park Service, www.nps.gov/fosm/learn/historyculture/mississippiperiod.htm.

23 The Huron, whose population numbered: James F. Pendergast, "The Confusing Identities Attributed to Stadacona and Hochelaga," *Journal of Canadian Studies* 32, no. 4 (Winter 1998), 149–67, utpjournals.press/doi/10.3138/jcs.32.4.149.

23 The French hoped to take up dealing in furs: Michael McDonnell, *Masters of Empire: Great Lakes Indians and the Making of America* (New York: Hill and Wang, 2016), 29.

25 The canals they dug would be in use: Jack Page, *In the Hands of the Great Spirit: The 20,000-Year History of American Indians* (New York: The Free Press, 2003), 72.

27 *"one of the cleverest bits of passive solar architecture"*: Page, 81.

31 When the Americans arrived: Kehoe, *North American Indians*, 144.

31 In 1863 the military launched: Ojibwa, "The Navajo Long Walk," May 2, 2010, Native American Netroots, nativeamericannetroots.net/diary/487.

33 California was a place apart: Robert Petersen, "California, Calafia, Khalif: The Origin of the Name 'California,'" December 15, 2015, KCET, www.kcet.org /shows/departures/california-calafia-khalif-the-origin-of-the-name -california.

34 It is estimated that in 1770: A. L. Kroeber, *Handbook of the Indians of California*, Smithsonian Institution Bureau of American Ethnology Bulletin 78 (Washington, DC: Government Printing Office, 1925), 880–91.

34 By 1832 that number was fourteen thousand: Dorothy Krell, ed., *The California Missions: A Pictorial History* (Menlo Park, CA: Sunset Publishing, 1979), 316.

35 Farther inland, evidence is emerging: Loren G. Davis, "New Support for a Late-Pleistocene Coastal Occupation at the Indian Sands Site, Oregon," *Current Research in the Pleistocene* 25 (2008), 74–76, retrieved at wpg .forestry.oregonstate.edu/sites/wpg/files/seminars/2008_DavisCRP.pdf. See also "Paisley Caves," *Archaeology*, August 11, 2014, www.archaeology.org /issues/145-1409/features/2370-peopling-the-americas-paisley-caves; and "Paisley Caves," *The Oregon Encyclopedia*, oregonencyclopedia.org/articles /paisley_caves/#.Ww3jM6kh2i4.

35 Skeletal remains of (mostly) young men: Kehoe, *North America Before the European Invasions*, 106.

37 Coastal Indian populations that had been around two hundred thousand: Robert Boyd, *The Coming of the Spirit of Pestilence: Introduced Infectious Diseases and Population Decline Among Northwest Coast Indians, 1774–1874* (Vancouver: University of British Columbia Press, 1999).

39 They adopted the bow and arrow around 500 BCE: Page, 47–49.

40 Seventeen young children were spared: "The Aftermath of Mountain Meadows," www.smithsonianmag.com/history/the-aftermath-of-mountain -meadows-110735627/.

42 These tribes plied the lowlands of south and central Texas: "Coahuiltecan Indians," *Handbook of Texas Online*, tshaonline.org/handbook/online /articles/bmcah.

43 By that time, its population had dropped: S. C. Gwynne, *Empire of the Summer Moon: Quanah Parker and the Rise and Fall of the Comanches, the Most*

Powerful Indian Tribe in American History (New York: Scribner, 2011), 274.

45   By the 1920s, they were the wealthiest people in the world: "The Forgotten
      Murder of the Osage People for the Oil Beneath Their Land." www.pbs.org
      /newshour/arts/the-forgotten-murders-of-the-osage-people-for-the-oil
      -beneath-their-land.

45   about eighteen thousand years ago: Alan J. Osborn, "Paleo-Indians," *Encyclo-
      pedia of the Great Plains*, plainshumanities.unl.edu/encyclopedia/doc/egp
      .na.080.

46   It wasn't long, however, before the former: Francis Haines, "The Northward
      Spread of Horses Among the Plains Indians," *American Anthropologist* 40, no.
      3 (1938), 429–51.

50   *Somewhere between thirty and sixty million buffalo*: "Where the Buffalo No
      Longer Roam," *Smithsonian Magazine*, July 17, 2012, www.smithsonianmag
      .com/history/where-the-buffalo-no-longer-roamed-3067904/.

THE "INDIAN PROBLEM" 1891–1934

52   Kevin Washburn slips off his cowboy boots: All quotes from author interview
      with Kevin Washburn, March 11, 2016.

53   The Oneida, despite being a member: "The Revolutionary War, Oneida's
      Legacy to Freedom," Oneida Indian Nation, www.oneidaindiannation.com
      /revolutionarywar/.

54   in recognition of their contributions to American victory: Joseph T. Glatthaar
      and James Kirby Martin, *Forgotten Allies: The Oneida Indians and the Ameri-
      can Revolution* (New York: Hill and Wang, 2010), 5.

53   *Han Yerry Tehawengaragwen led a band of Oneida*: "Oneidas Played Vital
      Role in the Battle of Oriskany," www.oneidaindiannation.com/oneidas
      -played-vital-role-in-the-battle-of-oriskany/

54   "The United States acknowledges the lands reserved to the Oneida": "The
      Revolutionary War, Oneida's Legacy to Freedom."

54   established by an act of Congress in 1796: "The United States Factory System
      for Trading with the Indians, 1796–1822." *Oxford Journals*, Oxford University
      Press, https://www.jstor.org/stable/pdf/1889430.pdf.

55   A Seneca, he was born and raised: "Ely Parker 1770–1844: Parker Family Tree,"
      A Warrior in Two Worlds: The Life of Ely Parker, PBS, www.pbs.org/warrior
      /content/timeline/crisis/parents.html.

56   "what should be the legal status": "Instructions to the Board of Indian Com-
      missioners," in Francis Paul Prucha, ed., *Documents of United States Indian
      Policy*, 3rd ed. (Lincoln: University of Nebraska Press, 2000), 126.

56   "the first aggressions have been made by the white man": Arthur C. Parker,

The Life of General Ely S. Parker: Last Grand Sachem of the Iroquois and General Grant's Military Secretary (Buffalo, NY: Buffalo Historical Society, 1919), 139, retrieved at https://babel.hathitrust.org/cgi/pt?id=hvd.32044014840516&view=1up&seq=7.

57   In 1871 Ely Parker resigned: Parker, 156.

57   "No Indian nation or tribe within the territory": U.S. Title Code 25, Section 71, "Future Treaties with Indian Tribes," Legal Information Institute, Cornell Law School, www.law.cornell.edu/uscode/text/25/71.

58   "the Indian agent had, in effect": Sharon O'Brien, *American Indian Tribal Governments* (Norman: University of Oklahoma Press, 1993), 272.

58   ". . . The [Indian] women gathered": Richard Harding Davis, "The West from a Car Window," *Harper's Weekly*, May 14, 1892, 461, babel.hathitrust.org/cgi/pt?id=mdp.39015014126026;view=1up;seq=439; and *The West from a Car-Window* (New York: Harper & Brothers, 1892), 158, 160.

58   "Their supplies had been limited": Clark Wissler, *Red Man Reservations* (New York: Collier Books, 1971), 64, quoted in Fixico, *Bureau of Indian Affairs*, 61.

59   "It has become the settled policy": Thomas Jefferson Morgan, in *Fifty-ninth Annual Report of the Commissioner of Indian Affairs to the Secretary of the Interior* (Washington, DC: Government Printing Office, 1890), vi.

59   "wear civilized clothes": Henry Dawes, quoted in Gerald E. Shenk, *"Work or Fight!" Race, Gender, and the Draft in World War One* (New York: Palgrave Macmillan, 2005), 54.

61   "I want the white people to understand my people": In-mut-too-yah-lat-lat [Chief Joseph], speech at Lincoln Hall, Washington, D.C., 1879, published in *North American Review* 128, no. 269 (April 1879), 412–34. Courtesy Cornell University's Making of America, psi.mheducation.com/current/media/prints/pr_105.html. "Clarke" in the online document has been edited to "Clark" here.

63   "I seem to be standing on a high bank of a great river": "Standing Bear's Speech," from *The Indian Journal*, Timeless Truths, library.timelesstruths.org/texts/Stories_Worth_Rereading/Standing_Bears_Speech/.

64   "an Indian is": *Standing Bear v. Crook* (1879), in Francis Paul Prucha, ed., *Documents of United States Indian Policy*, 3rd ed. (Lincoln: University of Nebraska Press, 2000), 150–52.

65   "Look upon your hands": Helen Hunt Jackson, *A Century of Dishonor* (Norman: University of Oklahoma Press, 1995), xiii.

65   It and *Ramona*: "Helen Hunt Jackson Tries to Write Her Uncle Tom's Cabin," New England Historical Society, www.newenglandhistoricalsociety.com/helen-hunt-jackson-tries-write-uncle-toms-cabin/.

66   "Kill the Indian in him, and save the man": *Proceedings of the National Con-*

ference of Charities and Corrections (Denver, June 23–29, 1892), ed. Isabel C. Barrows, (Boston: Geo. H. Ellis, 1892), 58–59.

67   "The 'civilizing' process": Luther Standing Bear, recollections of 1879 experiences at Carlisle school, 1933, quoted at faculty.whatcom.ctc.edu/mhaberma/hist209/luthsb.htm.

67   "We would cower from the abusive disciplinary practices": Margaret L. Archuleta, Brenda J. Child, and K. Tsianina Lomawaima, eds., *Away from Home: American Indian Boarding School Experiences* (Phoenix: Heard Museum Publications, 2000), 42.

70   "it is essential that the pupils be old enough": Institute for Government Research, Studies in Administration, *The Problem of Indian Administration* (Meriam Report) (Baltimore: Johns Hopkins Press, 1928), files.eric.ed.gov/fulltext/ED087573.pdf; also found in "The Challenges and Limitations of Assimilation: Indian Boarding Schools," *The Brown Quarterly* 4, no. 3 (Fall 2001), 375.

70   "there is no individuality": *The Problem of Indian Administration*, 386.

71   "maintain a pathetic degree of quietness": *The Problem of Indian Administration*, 329.

72   "must be imbued": John Oberly, Bureau of Indian Affairs, *Annual Report of the Commissioner of Indian Affairs, for the Year 1888* (Washington, DC: U.S. Department of the Interior, 1888), lxxxix.

72   "We must make the Indian": Merrill E. Gates, "The Indian of Romance," address to 14th Lake Mohonk Indian Conference, 1896, *Proceedings of the 14th Annual Meeting of the Lake Mohonk Conference of Friends of the Indian* (Lake Mohonk, New York, October 14–16, 1896), ed. Isabel C. Barrows (Lake Mohonk Conference, 1897).

73   The General Allotment Act, also known as the Dawes Act: John P. LaVelle, "The General Allotment Act 'Eligibility' Hoax: Distortions of Law, Policy, and History in Derogation of Indian Tribes," *Wicazo Sa Review* 14, no. 1 (Spring 1999), 251–302.

78   The Court of Indian Offenses was governed by only nine provisions: Code of Indian Offenses (1883), en.wikisource.org/wiki/Code_of_Indian_Offenses. See also "Courts of Indian Offenses" (November 1, 1883), in Francis Paul Prucha, ed., *Documents of United States Indian Policy*, 3rd ed. (Lincoln: University of Nebraska Press, 2000), 159.

78   "hear and pass judgment upon all such questions": Code of Indian Offenses.

78   the "sun-dance," the "scalp-dance," or the "war-dance": Code of Indian Offenses.

79   The wording of the treaty: "The Old Crossing Chippewa Treaty and Its

Sequel," Internet Archive, archive.org/stream/pdfy-fa00v1iDcvybuUVD
/The%20Old%20Crossing%20Treaty_djvu.txt.

80   "We do not know any of our chiefs": Anton Treuer, *Warrior Nation: A History of
       the Red Lake Ojibwe* (Saint Paul: Minnesota Historical Society Press, 2015), 81.

80   "This property belongs to us": Treuer, 81.

80   "We wish to live alone on our premises; we do not wish any other Indians to
       come here." Treuer, *Warrior Nation*, 83.

81   "Your mission here is a failure . . .": Treuer, *Warrior Nation*, 95.

81   "I do not look with favor on the allotment plan": Treuer, *Warrior Nation*, 97.

82   "Start with the rising sun": Ronald L. Trosper, "Indigenous Influence on Forest
       Management on the Menominee Indian Reservation," *Forest Ecology and
       Management* 249 (2007), 134–35, courses.washington.edu/dtsclass/TEK
       -Menominee.pdf.

FIGHTING LIFE 1914–1945

86   He graduated from high school: Statistics are drawn from Patrick Stark, Amber
       M. Noel, and Joel McFarland, *Trends in High School Dropout and Completion
       Rates in the United States: 1972–2012*, Compendium Report, U.S. Department
       of Education, National Center of Education Statistics, NCES 2015-015, nces.
       ed.gov/pubs2015/2015015.pdf, and Christopher Hartney and Linh Vuong,
       *Created Equal: Racial and Ethnic Disparities in the US Criminal Justice Sys-
       tem*, National Council on Crime and Delinquency, 2009, www.nccdglobal.org
       /sites/default/files/publication_pdf/created-equal.pdf.

86   In Minnesota in 2015: "Incarceration Trends in Minnesota," Vera Institute of
       Justice. https://www.vera.org/downloads/pdfdownloads/state-incarceration
       -trends-minnesota.pdf

91   All in all, as much as 30 percent: Russel Lawrence Barsh, "American Indians in
       the Great War," *Ethnohistory* 38, no. 3 (Summer 1991), 277.

91   Fourteen Indian women joined the Army Nurse Corps: The Women's Memo-
       rial. www.womensmemorial.org/native-american-women-veterans.

91   *Cora Elm, a member of the Oneida Nation of Wisconsin*, "On the Western
       Front: Two Iroquois Nurses in World War I," www.americanindianmagazine
       .org/story/western-front-two-iroquois-nurses-world-war-i

92   such as carpenters' mates, shipwrights: Thomas A. Britten, "American Indians
       in World War I: Military Service as Catalyst for Reform" (Ph.D. diss., Texas Tech
       University, 1994), 111, https://ttu-ir.tdl.org/handle/2346/16718

92   Farther north at the Somme: C. N. Trueman, "First World War Casualties," His-
       tory Learning Site, April 17, 2015, www.historylearningsite.co.uk/world-war
       -one/world-war-one-and-casualties/first-world-war-casualties/.

93   "at night barehanded and alone": "An Indian Gets a Move on Himself: A Match

for Twenty Huns," *Word Carrier* 46 (October–December 1918), 20, quoted in Thomas A. Britten, *American Indians in World War I at Home and at War* (Albuquerque: University of New Mexico Press, 1997), 77.

93   During the fray he was shot: Britten, 77.

94   "If a battle was on": Herman Viola, *Warriors in Uniform: The Legacy of American Indian Heroism* (Washington, DC: National Geographic Press, 2008), 68.

94   recruits were administered "intelligence" tests: "IQ Tests Go to War—Measuring Intelligence in the Army," History Matters: The U.S. Survey Course on the Web, historymatters.gmu.edu/d/5293. See also Richard Conniff, "God and White Men at Yale," *Yale Alumni Magazine*, May/June 2012, yalealumnimagazine.com/articles/3456-god-and-white-men-at-yale?page=3.

94   they disproportionately served as scouts, snipers: Barsh, "American Indians in the Great War," 276–303.

95   "Not even all the men and women": Britten, *American Indians in World War I at Home and at War*, 160.

96   American Indian births outstripped Indian deaths: Nancy Shoemaker, *American Indian Population Recovery in the Twentieth Century* (Albuquerque: University of New Mexico Press, 1999), 75.

96   "Be it enacted by the Senate": Quoted in "Native American Citizenship: 1924 Indian Citizenship Act," Nebraska Studies 1900–1924, http://www.nebraskastudies.org/en/1900-1924/native-american-citizenship/citizenship-for-native-veterans.

98   The new General Council combined centuries-old hereditary Ojibwe chieftain: Treuer, *Warrior Nation*, 196.

99   Indians could vote on what worked best for their tribe: Wheeler-Howard Act (Indian Reorganization Act, June 18, 1934), Article 18, Sovereign Amonsoquath Band of Cherokee, www.amonsoquathbandofcherokee.org/ira1934_wheeler_howard_act.html.

101   He had already seen battle action: "Ira Hamilton Hayes, Corporal, United States Marine Corps," Arlington National Cemetery, www.arlingtoncemetery.net/irahayes.htm.

102   "I was sick": Viola, "Fighting the Metal Hats: World War II," *Warriors in Uniform*, 93–94.

102   "pomp and circumstance": H. Paul Jeffers, *The 100 Greatest Heroes: Inspiring Profiles of One Hundred Men and Women Who Changed the World* (New York: Citadel Press, 2003), 135.

MOVING ON UP 1945–1970

112   By 1900 there were fewer than two thousand: *Annual Reports of the Depart-*

ment of the Interior of Indian Affairs for the Fiscal Year ended June 30, 1900: Report of the Commissioner of Indian Affairs (Washington, DC: Government Printing Office, 1900), 1.

113   "I worked around stock my whole life": All quotations from Red Hall are from author interviews with him in October 2014.

115   More than half of those who lived on farms: S. Mintz and S. McNeil (2016), "Overview of the Post-War Era" (ID 2923), *Digital History*, www.digitalhistory .uh.edu/era.cfm?eraid=16&smtid=1.

115   nearly eight million WWII veterans: U.S. Department of Veterans Affairs, "Education and Training/History and Timeline," www.benefits.va.gov/gibill/history .asp.

115   By 1970 six million African Americans: "World War I and the Great Migration," History, Art & Archives, U.S. House of Representatives, history.house.gov /Exhibitions-and-Publications/BAIC/Historical-Essays/Temporary-Farewell /World-War-I-And-Great-Migration/.

117   The Indian Claims Commission expanded: Indian Claims Commission Act of 1947, in Charles Joseph Kappler, ed., *Kappler's Indian Affairs: Laws and Treaties: Compiled Federal Regulations Relating to Indians*, vol. 6 (Washington, DC: Government Printing Office, 1971), digital.library.okstate.edu/kappler /vol6/html_files/v6p0323b.html#mn3. Also available on the Library of Congress website: 79th Congress, section 2, chap. 959, www.loc.gov/law/help /statutes-at-large/79th-congress/session-2/c79s2ch959.pdf.

117   The last claim on the docket: "Lead Up to the Indian Claims Commission Act of 1946," US Department of Justice, www.justice.gov/enrd/lead-indian-claims -commission-act-1946.

117   "broad waiver of the United States' sovereign immunity": "Lead Up to the Indian Claims Commission Act of 1946."

119   "the freeing of the Indian": Renée Ann Cramer, *Cash, Color, and Colonialism: The Politics of Tribal Acknowledgment* (Norman: University of Oklahoma Press, 2005), 20.

119   Tribes in states not covered: Ada Pecos Melton and Jerry Gardner, "Public Law 280: Issues and Concerns for Victims of Crime in Indian Country," American Indian Development Associates, www.aidainc.net/publications/pl280. htm.

120   "subject to the same laws and entitled to the same privileges": House Concurrent Resolution 108, 67 Statute B122, August 1, 1953, Native Media Center, University of North Dakota, arts-sciences.und.edu/native-media-center/_files /docs/1950-1970/1953hcr108.pdf.

121   Never mind that they had no authority: "The McCumber Agreement," North Dakota Studies, www.ndstudies.gov/content/%E2%80%9C-mccumber -agreement%E2%80%9D.

121   "We're called the 'landless Indians of Montana'": All quotes from author interviews with Sierra Fredrickson, September 2015 and February 2018.

123   Their century-old petition for legal, federal recognition: "125 Years Later, Native American Tribe in Montana Gets Federal Recognition." *The New York Times*, February 1, 2020.

127   "I'm from Birch Creek, Montana, on the Blackfeet Reservation": All quotes from author interview with David Schildt, November 2017.

132   Under termination and relocation: Patricia K. Ourada, *The Menominee Indians: A History* (Norman: University of Oklahoma Press, 1979).

132   A total of 1,365,801 acres: "Land Tenure Issues," Indian Land Tenure Foundation, iltf.org/land-issues/issues/.

BECOMING INDIAN 1970–1980

134   "Welcome to my office": All quotations from Bobby Matthews are from author interviews with him, 2014–2015. Sections of this chapter first appeared in "Off the Land: What Subsistence Really Looks Like," *Harper's Magazine*, November 2014, harpers.org/archive/2014/11/off-the-land/.

138   "ensure the political, educational, social, and economic equality": Mission statement, NAACP, Washington, DC, Branch, naacpdc.org/dcbranch.htm.

139   *"sovereignty, civil rights, and recognition for all Indians"*: "The Founding Meeting of NCAI," National Congress of American Indians, www.ncai.org /about-ncai/mission-history/the-founding-meeting-of-ncai.

140   "white man tends to rate the Indian": Paul Chaat Smith and Robert Warrior, *Like a Hurricane: The Indian Movement from Alcatraz to Wounded Knee* (New York: New Press, 1996), 41.

140   "This is all I have to offer": Mark Hamilton Lytle, *America's Uncivil Wars: The Sixties Era from Elvis to the Fall of Richard Nixon* (New York: Oxford University Press, 2006), 308.

141   Their life expectancy was between fifty: S. Ryan Johansson, "The Demographic History of the Native Peoples of North America: A Selective Bibliography," in *Yearbook of Physical Anthropology* 25 (1982), 145.

141   And there were more than four times: C. Matthew Snipp, "The Size and Distribution of the American Indian Population: Fertility, Mortality, Migration, and Residence," in *Changing Numbers, Changing Needs: American Indian Demography and Public Health* (Washington, DC: National Academies Press [US], 1996), www.ncbi.nlm.nih.gov/books/NBK233098/.

142   In Oakland, California, a mere sixteen: Jessica McElrath, "The Black Panthers," retrieved at web.archive.org/web/20070407155740/afroamhistory.about .com/od/blackpanthers/a/blackpanthers.htm.

143   a ten-point plan: "History of the Black Panther Party: Black Panther Party Platform and Program" ("What We Want, What We Believe," citing *The Black Panther*, November 23, 1967, 3), The Black Panther Party Research Project, web.stanford.edu/group/blackpanthers/history.shtml.

144   Indians in Minneapolis endured: S. Mintz and S. McNeil (2016), "The Native American Power Movement" (ID 3348), *Digital History*, www.digitalhistory .uh.edu/disp_textbook.cfm?smtid=2&psid=3348.

144   founded the American Indian Movement in July 1968: "A Brief History of the American Indian Movement," www.aimovement.org/ggc/history.html.

151   "You can see the frustration here": Robert Treuer, "Seven Days in November," *The Washingtonian*, May 1978, 109.

151   One pro-Indian lawyer was lowered: Treuer, "Seven Days in November," 109.

152   "War paint traditionally means": Treuer, "Seven Days in November," 106.

152   The occupiers finally released the twenty-point memo: Congressional Record of April 2, 1973, www.gpo.gov/fdsys/granule/GPO-CRECB-1973-pt8/GPO -CRECB-1973-pt8-5-1; see also "Trail of Broken Treaties: 20-Point Position Memo," American Indian Movement, October 1972, www.aimovement.org /ggc/trailofbrokentreaties.html.

153   The money was transferred in cash to Vernon Bellecourt: Treuer, "Seven Days in November," 99.

155   Yellow Thunder dropped out of school: Stew Magnuson, "Remember Raymond Yellow Thunder's Life," *Native Sun News*, posted at Indianz.com, February 13, 2012, www.indianz.com/News/2012/004568.asp.

155   He was a hard worker: Smith and Warrior, *Like a Hurricane*, 112–13.

155   while joyriding around Gordon: *State v. Hare (State of Nebraska v. Leslie D. Hare, State of Nebraska v. Melvin P. Hare)*, 208 N.W.2d 264 (1973) 190 Neb. 339, June 8, 1973, Justia, US Supreme Court, law.justia.com/cases/nebraska /supreme-court/1973/38761-1.html.

155   "found him in an old pickup truck": *State v. Hare*.

155   The men then took off: *State v. Hare*.

156   By the end of the week: Smith and Warrior, *Like a Hurricane*, 115.

157   Leslie was sentenced to six years: Russell Means, *Where White Men Fear to Tread: The Autobiography of Russell Means* (New York: St. Martin's Press, 1995), 215.

158   replacing them with family members: Smith and Warrior, *Like a Hurricane*, 196.

158   six previous tribal chairmen: Smith and Warrior, *Like a Hurricane*, 195.

158   awarded $17.5 million . . . "The Indians residing in the Black Hills": Edward
       Lazarus, *Black Hills/White Justice: The Sioux Nation versus the United States,
       1775 to the Present* (New York: HarperCollins, 1991), 492/375–376.

159   "bums trying to get their braids": Terri Schultz, "Bamboozle Me Not at
       Wounded Knee," Harper's Magazine, June 1973, harpers.org/archive/1973/06
       /bamboozle-me-not-at-wounded-knee.

161   "The fact is, we as a group": Smith and Warrior, *Like a Hurricane*, 208.

162   "If any foreign official": Smith and Warrior, *Like a Hurricane*, 218.

164   He had worked for the Pine Ridge tribal police: Smith and Warrior, 259.

164   "war games without a war": Smith and Warrior, *Like a Hurricane*, 234.

165   Even now, Indians don't complete high school: "High School Dropout Rates:
       Indicators on Children and Youth," Child Trends, DataBank, November 2015,
       www.childtrends.org/wp-content/uploads/2014/10/01_Dropout_Rates.pdf;
       also see Patrick Stark, Amber M. Noel, and Joel McFarland, *Trends in High
       School Dropout and Completion Rates in the United States: 1972–2012*, Com-
       pendium Report, U.S. Department of Education, National Center of Educa-
       tion Statistics, nces.ed.gov/fastfacts/display.asp?id=16.

167   "Whatever the cause, our joint federal-local effort must pursue poverty":
       Lyndon B. Johnson, Annual Message to Congress on the State of the Union,
       January 8, 1968, retrieved from Gerhard Peters and John T. Woolley, *The
       American Presidency Project*, www.presidency.ucsb.edu/ws/?pid=26787.

169   "use the best available talents": *The Indian Education Act of 1972—A Brief His-
       tory, Analysis, Issues and Outlook* (Washington, DC: Department of Health,
       Education, and Welfare, Office of Education, 1973), 14–15, files.eric.ed.gov
       /fulltext/ED111553.pdf.

170   For the first time, school districts: *The Indian Education Act of 1972*, 18.

171   In 1999 Montana passed the Indian Education for All Act: "Indian Education
       for All, MCA 20-1-501," MontanaTribes, www.montanatribes.org/files/iefa-law
       .pdf.

172   The remains of the Anglo Christians: Thomaira Babbit, "NAGPRA as a Para-
       digm: The Historical Context and Meaning of the Native American Graves
       Protection and Repatriation Act in 2011," *Proceedings of the Native American
       Symposium*, November 2011, 61–70, www.se.edu/nas/files/2013/03/NAS
       -2011-Proceedings-Babbit.pdf.

172   "give me back my people's bones": David M. Gradwohl, Joe B. Thomson, and
       Michael J. Perry, "Still Running: A Tribute to Maria Pearson, Yankton Sioux,"
       Journal of the Iowa Archeological Society 52 (2005).

174   As of 2018, the remains of more than 189,415: Fiscal Year 2018 Report,
       National NAGPRA Program, National Park Service, U.S. Department of the

Interior, irma.nps.gov/DataStore/DownloadFile/620933.

174 Between 1973 and 1976: Timothy Williams, "Tribe Seeks Reopening of Inquiries in '70s Deaths," *The New York Times*, June 15, 2012, www.nytimes .com/2012/06/15/us/sioux-group-asks-officials-to-reopen-70s-cases.html.

174 The FBI found shell casings nearby: Scott Anderson, "The Martyrdom of Leonard Peltier," Outside, July 2, 1995, www.outsideonline.com/1835141 /martyrdom-leonard-peltier.

175 Those who see him as a hero: "Post-Trial Actions, Criminal," International Leonard Peltier Defense Committee website, www.whoisleonardpeltier.info /LEGAL/CRIMINAL.htm.

176 On June 26, Agents Coler and Williams: Douglas O. Linder, "Testimony of FBI Special Agent Gary Adams in the Leonard Peltier Trial" (March 17–18, 1977), *Famous Trials*, www.famous-trials.com/leonardpeltier/762-adamstestimony.

178 "These white people think this country": Quoted in Eric Konigsberg, "Who Killed Anna Mae?" *The New York Times*, April 25, 2014, www.nytimes .com/2014/04/27/magazine/who-killed-anna-mae.html.

178 "I came here to fight": Konigsberg, "Who Killed Anna Mae?"

178 In early June 1975: "Anna Mae [Aquash] Timeline I—Wounded Knee," *News from Indian Country*, January 1997 and ongoing, www.indiancountrynews .com/index.php/investigations/286-aquash-peltier-timeline-1975-2010/2101 -annie-mae-timeline-i-wounded-knee; and Chris Summers, "Native American Prisoner to Fight On," BBC News, April 24, 2004, news.bbc.co.uk/2/hi /americas/3654785.stm.

179 Both Aquash and Darlene Nichols: Konigsberg, "Who Killed Anna Mae?"

179 showed up at Marlon Brando's house: Dennis Banks, *Ojibwa Warrior: Dennis Banks and the Rise of the American Indian Movement* (Norman: University of Oklahoma Press, 2004), 301–2.

179 The famed actor lent them his RV, gave them ten thousand dollars in cash: Konigsberg, "Who Killed Anna Mae?"

179 "begging for his life, but I shot him anyway": Konigsberg, "Who Killed Anna Mae?"

180 "shortly afterward and puzzled what to do": Konigsberg, "Who Killed Anna Mae?"

181 "I don't know if I would participate": Konigsberg, "Who Killed Anna Mae?"

181 "If there's a burning house": Konigsberg, "Who Killed Anna Mae?"

THE SOVEREIGNTY SURGE 1980–2015

183 fewer than half (245 tribes) own and run gaming operations: "Indian Gross Gaming Revenues of $34.6B Set Industry Record and Show a 2.5% Increase,"

National Indian Gaming Commission, https://www.nigc.gov/news/detail/2019
-indian-gross-gaming-revenues-of-34.6b-set-industry-record-and-show-a
-2.5-increase.

184   By comparison, the Pechanga Band: Vince Beiser, "A Paper Trail of Tears: How Casino-Rich Tribes Are Dealing Members Out," *Harper's Magazine*, August 2006, harpers.org/archive/2006/08/a-paper-trail-of-tears/, retrieved at faculty.humanities.uci.edu/tcthorne/Hist15/disenrollmentatpechanga2000 .htm.

184   And the gaming compacts signed between tribes and states: "California Tribal Casinos: Questions and Answers," California Legislative Analyst's Office, February 2007, www.lao.ca.gov/2007/tribal_casinos/tribal_casinos _020207.aspx.

185   "I said it was wrong": Quoted in David Treuer, *Rez Life* (New York: Grove Press, 2012), 228–29.

186   Helen called them up: Treuer, *Rez Life*, 228–29.

187   There was nothing in PL 280 "remotely resembling": *Bryan v. Itasca County*, 426 U.S. 373 (1976), Justia, US Supreme Court, supreme.justia.com/cases /federal/us/426/373/case.html.

187   "That was $147 off my mind": Treuer, *Rez Life*, 236.

187   "I never got nothing from nobody": Treuer, *"Rez Life,"* 237.

187   the Seminole tribal chairman saw a big window of opportunity: Matthew L. M. Fletcher, "The Seminole Tribe and the Origins of Indian Gaming," *FIU Law Review* 9 (2014), 255–75, esp. 263–65, retrieved at digitalcommons.law.msu .edu/cgi/viewcontent.cgi?article =1543&context=facpubs.

188   The tribe promptly sued: See *Seminole Tribe of Florida v. Butterworth*, 491 F. Supp. 1015 (S.D. Fla. 1980), May 6, 1980, Justia US Law, law.justia.com/cases /federal/district-courts/FSupp/491/1015/1798786/.

188   Within a year of the Cabazon win: Charles Wilkinson, *Blood Struggle: The Rise of Modern Indian Nations* (New York: W. W. Norton, 2005), 335–36.

189   The first provision was that whatever forms of gaming: Indian Gaming Regulatory Act, National Indian Gaming Commission, www.nigc.gov/general -counsel/indian-gaming-regulatory-act.

190   more than thirty-three billion dollars in 2018: "2018 Gaming Revenues of $33.7 Billion Show a 4.1% Increase," press release, National Indian Gaming Commission, www.nigc.gov/images/uploads/newsrelease/20190906_GGR _PR_Announcement_draft_(00000002)_kic_cjt_ess_edits-1-1FINAL.pdf.

190   Blood Quantum and Disenrollment: This section on disenrollment includes the majority of my op-ed "How Do You Prove You're an Indian?" published in *The New York Times* on December 20, 2011, www.nytimes.com/2011/12/21

/opinion/for-indian-tribes-blood-shouldnt-be-everything.html.

190   As of 2017, more than fifty tribes: David E. Wilkins and Shelly Hulse Wilkins,
      Dismembered: Native Disenrollment and the Battle for Human Rights
      (Seattle: University of Washington Press, 2017), 67.

190   Many different rationales have been used to justify this: David E. Wilkins and
      Shelly Hulse Wilkins, 67–78.

191   In short order, the number of registered full-bloods: Melissa L. Meyer, *The
      White Earth Tragedy: Ethnicity and Dispossession at a Minnesota Anishi-
      naabe Reservation* (Lincoln: University of Nebraska Press, 1994), 170.

195   an "emerging litigation" capability: Wilkinson, *Blood Struggle*, 242.

195   As the Indian legal and professional class grew: Wilkinson, 241.

196   "authority to pass ordinances" . . . "any oil and natural gas": 18 Land & Water L.
      Rev. 539 (1983), Indian Law—Tribal Authority to Levy a Mineral Severance Tax
      on Non-Indian Lessees—*Merrion v. Jicarilla Apache Tribe*, HeinOnline, heinon-
      line.org/HOL/LandingPage?handle=hein.journals
      /lawlr18&div=25&id=&page=.

196   "avail themselves of the 'substantial privilege' ": *Merrion v. Jicarilla Apache
      Tribe*, 455 U.S. 130ff (1982), *Merrion v. Jicarilla Apache Tribe*, No. 80-11,
      Argued March 30, 1981, Reargued November 4, 1981, Decided January 25,
      1982, Justia, US Supreme Court, supreme.justia.com/cases/federal
      /us/455/130/case.html.

200   *We have a relationship with pot:* All previously unpublished quotations from
      Gabriel Galanda were recorded in June–July 2015.

200   Two months after the "pot summit," I sat across from Eddy Pablo: All quotes
      from author interview with Eddy Pablo, May 2015.

202   The median household income at Tulalip: "Tulalip Reservation Division WA
      Demographic Data and Boundary Map," washington.hometownlocator.com
      /counties/subdivisions/data,n,tulalip%20reservation%20division,id,53061935
      06,cfips,061.cfm.

202   The tribe opened a marijuana dispensary: Andrea Brown, "Retail Cannabis
      Is the Newest Money-Maker on the Reservation," Herald Net, September 2,
      2018, www.heraldnet.com/business/retail-cannabis-is-new-money-maker
      -on-the-reservation/.

203   four-hundred-thousand-dollar skate park: Kari Bray, " 'Worth the Wait': Lake
      Stevens Skate Park Could Open by August," Everett, Washington, *HeraldNet*,
      December 9, 2016, www.heraldnet.com/news/plans-for-skate-park-in-lake
      -stevens-finalized/.

203   "approximately" 326: Bureau of Indian Affairs, FAQ, "What is a federal Indian

reservation?" www.bia.gov/frequently-asked-questions.

204 Fifteen percent of American Indians have diabetes: "National Diabetes Statistics Report, 2017: Estimates of Diabetes and Its Burden in the United States,"
National Center for Chronic Disease Prevention and Health Promotion,
Division of Diabetes Translation, Centers for Disease Control and Prevention,
www.cdc.gov/diabetes/pdfs/data/statistics/national-diabetes-statistics
-report.pdf.

204 For some reason we don't get it as often: Steven Parker, "Native Americans:
The Facts," HealthGuidance for Better Health, www.healthguidance.org
/entry/6323/1/Native-Americans-The-Facts.html.

205 According to the Tribal Employment Rights Organization: "Native American
Owned (NAOB) Registry," http://www.tulaliptero.com/Contractors/NAOB
Registry.

209 The tribe is currently negotiating: "Recent Transportation Revenue Pack-
ages," *Transportation Resource Manual*, Washington State Legislature, 2017,
27, leg.wa.gov/JTC/trm/Documents/TRM%202017%20Update/5%20-%20
Recent%20Revenue%20Package%20-%20%20Final.pdf.

209 "They're having booms in other places": Author interview with Terri Goban,
May 2015.

DIGITAL INDIANS 2015 ONWARD

214 "chefs, ethnobotanists, food preservationists, adventurers, foragers": "The
Sioux Chef Mission," the Sioux Chef, www.Sioux-chef.com/about.

214 opened the Indigenous Food Lab: "The Sioux Chef's Indigenous Food Lab
Opens in Midtown Global Market," *The Star Tribune*, August 19, 2020, www
.startribune.com/the-sioux-chef-s-Indigenous-food-lab-opens-in-midtown
-global-market/572161302/?refresh=true.

219 "The U.S. government spent two hundred years trying to kill us": Author interview with Anton Treuer, 2015.

220 Manuelito Wheeler, a Diné language activist: Matt Hansen, "The Future of
America's Endangered Languages," *The Week*, June 29, 2015, theweek.com
/articles/563549/future-americas-endangeredlanguages.

220 Sarah Agaton Howes is one of those fighting not just against a system: All
quotes from author interview with Sarah Agaton Howes, April 2015.

223 Chelsey Luger is also part of the force that's creating the shift: All quotes from
author interview with Chelsey Luger, March 2014.

227 In 2013 the Violence Against Women Act: Jennifer Bendery, "At Last, Violence
Against Women Act Lets Tribes Prosecute Non-Native Domestic Abusers,"
The Huffington Post, March 6, 2015, www.huffingtonpost.com/2015/03/06
/vawa-native-americans_n_6819526.html.

227 According to the National Institute of Justice: André B. Rosay, "Violence Against American Indian and Alaska Native Women and Men," National Institute of Justice, June 1, 2016, nij.ojp.gov/topics/articles/violence-against-american-indian-and-alaska-native-women-and-men.

228 I grew up in Minneapolis and went to Roosevelt High: All quotes from author interview with Nicole Matthews, May 2022.

234 "By the time the company finally settled on a construction path": United States District Court, District of Columbia, *Standing Rock Sioux Tribe, et al., Plaintiffs, v. U.S. Army Corps of Engineers, et al., Defendants*, Civil Action No. 16-1534 (JEB), signed, September 9, 2016, retrieved from National Indian Law Library, www.narf.org/nill/bulletins/federal/documents/standing_rock_v _army_corps.html.

234 "their limited scope": United States District Court.

238 over 1,172 miles, across four states, and under the Missouri and Mississippi Rivers: Gregor Aisch and K. K. Rebecca Lai, "The Conflicts Along 1,172 Miles of the Dakota Access Pipeline," *The New York Times*, last updated March 20, 2017, www.nytimes.com/interactive/2016/11/23/us/dakota-access-pipeline -protest-map.html.

239 According to a report released by the Centers for Disease Control and Prevention: "COVID-19 Among American Indian and Alaska Native Persons—23 States, January 31–July 3, 2020," Centers for Disease Control and Prevention, August 28, 2020, www.cdc.gov/mmwr/volumes/69/wr/mm6934e1.htm?s _cid=mm6934e1_w.

240 Thirty-one Native women campaigned: Julie Turkewitz, "Native American Women Running for Office, Including a Seat in Congress" (from *The New York Times*), *The Seattle Times*, March 19, 2018, www.seattletimes.com/nation -world/nation/theres-never-been-a-native-american-congresswoman-that -could-change-in-2018/.

240 In the 2020 elections: Aliyah Chavez, "12 Native candidates for Congress: If elected . . . 'It will be a great day,'" *Indian Country Today*, February 18, 2020, indiancountrytoday.com/news/12-native-candidates-for-congress-if-elected -it-will-be-a-great-day-GovPIjk3rkmqOvGFI0s1tA.

241 The numbers tell part of the story: "About Tribes: Demographics," National Congress of American Indians, www.ncai.org/about-tribes/demographics; and "U.S. Census Marks Increase in Urban American Indian and Alaska Natives," Urban Indian Health Institute, February 28, 2013.

EPILOGUE

245 "Power always thinks it has a great Soul": John Adams to Thomas Jefferson, February 2, 1816, Founders Online, National Archives, https://founders

.archives.gov/documents/Jefferson/03-09-02-0285.

245   "We are not children": Peter Nabokov, *Native American Testimony* (New York: Penguin Books, 1999), 137.

246   "I am very sorry that you could not have seen": Brenda J. Child, *Boarding School Seasons: American Indian Families, 1900–1940* (Lincoln: University of Nebraska Press, 1998), 65–66.

PHOTO CREDITS

Front cover (top left and right), 69: Archives and Special Collections, Dickinson; front cover (bottom): Istock; 17, 44, 53, 56, 61, 75, 144: Library of Congress; 27: National Archives/Department of the Interior, National Park Service; 36: University of Washington Libraries, Special Collections, photographer Howard Clifford, AWC5193; 49: Wikimedia: Burton Historical Collection, Detroit Public Library; 76: Osage Nation Museum, catalog #P01-0376; 90: Wikipedia: indigenouswarhero.org; 91 Carlisle Indian School Digital Resource Center; 93 Oklahoma Historical Society, Czarina Conian Collection; 97, 151, 160: Bettman Archives/Getty Images; 102, 126, 147: Associated Press; 128: National Archives and Records Administration; 139: National Congress of American Indians and Alaska Natives, Inc.; 141: Museum of History and Industry (MOHAI), Seattle, WA; 149: National Museum of the American Indian, Smithsonian Institution and Oakland Museum of California; 166, 197: Minnesota Historical Society; 168, 193, 198: courtesy of the author; 173: Ames History Museum; 194: courtesy of Nedahness Rose Green; 203: Wikipedia: ©Brianhe; 228: courtesy of Nicole Matthews; 232: Flickr: © Anthony Crider; 235: Getty Images; 240: Johns Hopkins Center for American Indian Health; 241: U.S. Department of the Interior.

INDEX

❖❖❖❖❖❖❖❖❖

PAGE NUMBERS IN *ITALICS* INDICATE PHOTOS